## Not Only for Myself

<>

ALSO BY MARTHA MINOW:

<>

*Law Stories*
(coeditor with Gary Bellow)

*Family Matters: Readings on Family Lives and the Law*
(editor)

*Narrative, Violence and the Law: The Essays of Robert M. Cover*
(coeditor with Michael Ryan and Austin Sarat)

*Making All the Difference: Inclusion, Exclusion, and American Law*

# NOT *Only*
# *for* MYSELF

<>

*Identity, Politics, and the Law*

Martha Minow

The New Press > New York

Library of Congress Cataloging-in-Publication Data
Minow, Martha
Not only for myself: identity politics and the law / Martha Minow.
p. cm.
Includes bibliographical references.
ISBN 1-56584-374-6
1. Minorities—Legal status, laws, etc.—United States.
2. Group identity—United States. 3. Discrimination—United States.
4. Equality before the law—United States. I. Title.
KF4755.M56    1997
342.73'087—dc21    96-295878
CIP

Published in the United States by The New Press, New York
Distributed by W.W. Norton & Company, Inc., New York

The New Press was established in 1990 as a not-for-profit alternative to the large, commercial publishing houses currently dominating the book publishing industry. The New Press operates in the public interest rather than for private gain, and is committed to publishing, in innovative ways, works of educational, cultural, and community value that might not normally be commercially viable.

BOOK DESIGN BY ANN ANTOSHAK

PRODUCTION MANAGEMENT BY KIM WAYMER

PRINTED IN THE UNITED STATES OF AMERICA

9 8 7 6 5 4 3 2 1

*For*
Josephine Baskin Minow
*and*
Newton N. Minow

# Contents

<>

*Not Only for Myself*

<>

# PREFACE

<>

I wrote this book for three reasons. First, an immediate inspiration
came after Sheldon Hackney, chair of the National Endowment for
the Humanities, asked me to join with other scholars to advise the
NEH on its new initiative, the National Conversation on being an
American. The discussions that ensued among the scholars were
engaging, intense, and only occasionally vituperative. I would like to
thank Chairman Hackney, other participants in our sessions, and
Catherine Stimpson of the MacArthur Foundation for getting me into
rooms with smart, well-intentioned people who, despite their disagreements with one another, all triggered further disagreement
from me. And thanks to The New Press, I have had the freedom and
support to write what I think, not (necessarily) what will sell.

Second, as a member of a university community for sixteen years, I
have experienced in a vivid, daily way many fights over the appropriate places of racial, gender, and other group-based identities in hiring, admissions, curriculum, and teaching. Some of these fights have
been illuminating; many have not been. This book reflects, I hope,
what I have learned from these experiences but also a sense of perspective that locates academic fights as a relatively small spot on the
map of what matters. Topics more worthy of public attention are rules
about voting in the larger polity, how young people do and do not
encounter people different from themselves in elementary and high
schools, and the response of this "nation of immigrants" to the newest

immigrants, and to the oldest, involuntary ones. These and other social issues receive attention in the book. Yet, this is not a book of policy analysis or prescriptions; instead, I am reaching for a stance, a productive approach to problems informed by a deep respect for paradoxes and conflicts that resist neat solutions. Hence, the book explores works of fiction as much as it examines lawsuits and legislative debates. Rabbi Hillel's paradoxical questions ("If I am not for myself...") exemplify the stance I seek, and thus give me the title for the book.

My first and most remarkable teachers, my parents, taught me to be for myself but not only for myself, and my life-long discussions with them give the third, and most important impetus for this book. Josephine and Newton Minow have taught their daughters, sons-in-law, grandchildren, extended family members, friends, and colleagues by example how to combine self-respect with genuine and abiding concern for others. They have given their children the even more striking gift of their profound belief in each of us, matched in power only by their relentless honesty and curiosity in interrogating our views about matters of public import. Exemplified in my mother's recent children's book, *Marty the Broken-Hearted Artichoke*, is their life-long practice of overcoming prejudices of others by exhibiting their own capacities for caring across differences. I deeply appreciate their engagement with this book, their constant supply of clippings in support and in opposition to its arguments, and their clear-sighted reminders to try to write so people outside academic walls can get something out of it.

I would like to thank Sameer Ashar, Gary Bellow, Larry Blum, Alexi Lahav, Newton Minow, Todd Rakoff, Joe Singer, Avi Soifer, and Vicky Spelman for reading the entire book and giving generous and vigorous comments. Many ideas here reflect extensive discussions with my "Pentimento reading group"—Anthony Appiah, Larry Blum, Richard Ford, José Garcia, Maneesha Sinha, David Wilkins, and David Wong—and I am grateful to each of these people for their unique and collective insights. Individual chapters, or their previous incarnations, received considerable help from Anita Allen, Jack Balkin, Einer Elhauge, Katie Fallow, Lisa Fishbayn, Jodi Freeman, Mary Ann Glendon, Lani Guinier, Moshe Halbertal, Randall Kennedy, Tom Kim,

Frank Michelman, Richard Parker, Jon Rieder, Jane Schachter, Joan Scott, Cass Sunstein, Susan Sturm, Dennis Thompson, Mary Minnow, Nell Minnow, Richard Weissbourd, David Wiseman, and Zipporah Wiseman. Bonnie Honig, Craig Lamay, André Schiffrin, and Joan Scott each challenged me to think harder in ways I hope they see reflected in the book.

Thanks to the Cleveland-Marshall Law School for inviting me to give a lecture; some of the resulting work appears now in chapter 1. Congregation K.A.M.-Isaiah and Indiana University Law School each hosted my early thoughts on Kirya Joel; the comments from members of those communities greatly enriched the ideas that now appear in chapter 5. Thanks also to the University of Oregon and Jim O'Fallon, for inviting me to give the Colin Raugh Thomas O'Fallon Memorial Lecture on Law and American Culture, which has been reworked here as parts of chapters 2 and 4, and to Catherine Stimpson and Richard Sennett for inviting me to present that lecture to an amazing and stimulating collection of American and European scholars in the stunning setting of Bellagio, Italy.

Throughout the last six months, Ann Harkevy has been a research assistant from heaven. Laurie Corzett also did research, word processing wonders, and other magic to organize the hectic schedule competing with this book. Ola Myles similarly straightened out messes on the home front while providing steady and fun-filled care for my daughter, Mira. Ellen Kelley, Kathy Wheeler, Lisa Beth Calvo, and other remarkable people at the Cambridge-Ellis School have taught Mira, and me, daily about avenues for embracing differences. Chris Desan, Richard Fallon, Frank Michelman, Todd Rakoff, and Carol Steiker make a real community just outside my office door, a community in which people really are for others as much as for themselves. And yes, it is located within the Harvard Law School. I also cherish how much I learn each time I meet with Margot Strom and the other people behind Facing History and Ourselves, an educational resources program developing materials to teach young people about the Holocaust, slavery, and the obligations of political vigilance against group-based oppression.

My debts to Vicky Spelman include what I have learned from her work on the uses and abuses of other people's suffering, on the neglected subject of repair, and on the ways to make the arts part of everyday living. And Joe Singer and Mira Judith Minow Singer, thank you for being so privately accommodating and so constantly able to instruct me about how being for others is being for oneself.

My grandmother Doris Minow and my uncle Burton Minow both passed away while this book grew. May their blessed memories continue to inspire all who had the honor of knowing them.

<>

MARTHA MINOW
*Cambridge, Massachusetts*

# CHAPTER 1
## *Knots*

<>

### I. SETTING THE STAGE

In August 1990, the producer of *Miss Saigon*, the hit London musical, decided to cancel its Broadway production because the actors' union denied permission for the English lead actor to perform the play in New York.[1] Actors' Equity, the union, issued a statement saying that it could not "appear to condone the casting of a Caucasian in the role of a Eurasian."[2] The conflict between the union and the producer triggered a cause célèbre debated in the theater community, in the press, and inside Actors' Equity itself. A week after its initial decision, the union reversed itself, concluding it had "applied an honest and moral principle in an inappropriate manner."[3] After weeks of negotiations securing complete casting freedom to the producer, plans for the play revived, but the issue continued to produce controversy and wide media coverage for months thereafter.

Several contexts help explain the controversy. Advance ticket sales put $25 million at stake.[4] New York had recently elected an African-American mayor who wanted both to remedy discrimination and to preserve the theater industry.[5] Further, conservative American officials and commentators had assaulted controversial art in a battle over federal subsidies.[6] Pundits and public intellectuals debated "politically correct" sensitivities about racism, sexism, and homophobia.[7] The U.S. Supreme Court seemed on the brink of repudiating most public affirmative action programs.[8]

As I read about the casting of *Miss Saigon*, I could not help but draw connections to another "casting" debate, closer to my home.[9] The ongoing debate over why law school faculties remain largely white and male intensified with Professor Derrick Bell's decision to take a leave without pay until Harvard Law School hired a female law professor of color for a tenured or tenure-track position. Further escalating the issue at Harvard, a group of law students sued the school and claimed that discriminatory hiring practices hindered their education.[10] Both *Miss Saigon* and Harvard Law School generated arguments about merit and symbolism, about overcoming discrimination and about risks of new forms of discrimination, about fairness and representation. In both contexts, one side argued that there must be someone hired from the minority community while the other side maintained that hiring must be color-blind and merit based.[11]

The casting of *Miss Saigon* and the hiring at Harvard Law School thus exhibited clashes over identity politics—political claims made or resisted in terms of group-based identities, such as race, ethnicity, religion, gender, sexual orientation, and disability. The comic version is epitomized by a cartoon by Jeff McNelly, showing one bird at a bar muttering, "Seagull-Americans, peacock-Americans, mallard-Americans." In the next frame, the bird announces, "We all have something in common." "Yea," replies the bartender bird, "hyphens." The less comic versions appear not only on college campuses torn by fights over dorms for lesbians or majors in ethnic studies, but also in polarized responses to criminal trials in which a viewing public believes that lawyers and juries put racial loyalty ahead of evidence, and in urban violence sparked by conflicts among ethnic groups.

This book explores current knots of identity politics in hopes of framing more constructive approaches to the underlying issues. The knots entwine two strands of mistakes. We tend toward ignorance about the mistreatments along group lines—and nonetheless participate in the constant, unthinking use of group categories.

IGNORANCE: Even highly educated people show remarkable ignorance about such histories. "What were Japanese internment camps?" a student with an advanced degree asks during a law school class. "Why didn't Martin Luther King get a parade permit before marching in Birmingham?" asks another. Ignorance about the present is also widespread. Law students return to school shocked by incidents of sexual harassment and anti-Semitism found at summer jobs. Some are stunned by the views expressed by their own fellow students. "I was happily talking the first week of school with others in La Alianza," the Hispanic student group, one student told me, "until they joined in gay bashing." "My classmates think that because I'm black, I grew up poor," says another. "Just because I have a Southern accent doesn't mean I'm a bigot" objects a white student. Higher education and workplaces permit daily exposure and encounters among diverse groups of people, who in turn often discover the depth of their ignorance about one another.

ROUTINE CATEGORIZATION: Each new human life is a bundle of possibilities and has miraculous potential; something terribly wrong happens when a society determines life chances by membership in groups of which the infant is not even yet aware.

Yet, sort we do. Parents, teachers, neighbors, strangers, the mass media, and advertisers all register and sort people by group traits. Old-style sorting, still present in many places, implements long-standing prejudices and privileges of white, able-bodied heterosexual male Christians. An old-style identity politics attacks others based on *their* identities; it resurges in the burnings of black churches, and in right-wing fundraising campaigns predicated on demonizing gays and lesbians who would like to formalize their committed relationships.

New-style sorting often emerges in response. Many of the routine categories are part of large-scale social efforts to redress discrimination along group lines. Using policies to remedy group-based harms makes the group identities seem all the more real and entrenched, but denying the significance of group-based experiences leaves legacies of harm and stereotyping in place. By now, Americans take for granted that they identify themselves, and others, in terms of group categories. The census, mortgage applications, student financial aid forms, consumer surveys, and public opinion polls ask for information on race, gender, and ethnicity. Government and other institutions make these categories the building blocks for perceiving and sorting people.

When are the uses of group categories a valuable remedy, and when a further mistake? Consider the example of education. The all-male Virginia Military Institute resisted applications from women and lost in the Supreme Court because it failed to show a strong reason to maintain its exclusion along gender lines.[12] When school reformers planned an all-girl school for disadvantaged girls in Harlem, civil rights activists challenged the plan as a violation of constitutional and statutory guarantees of equality while other activists defended it as a thoughtful response to inadequate educational opportunities for poor, African American girls.[13] In another case, Asian-American students sued a competitive-admission public high school for using higher test cutoffs for their racial group than for others.[14]

A college appointed a new director of its Jewish Studies program who resigned under pressure of attacks that he should not serve because he is not himself Jewish.[15] An appellate court decision rejected the affirmative action effort of the University of Texas law school— but observers worry that the school could quickly return to its not so distant all-white past.[16] Learning-disabled students sue a university for creating a hostile learning environment by requiring recent expert assessments of their conditions before they can receive services;[17] meanwhile, the numbers of students claiming services because of learning disabilities grows exponentially. At the same time, civil rights advocates investigate why such a disproportionate number of nonwhites are placed in special education classrooms.[18]

Beyond the context of education, people turn to group identities to answer vexing problems. How should we frame elections of government representatives? How should juries be composed? How can claims be aggregated in class action lawsuits—along what lines of commonality? How should a university, workplace, or a city respond to incidents of hate speech? Who should be eligible for United States citizenship? Who should be selected to adopt a child whose skin is "brown" or "black"—or "white"?

If we do not sort people when we answer these questions, historic mistreatment along group lines will go unremedied. Denied the vote by this country's founding law and, in some parts of the country, by practices continuing into the present, African Americans cannot gain basic rights of participation without being recognized as a group. This does not dictate the form that recognition should take or the voting arrangements best designed to rectify exclusions, yet some explicit attention is needed if the exclusionary patterns are not to continue.[19] Accommodating persons with disabilities in the workplace similarly requires identification.

At the same time, uses of race, ethnicity, religion, gender, and other identity categories make leading public figures warn of the "disuniting" of America,[20] or of distraction from more serious economic injustices. The sorting impulse is contagious. Identity politics seems to breed identity politics. "Kiss me, I'm Irish" once responded to "Black is Beautiful"; now "white men" become an identity group, confident of their desert and unembarrassed by their self-interest. As cultural politics take center stage, economic disparities recede from public view. Cynical politicians may even foment conflicts among groups to advance their own power. If this is true, then proud defenses by groups against group hatred may play right into the hands of those who would divide for their own selfish gain. Resources for personal meaning include group affiliations, but those affiliations also provide predicates for violence and subordination.

A close examination of identity questions in social and legal settings can illustrate the insights and limitations on each side of disputes. I will explore potentially more constructive approaches to the underlying concerns of equality, liberty, and overcoming old and new forms of oppression. The aim is not so much to advocate a new set of policies as to articulate a more productive philosophy about policies and problems surrounding identity themes.

## II. IDENTITY QUESTIONS IN CASTING, HIRING, AND ELECTORAL POLITICS

Looking at the parallels between the law school hiring context and the *Miss Saigon* casting controversy reveals the passions as well as the conceptions that operate in conflicting arguments. Both settings occasion disagreements over the assumption that group membership serves as a proxy for shared experiences, and especially common experiences as victims of societal prejudice. Proponents of group consciousness at times advocate this strategy as a response to historic exclusion; another goal is to offer role models for members of historically excluded groups.

Opponents, styled as defenders of neutrality, resist such arguments because they undermine the commitment to treating individuals as individuals.[21] Some opponents further charge that the call for hiring members of racial minorities is incoherent if the advocates' real motives are to hire someone who holds a particular, "politically correct" view. Skin color is no determinant of such views, this argument continues, and political litmus tests for hiring violate academic freedom. As for the role model argument, any individual should be able to inspire the next generation, claim the defenders of neutrality. Thus, Jonathan Pryce, the white English actor cast by the producer for the role in *Miss Saigon*, commented: "What is appropriate is that the best person for the job play the role, and I think it's completely valid that I play the role."[22] Translated for law school hiring, this argument sounds like: "What is appropriate is that the best person for the job get the job; excellence must not be sacrificed for other considerations."

About *Miss Saigon*, arts critic Frank Rich commented: "By refusing to permit a white actor to play a Eurasian role, Equity makes a mockery of the hard-won principles of non-traditional casting and practices a hypocritical reverse racism."[23] Similarly, though perhaps less vividly, professors have argued that demanding the appointment of a professor because of his or her sex and race contravenes hard-fought principles of equal opportunity and color-blindness.[24]

Even more directly on point were arguments over a hiring controversy at Harvard a few years back: when the administration invited one white civil rights lawyer and one black civil rights lawyer to visit the school and teach a course on civil rights, students protested the school's failure to hire a full-time faculty member of color for such a course. In its defense, the Harvard administration challenged the idea that a white person who had devoted his life to the subject could not teach about civil rights.[25]

In contrast, Ellen Holly, a black actress, commented about the *Miss Saigon* casting debate:

> Racism in America today is nothing so crass as mere hatred of a person's skin color. It is rather an affliction of so many centuries' duration that it permeates institutions to the point of becoming indivisible from them. Only when the darker races attempt to break out of the bind—and inconvenience whites in the process—do whites even perceive

racism as an issue. Only when a white is asked to vacate a role on racial grounds does the matter become a front-page issue.[26]

Analogously, in law school faculties around the country, individuals argue about institutionalized racism. Some observers argue that implicit preferences for people who are part of the "old-boy network" go unnoticed, while preferences for someone from a traditionally excluded group provoke an uproar. Advocates for change assert that only changed demographics in hiring should count as evidence that historic exclusions are being overcome.

From this point of view, what may look like a preference for a member of a racial minority is really an effort to counteract a preference for whites. But another argument for preferring members of racial minorities simply views them as specially qualified people for the job at hand. In the wake of the *Miss Saigon* controversy, the distinguished playwright August Wilson defended his demand for a black director for the film production of one of his plays. He explained:

> We are an African people who have been here since the early 17th century. We have a different way of responding to the world. We have different ideas about religion, different manners of social intercourse. We have different ideas about style, about language. We have different aesthetics. Someone who does not share the specifics of a culture remains an outsider, no matter how astute a student or how well-meaning their intentions. I declined a white director not on the basis of race but on the basis of culture. White directors are not qualified for the job.[27]

Similarly, an African American professor is needed, many argue, because that person will bring cultural perspectives otherwise missing from the law school community. That perspective will enrich the classroom, the scholarship, the counseling of students who share that background, and the counseling of students who do not share that background. Similarly, some law school faculty members conclude that their school should hire a Hispanic professor, because the increasing numbers of Hispanic students need the knowledge held by that person and because white, Asian, and African American students need to see a Hispanic person in the respected position at the head of the class. Hence the slogan, "No education without representation."[28]

An additional argument is that professors are role models, and only members of historically excluded groups can serve adequately as role models for students of those groups.[29] This issue surfaced vividly when at Galludette University (for deaf and hearing-impaired students) students' protests over the nomination of a hearing president led to the hiring of its first hearing-impaired president.[30] Some who support this role model idea maintain, somewhat differently, that only a variety of role models can serve the needs of all students. Thus the special pedagogical needs of students who are members of minority groups are distinct from and yet complementary to the benefit all students derive from diversity among the faculty. Further, in a distributive justice sense, the focus on race and sex in hiring should serve to shift resources, including the resource of academic attention, to new agendas for legal scholarship and teaching.[31] Similarly, the presence of actors of color in a play can encourage young people of color to consider acting as a career, just as professors of color can inspire nonwhite students to pursue academic careers. Yet individualists would object that any person, regardless of race, gender, or other group trait, should be able to inspire members of the next generation to achieve, whether through academic study or artistic accomplishment.

Even more striking than these parallels in opposing arguments is the parallel between those who find the entire framework of debate unacceptable, whether in the context of *Miss Saigon* casting or law school hiring. Playwright David Henry Hwang, one of the first to complain about the casting choice in *Miss Saigon*, later said that he could not choose between minority casting and the producer's right to cast whom he wants, because that is "like asking me to pick between my father and my mother; I can't. It's real hard for me to pick between artistic freedom on the one hand and discrimination on the other."[32] Similarly, some law professors argue that the choice cannot be between excellence and diversity because both are critical. In addition, many reject the implication that schools must trade or sacrifice some excellence in order to achieve diversity.

One person struggling with these tensions concluded that at least the debate over the casting in *Miss Saigon* brought the chronic difficulties facing actors of color to public attention. Shirley Sun, director, producer, and writer of the recent film *Iron and Silk* concluded that "'Artistic freedom' should not be used to exclude any group. If the stage is a sublime place where any actor can play any role, why can't an Asian or Asian-American play a Eurasian role?"[33] If theater offers the possibility that actors can entice audiences to suspend their disbelief and be transported by crafted illusions, why cannot more actors have this chance to transport the audience?[34] The casting decision in *Miss Saigon*, on this view, was not about matching the actor's race with the character's race, but about the magical creation of an illusion of reality by whichever actor gains the chance to play the role.[35]

Some producers specifically endorse cross-racial casting, not only to give the best candidate the chance with the role, but also to enrich and challenge the plays with the different dimensions that casting may afford.[36] Similar arguments are offered for entire cross-cultural productions, such as the Cleveland Play House presentation of *The Glass Menagerie* with a black cast.[37] Here, the parallels to law school hiring may become somewhat strained, yet faculties often consider it a "plus" to hire a woman or a person of color to teach business-related subjects, such as corporations, securities law, and taxation, as contrasted with civil rights and family law courses.

Arguments over the place of group identity also animate other debates. Should juries be selected to mirror the diversity in the population, with individuals representing specific constituencies, or should the selection be random, even if particular juries end up with members who all share a race, a gender, or an ethnic background? Should lawyers be able to exclude candidates for a jury because of group membership, and thus treat that membership as a proxy for viewpoint? Or should groups be protected from such jury exclusion, and if so, which groups—based on race, gender, religion, occupation, primary language? Should a client pick a lawyer based on group membership? Should a gay attorney argue a case involving gay rights or would it be better, strategically, to select a heterosexual attorney? Should a male defendant charged with rape select a female attorney, and should a female attorney be willing to market her gender as part of the persuasive strategy of defense?

Perhaps most analogous to the casting and hiring debates are disagreements over electoral politics and voting rules. Should electoral processes seek to produce representatives who match their voting districts by race, or other features?[38] The Voting Rights Act has inspired efforts to redraw district lines to prevent dilution of the effect of votes cast by members of racial minorities. Civil rights activists had supported enforcement of these provisions with the particular hope of increasing the number of minority representatives elected to office. Critics of race-consciousness attack the Act and its implementation for focusing on race rather than seeking racial neutrality.

Gender, ethnicity, and other group traits also trigger clashes in the design of electoral processes. In *The Politics of Presence*,[39] Anne Phillips observes and defends a recent trend stressing a range of personal characteristics of representatives, along with, or even instead of, the ideas they advance. Differences among people involve not only ideas and beliefs, but also identities reflecting group experiences. These differences deserve representation.

As a result, "[a]dequate representation is increasingly interpreted as implying a more adequate representation of the different social groups that make up the citizen body."[40] Representatives should "mirror" or resemble those they represent.[41] The strategy pursued by some states under the federal Voting Rights Act carves up geographic boundaries for voting districts to produce districts with a majority of nonwhite voters in order to increase the chance of electing nonwhite representatives. Several European political parties use quota systems to produce gender parity in elected assemblies.[42] Demands for political presence, as Phillips would describe it, grow from social movements against inequalities arising from traits other than class.[43] Political presence becomes a growing concern in the wake of global migration patterns, producing more diverse local populations, and apparently waning national and class-based identities.[44]

Leaders of identity-based social movements acknowledge that they cannot fairly speak for the interests of members until engaging with those members to discover who they are and what matters to them. Once again, actual presence is crucial; leaving it to others will not work. Yet the problem of "too many meetings" for too many people yields to the solution of representatives, matched by identity group. The mechanisms for consulting with group members remain far from perfect.

Those who demand attention to group difference anticipate and reject the alternatives of neutrality and indifference to group identities. Claims to neutrality in the past have accompanied group-based exclusions and degradations. Apparently neutral, abstract norms governing selection of representatives, and other features of government in operation, have frequently failed to reflect, or represent, the experiences, interests, and needs of the full variety of human beings. Equality under the law itself has been construed to benefit some, but not all, people.[45]

Thus, equal protection against discrimination on the basis of sex is not violated, according to the Supreme Court, when an employer refuses to include pregnancy in its insurance coverage, because not only men but also some women are not pregnant at any given time.[46] Criminal statutes traditionally defined rape to require a victim to fight back physically, rather than merely say "No"; this reflects a traditionally male conception of sexuality and self-defense.[47] A statutory guarantee of freedom of contract may look neutral. But if it lacks any prohibition against racially discriminatory treatment within those contracts, anyone in jeopardy of discrimination on the basis of race would view this as a perversely crabbed interpretation—even if it is the one adopted by the Supreme Court.[48] Buildings open to the public but inaccessible to people who use wheelchairs are not neutral, but disabling; mass transit systems that are hazardous to people with visual or hearing impairments are also not neutral but instead prefer some people over others.[49] The Americans with Disabilities Act, the Civil Rights Restoration Act, and some judicial opinions [50] look behind apparently neutral practices to find discriminatory effects and to advance a vision of equality as inclusion. Although these developments have in turn triggered opposition and resistance, questions about exclusion along group lines resonate and reverberate in public debate.

These questions are especially pointed in the context of electoral representation. Members of an historically excluded group therefore say to those outside their group who claim to speak for them: "You don't know, and you get it wrong." Or worse, "You *do* know, and you do us wrong," as in deliberate racism. Moreover, "we want to speak for ourselves"; or "only with a representative of our own group can we each have the vicarious experience of speaking and being there." At its base, the focus on group differences assumes sharp divisions among groups organized around sociological identities, and also expresses doubts about claimed comprehension or solidarity across these divisions.

Of course, others disagree.[51] Color-blind individualists oppose race-based thinking, and assert that people can well represent those who look unlike themselves. For those with this view, concerns about equality are better handled by treating each individual as equal than by proceeding along group lines. According and enforcing rights to each individual through general commitments to neutrality and equality, in the best scenario, will overcome past group-based mistreatments. Using group-based categories would violate this vision.[52] Many take the same position when addressing questions about ethnic and language minority groups. In this view, electoral districts should not be drawn along racial lines.[53] Even worse would be proportional representation, for it would require identifying and installing group categories in the process of politics. Similarly, advocates of individualism and neutrality oppose gender distinctions in electoral rules with the added emphasis on women's position as often near, or more than, a majority across electoral districts.

Besides the defenses of neutrality and treating each individual as an individual, resisters to group-based electoral rules can draw on evidence of people's capacities to empathize, and change, regardless of group membership. People are malleable and can learn to share and behave altruistically in environments promoting those goals.[54] Accordingly, representatives do not have to look like or even share experiences with those they represent. The messages from this perspective to those who emphasize group differences are (1) don't be so sure others don't care to understand or can't understand you; (2) people who don't look alike can still work together, even to advance the interests of those who have been excluded in the past; (3) people can learn from one another; and (4) the rules we adopt will influence whether we grow more self-interested or instead more altruistic and capable of empathy. Rules of representation therefore should promote intergroup dealings and deliberation.

Group-based categories thus offend those who are committed to individualism and also offend some who are committed to a deliberative community. For others, group-based categories are too large and crude to capture the variety and multiplicity of individuals' identities. A cascade of objections to proportional representation or other group-based strategies emerge from this perspective. How many differences now need to be represented? Can a Latina represent Hispanic men as well as women? Must the African American caucus divide along gender lines, and country-of-origin lines, and class lines? Must the gender caucus divide along racial lines, and then, ethnic, sexual orientation, religion, and disability lines? If so, how can any political movement emerge?[55] Why should we assume that sociological traits of a person, traits like race or gender, match interests or preferences? Why, indeed, assume that an individual's identity is natural or fixed rather than chosen, constructed by society, or in flux?[56]

With this last set of objections, debates over group identity come full circle. For worries that race and gender are too general to capture important dimensions of identity are inflected by contemporary preoccupations with identity, difference, and distrust. They do not reflect faith in neutrality or a focus on each unique individual; nor do they indicate Edmund Burke's confident elitism or faith in the objectivity of interests. Indeed, these questions express emphatic distrust along lines of difference—but because the differences are multiple and shifting, conventional groupings are inadequate. Given the criss-crossing arguments for and against group-based thinking in casting, hiring, and voting rules, is it possible to articulate what seems powerful, and what seems mistaken, in all the positions in this debate?

## III. Both Right, Both Wrong

An old story is told of disputants who consulted a rabbi. He listened intently to the first person's story, and then announced, "You're right." Then the rabbi heard the second person's completely opposing version, and concluded, "You're right." The rabbi's wife was listening through the door, and shouted back, "They can't both be right." The rabbi replied, "You're right, too."

The critics and the advocates of identity politics each have important and valid perceptions. On the one hand, there are dangers from using group categories in politics and law, hiring and voting. Errors will be made in efforts to assign people to group categories because people do not "fit" categories. Some people fall between categories.[57] All people are artificially reduced to one feature when typed by race, disability, or any single category. Any given trait is both too limiting and too general to do justice to an individual. Every person has a race, and a gender, along with perhaps countless characteristics, and each modifies and inflects the others. A Caribbean American heterosexual male whose family has lived in Louisiana for two generations, an African American lesbian in Los Angeles, and a recent immigrant mother who left her children in Liberia may share some interests but not others; a first-generation Catholic Cambodian girl who is blind and lives in Minneapolis has some, but not many, things in common with the fourth-generation Chinese American boy who is a gymnast and an atheist, or the Chinese infant girl recently adopted by the Jewish couple in Ohio. Yet, in much of contemporary America, the fact that all of these people are not white will deeply influence their reception in dominant institutions—and affect how they themselves react to a range of potential self-affiliations.

Being assigned to categories and choosing to embrace a category involve complex interactions among people, historical settings, and events. No clear answer can be found to resolve who is in and who is out of any given category once we compare how people identify themselves, how groups identify their own members, and how nonmembers attribute traits to others. "Race" lacks any coherent definition. Ethnicities change, subdivide, and merge. An individual can shift, through his or her lifetime, across different stages of able-bodied and disabled experiences; some people also move through different sexual orientations, genders, and religions.

On the other hand, the weight of group identities is undeniable. Social institutions, such as law, work to make them seem real. So do long histories of enslavement, subordination, or other sustained maltreatment based on national origin, skin color, religion, and other group traits. Identity politics centrally responds to mistreatment along group lines—mistreatment that has been and, too often, remains real. There is no rush to the front of the line by political voices from outside affected groups to name and fight discrimination and group-based mistreatment. Local and national black leaders initially mobilized the nation in response to recent terrorism against black churches; the National Council of Churches and the Anti-Defamation League of B'nai B'rith, representing other identity groups, organized an early response, and later Congress and white fundamentalist church groups joined in response.[58]

It is no mistake to perceive a political landscape marked by countless people who deny, do not care about, or even endorse versions of racism, sexism, anti-immigrant, and anti-gay feelings, as well as tensions across religious and ethnic group lines. As long as race seems a problem for blacks, Hispanics, and Asians but not for whites; gender a problem for women but not for men; anti-Semitism a problem for Jews but not for gentiles; homophobia a problem for gays and lesbians but not for straights; then more intensive remembering, acknowledging, and raging will be pursued by those who feel they cannot leave the issues any more than they can leave their skins.

Moreover, it does little good to tell people to halt the preoccupation with group identity and past pain, defer to the common good, unite around economic issues, or let go of rage over racism. Such an approach does not work. Rather, it sounds like indifference to or complicity with historic and ongoing oppression drawn of particular groups. Those who feel continually demeaned and excluded cannot trust calls for neutrality, universality, and the common good.

Wishing away identity politics also neglects the hunger for memory and acknowledgment that people know—or believe—afford a sense of place and meaning. Satisfying that hunger gives energy for joining with others. Finding a place where community and reciprocal affiliation seem obvious affords comfort and strength.

Against implicit and explicit put-downs, some people seize on the identity group as a source of pride. "Lo and Behold, here in our midst is dissimilarity that simply could not be squelched, and that now is insisting on its right to flourish"; an observer of the conflict between French-speaking and English-speaking Canadians could be speaking of the United States.[59] Asserting an identity group can give people a sense of place and connection that otherwise feel absent or beyond their control. For example, an Asian American student group forms, although one member says he never cared to identify as Korean American before leaving home, and another says she never felt any commonality between Japanese and Chinese Americans until so many people assumed she was one when she was the other. Not only do people find they share common experiences, they invent commonalities against the anonymity of larger institutional settings.

Meeting and working within groups that share a race, or gender, or other trait, does not end or reduce disagreements for those in the group. For example, women disagree intensely about regulating pornography.[60] People of color disagree about restricting hate speech.[61] Gays and lesbians disagree about authorizing same-sex marriage.[62] In these disagreements, participants aver they are *for* the good of the entire group. They simply disagree about how to advance it. Yet members of groups also often disagree about who else should be a member, and about the meanings of group membership itself. American Indian tribes struggle over definitions of membership, and debate questions such as should blood, and to what degree, matter; how should intermarriage be treated; and should assimilation to the dominant culture affect one's status as an Indian.[63] Jews have similarly disagreed among themselves about who is a Jew, with questions over whether the traditional prerequisite of a Jewish mother can be supplemented with the alternative of a Jewish father, as well as questions about whether Jews should accept external, and genocidal, attributions of Jewishness by the Nazis.[64] Tactical judgments about dealings with outsiders may be part of the debates here, alongside issues of meaning, culture, and continuity.

## IV. The Rest of This Book

This book explores issues of identity politics not as questions of tactics but instead as clues to collective social experiences in the United States as the twentieth century closes. Amid assertions and rejections of group membership and struggles for both liberty and equality, some people worry about a fragmenting, disuniting America while others urge a more finely categorized collection of subgroups.[65] Both approaches imply that some notion of identity—whether broad like "American" or narrower like "bisexual biracial"—can do important work in addressing issues of politics, justice, and orderly social change.

I will suggest instead that preoccupations with identity replicate, rather than resolve, conflicting conceptions of individual freedom and social meaning, self-creation and patterns beyond personal control. For none of us have individual identities except by reference to collective social experiences, and yet all of us retain some degrees of freedom for self-invention out of the found materials of biographical and social life.

The questions worth attention, I suggest, do not concern fixing or selecting the right identities for use in politics and law but instead ask how to strike a productive stance toward the paradoxes of individual and social meaning.[66] Practice with paradox can decrease a tendency to seize one or another side, only to be hit by the other side in arguments with others, or with ourselves.[67] Noticing and thinking about paradoxes of identity can reduce the likelihood of polarized discussions while also reorienting attention from desires to fix or solve issues of identity toward attending to the circumstances that make identities seem so salient.

One paradox of identity is that individual efforts to express unique experiences, based on membership in oppressed groups, resonate with broad audiences as universal, familiar tales. For example, David Mura, a Japanese American poet and author, has written a vivid, sensitive examination of his childhood and early adulthood as a "model minority" and "honorary white."[68] Interspersing this narrative with evocative re-creations of his parents' experiences in the Japanese internment camps, the book struggles to attain an honest confrontation with the author's own self-confessed errors. These are compulsive sexual promiscuity and obsession with pornography, which Mura comes to understand at least in part as responses to a culture that equates beauty with whiteness and in part a response to his parents' silence about their pasts.

As Mura traces his own recognition that assimilation is impossible when a Japanese body has defined criminality, he makes peace with his parents, whose rigid efforts to promote their children's assimilation had so enraged him. He rebuilds, through therapy, a sense of a self after regaining a sense of Asian American culture and claiming an identity as a person of color, not an "honorary white." Yet a sympathetic reviewer for an international newspaper, in an admiring review of the book, concludes,

> Readers may be struck, as I was, not by the ethnic uniqueness of Mura's experience but by its universality. His 1960s tug of war against a conformist father who forces him to cut his hair, his 1970s search for redemption in drugs and promiscuity, his 1980s marriage and flight from excess, his 1990s born-again multiculturalism: Far from distinguishing him from mainstream America, these are all, for his generation, its very essence. In deciding he is different, he has finally joined the crowd.[69]

A related paradox of identity joins the recognition that each person is ultimately unique and alone with an acknowledgment of this as a universal, common human condition. An illustration appears in the words of a leading American advocate and theorist of rights for women. After a lifetime of advocacy for women's rights—and efforts both to assert women's similarity to men and women's special vulnerabilities and strengths[70]—Elizabeth Cady Stanton testified at congressional hearings on women's suffrage in 1892. She asserted that

> The talk of sheltering woman from the fierce storms of life is the sheerest mockery, for they beat on her from every point of the compass, just as they do on man, and with more fatal results, for he has been trained to protect himself, to resist, to conquer. . . . Rich and poor, intelligent and ignorant, wise and foolish, virtuous and vicious, man and woman, it is ever the same, each soul must depend wholly on itself.[71]

As another, more recent example, Gary Larson, who entitles his cartoons "the Far Side," drew a picture filled with penguins, crowded together and looking identical. One in the back has a balloon coming from his mouth in which these words appear surrounded by musical notes: "I gotta be me, oh I just gotta be me." Larson's distributor decided to reprint the cartoon as a color poster, but the printer decided to color the shouting penguin, and only that one, a distinctive shade, until Larson could correct this mistake in a later printing. Larson's point was to illustrate the paradoxical quality of individual identity as unique and universal. "The entire point of the cartoon had been reversed. In the original version, I was being cynical about the futility of trying to be unique in a sea of commonality. But by making the singing penguin yellow, the publisher made him stand out, and the cartoon then made the same point the song orginally intended."[72]

Mirroring paradoxes of identity are paradoxes of political pluralism, the forms of society and government that permit the flourishing of multiple identity groupings:

> —a tolerant political system must, to some degree, tolerate the intolerant;[73]

> —a pluralist political system enables apparent autonomy for subcommunities while subjecting them all to centralized permission, setting the scope for their autonomy.[74]

Often, as I struggle with these issues, my eyes wander to the wall where I have hung these famous, and paradoxical, words of Rabbi Hillel:[75]

> If I am not for myself, who will be for me?
> If I am not for others, what am I?
> And if not now, when?

These simple words from a first-century rabbi inspire many commentaries. Inside the rabbinic tradition, Hillel's words refer to the duty of every Jew to be self-reliant in fulfilling the religious commandment to do good deeds while also teaching others to do the same.[76] Yet among ordinary Jews as a group, Hillel's teachings take on political meaning. If we do not stand up for ourselves, we should not expect anyone else to do so. Hillel's admonition inspired Zionists to seek a nation state for Jews.[77]

I think Hillel's words rightly summon up a more profound challenge, relevant to every human being. How can we each have self-respect but also regard for others? How can we have a proper sense of urgency about doing what is right? These questions compel me as an individual. If I don't assert myself, protect my own interests, who will? Maybe no one. I cannot count on others respecting me if I do not respect myself. If I should be for myself as a unique and separate person, I should also be for myself as a member of groups. I should stand up as a Jew, as a woman, as an American.

If we are not for ourselves, who will be? This question, and the fear that no one will reply, echoes in campus politics, office politics, American electoral politics, and world politics. Hillel's first question may not always tell us how best to stand up for ourselves, but it is a familiar warning about the indifference of others, and reminder of the interdependence between self-respect and communal respect.

The second question, though, seems less familiar. What are we if we are only for ourselves? Sometimes claims of universal good push in this direction: why don't we all come together, or, in Rodney King's phrase, "Why can't we all just get along?" Why can't we emphasize our commonality rather than our differences? asks the universalist. Yet put in these universal terms, the appeal often is heard as a denial of differences. Then those who think differences matter cannot hear it, or do not respond. Too often, the denial of differences is an implicit assertion of majority superiority, telling minority group members to put *their* differences aside.

"If I am not for others, what am I?" Hillel's second question acknowledges differences and does not submerge them under unity or commonality. It starts with the divide between self and others and urges a more direct connection with other, real human beings than a universal call for unity implies.[78] Indeed, this question points attention to the uniqueness of other people even while eliciting a sense of connection with them.[79] Being for others can involve not only caring about but also caring for them.[80] Interestingly, Hillel returns attention to the "I"; one's own self remains at the heart of the question in testing one's attention and concern for others. Is this a case of the self-absorbed conversationalist who says, "enough about me, what do *you* think of me?" I think instead that it is an acknowledgment of the lens of the self through which we each, unavoidably, sense, evaluate, and know.[81]

Hillel's second question could also be heard in terms of the divide between my group and others. If we are not for others, what kind of group are we? Implied are unacceptable answers. What are we? We are fools.[82] Being only for ourselves could mean we are unable to see the threat to Jews when black churches are burned, or too limited to imagine the danger to our own old age when we mistreat the current elderly. Here the mistake is a failure of moral imagination; we should be for others because we might need others' help next time and because evil and harm do not visit only people unlike ourselves. A German pastor who voted for the Nazi party in 1933 but found himself in a concentration camp in 1938 after opposing Hitler, is believed to have said:

> In Germany, the Nazis came for the Communists, and I didn't speak up because I wasn't a Communist. Then they came for the Jews, and I didn't speak up because I wasn't a Jew. Then they came for the trade unionists, and I didn't speak up because I wasn't a trade unionist. Then they came for the Catholics, and I didn't speak up because I was a Protestant. Then they came for me, and by that time there was no one left to speak for me.[83]

Hillel's second question implies another answer. If we are not for others, then we are monsters. We have made "myself" into a kind of being we should not want to be. It is not just that we should not want to be, or be seen to be, selfish and self-absorbed. Failing to be for others makes us capable of monstrous acts.

An episode of the television show "Star Trek: The Next Generation" explored this theme. Data, the android, is a unique being: he has remarkable capacities for storing and processing information, but he also continually struggles to overcome the limits of his programming and to understand such human qualities as humor, surprise, and friendship. A scientist requests permission from the ship's captain to take Data apart and study his inner workings. The scientist cannot guarantee, however, that when Data is reassembled, the android will retain what he has learned beyond his programmed instructions. Data refuses to agree to the scientist's request. He is afraid he will lose what he has learned about humor, surprise, and friendship—and lose his emerging capacities to laugh and to befriend. The ship's captain also refuses consent. The scientist argues that Data is Starfleet property and brings the matter to an adversarial hearing.

Within these confines, an intriguing debate emerges. One side argues that Data is merely property, and supports this claim by detailing the circumstances of his invention and construction, and by dramatically shutting off Data's power, leaving "it" limp in the witness chair. The other side struggles first to argue that Data is a person, given "his" affection for others, "his" memories, and "his" cultivated sense of humor.

But then, in a startling shift of strategy, the defense tells the court that the question is not whether Data is a person or property, but instead, whom do we want to be? Do we want to be the kind of people who create an android and then subject "it" to a potentially destructive exercise in which it expressly declines to participate? Do we want to be the kind of people who invent a creature capable of consciousness and then convert that consciousness for our own use and exploitation? Do we want the scientist to learn to disassemble and then mass-produce other androids while thinking of them as "things" with no entitlement to self-determination? The allusions to slavery are rife. The court concludes that Data itself/himself should have the power to decide whether to participate in the experiment. The court decides that the community should be the kind that embraces the integrity of individual consciousness and respects the autonomy of other conscious beings.

If we are not for others, suggests Hillel, we are fools, or monsters. Identity politics takes one big step from the individual toward others—but limits concern to those who match the individual's own identity trait. I am for others, but only those like myself. If we foreshorten concern along group lines, what are we? But, to return to Hillel's first question, if we are not for ourselves, who will be for us?

Psychological research suggests that taking perspective of others requires some cognitive development, normally available by the time a child is six or seven.[84] Most adolescents and adults readily have the capacity. What is more often lacking is the motivation to exercise it. I write this book with hopes of stirring such motivation, and also shifting the debate from the tired attack and defense of identity politics. Drawing on law, popular culture, literature, and politics, I tell a story about where we are and what we could become.

I turn next, in chapter 2, to identities. What are the strengths and limitations of thinking, advocating, litigating, and politicking along lines of group differences? How, if at all, can identity politics withstand growing demonstrations of the complexity of each person's identity and the shortcomings or total incoherence of particular group categories?

Chapter 3 examines the role of American law in bolstering the apparent solidity of group identities, despite ambiguities and contests over identities. I explore then alternative stances toward identity that advocates and judges could pursue while also considering the limitations of law in struggles over identities.

Needs for acknowledgment, memory, and redress animate many legal and political claims framed by group identities. Chapter 4 asks how such claims can receive proper responses that also sustain vital possibilities of individual self-definition. No remedies can fully resolve the double-sided problem of ignorance of group-based harms and unthinking group categorization. What combination of strategies can deepen our understanding of this persistent tension rather than lulling us into pretending it has disappeared?

Chapter 5 focuses on the special issues raised by schooling. Who should control the power of educational institutions to influence group identities and the teaching about groups? How much should parents and how much should the state have to say about the kinds of schools children attend and the kinds of peers they encounter? Parents' opportunities for self-definition should include control over their children's identities, but public power should also be deployed to open children's chances to invent themselves, and to overcome the segregation effect of past generations' choices.

Chapter 6 addresses the charges that America risks new and dangerous fragmentation because of identity politics by evaluating both the charges and the conception of unity that animates them. After considering debates over affirmative action, the book closes by returning to the paradoxical possibility of forging commitment to others without relinquishing commitment to oneself.

# CHAPTER 2
## *Identities*

<>

There are two kinds of people in the world, the saying goes: those who think there are two kinds of people, and those who do not. But do those who *do not* think there are two kinds of people divide further, perhaps over their reasons for rejecting the halving of humanity? Some are likely to emphasize the commonality or unity of all people, and reject dualism for that reason. Others are likely to find two groups or kinds inadequately plural, and to emphasize—with fear or with delight—the multiplicity of groups of people. Of course, taken at their extremes, these two views may converge. A thoroughly pluralist view would see the uniqueness, and individuality, of each person, and then, perhaps, the commonality of uniqueness uniting all people. But most contemporary debates over identity politics in the United States fix on a curious mixture of racial, ethnic, gender, and sexual politics, and focus on African Americans, Hispanics, Asian Americans, women, and gays and lesbians.[85]

American discussions of identity teeter between two topics: how does and should a particular individual affiliate with one or more groups, such as racial, ethnic, gender, and religious groups; and how can individuals express their own self-definition beyond group affiliation. The two topics diverge over the importance of group membership in defining the individual, but converge in the tension between freedom and constraint—between the invented and the always already there. This chapter explores this tension in criticisms of group-based thinking, and proposes a conception of identity as a process of negotiation through social relationships of power and culture. But first, let us consider why identity has come to seem such a prevalent preoccupation— either as a supposed answer to disputes over representation and politics, or a supposed threat to unity and democracy.

Complex questions of identity appear in biblical stories and classical Greek dramas. Moses struggled with the tension between his royal Egyptian upbringing and his impoverished Jewish roots; Oedipus sought to flee a familial destiny only to be ensnared by it.[86] Nonetheless, our distinctively contemporary preoccupation with identity imbues scholarship, art, and popular culture.[87] After world wars, industrial dislocation, and exposure to mass communications, people may have a greater sense of the mutability of their identities. Encounters with people of more varied ethnic, racial, religious, and class backgrounds challenge an individual's sense of self and community. Moving from a small town can open avenues for different self-presentations in terms of gender roles and sexual orientation. Perhaps identity becomes important when it becomes a question. It often becomes a question when individuals and groups are mobile and able to change some of their identifying traits. When people come into frequent contact with others unlike themselves, they can both heighten and put in jeopardy their sense of distinctiveness.[88]

The salience of group-based identities in particular also emerges from social movements organized against group-based oppression or discrimination. In the United States, the civil rights movement of the 1960s became a model; multiracial coalitions organized against race discrimination, but then many African Americans specifically sought all-black organizations to promote racial pride and power.[89] The women's movement, the disability rights movement, and the gay-rights movement followed; members of particular ethnic groups pursued similar approaches and sought specific political and legal reforms to benefit members of their groups. Rather than seeking assimilation to an established American culture, people participating in these movements seek to validate their different cultural practices and to challenge institutions that exclude or degrade people who claim them.[90] In the historical rights movements waged by particular groups, people have discovered common experiences and interests, organized against the imposition of inferiority or outsider status, and reclaimed aspects of the previously degraded traits as valuable sources of pride.[91] In addition, many people cherish religious and ethnic affiliations not, or not only, because they seek to resist past oppression but because they find value in the internal practices and traditions of those affiliations. For them, the group membership is a given, but they may newly choose to use that trait as a public, political face.

This process in the United States has come to be called "identity politics." Yet it, or versions of it, are hardly restricted to the United States.[92] Political and cultural developments around the globe often include mobilization around group-based identities; some are ethnic groups that resurge after the toppling of communist or repressive regimes; others are religious movements. Women's movements within and across countries make gender a crucial category. Some groups organize around expatriate nationalities or nationalities in search of sovereignty or territory.

For many people, identities framed by nation-states claim less allegiance than in the past because of global economic developments and geopolitical changes, with resulting room for other group identities, such as religion and ethnicity.[93] Global corporate entities develop advertisements that appeal to specific group-based identities while also marketing commodified versions of them.[94] Especially in secular cultures, some people feel a loss of meaning and affiliation, and turn to group-based identities in response. And continuing patterns of group-based mistreatment, such as racism, ethnocentrism, homophobia, and sexism, give many people reasons to organize, as group members, in resistance. Identity politics can help people overcome a sense of anonymity and anomie while also giving shape to perceptions of unequal power and recognition.[95] Identity politics also provides a lightning rod for those who think the United States is in serious trouble.

## I. Objections to Identity Politics

The prominence of group identities, and the politics of identity, make some people very worried or angry. Some place the individual at the center of political and moral discussion and worry about any emphasis on groups.[96] Arthur Schlesinger, Jr., for example, warns that the multicultural trends, and a virus of tribalism, threaten national cohesion.[97]

He tries to revive the earlier conception of America as a melting pot, and urges Americans to acknowledge the global attraction of a once vibrant American civic culture, symbolized by the Statue of Liberty. Schlesinger is clear that the dangers stem not only from the self-segregation of minority groups but also from growing inequalities and failures to desegregate from all sides. In this context, Schlesinger argues, sensitivities to group differences should not be so acute as to threaten unity with a Tower of Babel.

> If we now repudiate the quite marvelous inheritance that history bestows on us, we invite the fragmentation of the national community into a quarrelsome spatter of enclaves, ghettos, tribes. The bonds of cohesion in our society are sufficiently fragile that it makes no sense to strain them by encouraging and exalting cultural and linguistic apartheid.[98]

Of course, Schlesinger is not merely pointing to an already defined "inheritance"; he is crafting it, shaping it, redescribing it in the service of the nationalist's cause of unity.

Another influential work in this vein is Jean Bethke Elshtain's *Democracy on Trial*.[99] In addition to concerns about balkanization from identity consciousness, Elshtain attacks the tendency of identity groupings to enable "sweeping and often negative generalizations about groups and the ways all group members supposedly think and believe."[100] (Elshtain would strengthen her argument, if not her political stance, by acknowledging the tendencies of the power elite, white ethnics, and tradition-minded academics to type and stereotype groups other than themselves.) Thus, not only national cohesion but even individual freedom is undermined by identity group thinking.[101] Elshtain could find perhaps surprising evidence for her argument in the constricted public voices of African Americans when President Bush nominated Clarence Thomas for Supreme Court office. Cornel West later noted, "The very fact that no black leader could utter publicly that a black appointee for the Supreme Court was *unqualified* shows how captive they are to white-racist stereotypes about black intellectual talent."[102]

Others warn that the focus on ethnic, racial, and gender identities distracts attention from economic disparities and splinters coalitions that could otherwise work for greater economic justice.[103] Whether motivated by practical concerns about balkanized politics or theoretical interests in individualism, these opponents of identity politics resist group-based thinking from the start.

Many of the claims by opponents of multiculturalism deserve empirical investigation; others reflect different tastes, fears, biographies, or affections that seldom respond to inquiry and argument. But most striking to me is the lack of engagement between these critics of group-based thinking and another group, more sympathetic to identity *politics*, who nonetheless find real difficulties with identity *categories*. In a recent essay reviewing books on gay and lesbian rights, Professor Jane Schacter notes that people who otherwise disagree may share both skepticism about identity categories used in antidiscrimination laws and concerns about the cultural effects of such categories.[104] Admittedly, a skeptic who proceeds with liberalism's focus on the autonomy of each individual would view identity categories as too particular in ways that undermine liberal conceptions of equality, while a skeptic who is influenced by post-modern assaults on the unity of the subject self would treat identity groupings as too crude to capture the complexity and mutability of any one person's identity. Yet some commerce among these criticisms could illuminate the subject. Three objections explode within critical discussions about identity categories; they converge with some of the worries expressed by liberals and traditionalists while raising further difficulties for the use of identity categories.

## A. *Reducing a Person to One Trait, One Viewpoint, and One Stereotype*

The first is the tendency to reduce a complex person to one trait—the trait drawing that person into membership in a particular group—and then to equate that trait with a particular viewpoint and stereotype. Taken together, this process of reduction can be said to "essentialize" the group trait.[105] This tendency leads people to treat a particular trait as the equivalent to a particular viewpoint and set of experiences, even though the trait, such as race or gender, is at best a rough proxy for those views or experiences. To be a lesbian does not mean one hates men, or wants to be one; to be Chicano does not entail being a supporter of bilingual education. Reducing a person to one trait produces stereotypes that are often stigmatizing. Is a woman only concerned with marriage and children? Is a gay man only concerned with sexual activity?[106] Thinking about an individual in terms of one characteristic invites such distortion. Such distortions, in turn, yield harms and mistakes; a woman is denied a promotion, a gay man is refused a position as a teacher based on false assumptions about the particular individuals involved.

Identifying a particular person to represent any group exposes faults of reductionist thinking. Justice Clarence Thomas does not express the viewpoint of many who seek to advance African American interests, nor does Margaret Thatcher embody the standpoint of women advocated by most feminists. People who share a trait, like race or gender, may differ in many other ways. Some have more, some have less power to injure others who share that same trait.[107] The gap between the representative who shares the group trait and the interests and needs of people in the group may lead to painful disputes over authenticity and over the relationship between identity and experience. Those disputes immediately challenge the simplicity of the identity category as a focus for mobilization and representation.

On this point, social theorist Judith Butler has commented:

> The minute that the category of women is invoked as describing the constituency for which feminism speaks, an internal debate invariably begins over what the descriptive content of that term will be . . . In the early 1980s, the feminist "we" rightly came under attack by women of color who claimed that "we" was invariably white, and that the "we" that was meant to solidify the movement was the very source of a painful factionalization. The effort to characterize a feminine specificity through recourse to maternity, whether biological or social, produced a similar factionalization and even a disavowal of feminism altogether. For surely all women are not mothers; some cannot be, some are too young or too old to be, some choose not to be, and for some who are mothers, that is not necessarily the rallying point of their politicization in feminism.[108]

The defect in identity claims signaled by the charge of "essentialism" produces both the mistaken reduction of any individual to one trait and the faulty assumption that any given trait of an individual determines viewpoint, experience, or political interest and commitment. Identity groups do not always, or perhaps even often, inspire political solidarity and action.[109] June Jordan put it this way: "So far as I can see, the usual race and class concepts of connection, or gender assumptions of unity, do not apply very well. I doubt that they ever did. Otherwise why would Black folk forever bemoan our lack of solidarity when the deal turns real. And if unity on the basis of sexual oppression is something natural, then why do we women, the majority of people on the planet, still have a problem?"[110]

Philip Roth explores subtle dimensions of this question in his short story "Defender of the Faith."[111] What does, or should, it mean to be a defender of a religious faith? Does it mean sticking by, or even preferring, co-religionists? Or does it mean adhering to some ideals even to the detriment of a fellow member? In the story, Nathan Marx is assigned to a training camp in Missouri after serving two years in battle in World War II. A trainee named Grossbart approaches him just after Marx's arrival to request help for Jewish soldiers who want to attend religious services on Friday nights but who also do not want the other soldiers to think this is an excuse to avoid the weekly barracks cleaning scheduled for Friday nights. The trainee tries to establish that Marx is also Jewish. Marx at first resists the identification, and then accepts it. He shows no intention to help the Jewish trainees, but in fact he does smooth the way for them by talking with the Captain. Marx then finds himself walking to the Friday night services where he sits in the back row and watches the trainees from his company. He notices that Grossbart is entirely disengaged from the religious ritual.

Grossbart wheedles Marx for more favors, including assistance in obtaining Kosher food and a leave to attend a Passover Seder. In each instance, Marx at first resists, and then grants the favor. He is most moved by the almost forgotten memories of his own childhood and his own family that are evoked by the young Jewish trainees. But in Grossbart's case, the claims of religious need are apparently lies. He returns from the supposed Passover Seder with a Chinese eggroll for Marx, and a story about why the Seder did not work out. When Grossbart then asks Marx to help him avoid combat duty overseas, Marx refuses, only to find that Grossbart was able to pull strings with someone else. Marx then uses his own position to change Grossbart's assignment. He lies to another officer that Grossbart wants to see combat duty, and secures a reassignment to assure that he will.

The story is ambiguous about Marx's motives. Perhaps there is some vindictiveness, some anger about being used by Grossbart, and being claimed as a co-religionist. Perhaps Marx finally seeks to protect the truly religious Jews from the bad reputation of a manipulative, deceitful, and self-interested coward like Grossbart. In that way, Marx accepts and defends his own identity as a Jew. The end of the story suggests both possibilities. Marx watches as the trainees learn of their orders to ship out; he hears Grossbart weep, swallow hard, and try to accept his fate. "And then, resisting with all my will an impulse to turn and seek pardon for my vindictiveness, I accepted my own."[112]

Roth describes his story as "about one man who uses his own religion, and another's uncertain conscience, for selfish ends; but mostly it is about this other man, the narrator, who because of the ambiguities in his particular religion, is involved in a taxing, if mistaken, conflict of loyalties."[113] The character of Marx is also involved in a construction of loyalties; a process of claiming, resisting, and remaking his own identity.

Roth's story demonstrates ways in which people remain interdependent even as they test out new versions of themselves. The story also suggests how an identity is founded on both the views of others and the individual; Marx is treated as a Jew both by his non-Jewish fellow officers and by the Jewish trainees. Both kinds of treatment influence his sense of himself as a Jew. Although he resists both, he defines himself in the course of that resistance. Whatever it means to be a Jew, the meaning is contingent on relationships with other Jews and non-Jews. Being a Jew takes meaning and shape depending on shifting ties and animosities within and between both groups.[114]

"Defender of the Faith" suggests the power that memory and history can wield in the process of defining a person's identity, even as the person retains the ability to affirm or repress that identity.[115] The Jewish trainees are able to appeal to Marx in part because they remind him of his own past that which have remained part of him, although he has put aside all forms of affiliation with Judaism. Marx feels Gross-bart used their shared Jewishness to secure benefits he could not obtain from a non-Jewish officer. Marx's response, making sure that Grossbart is sent along with the other soldiers to combat duty, in one way acknowledges his Jewish identity, defined not as a primitive tribal loyalty, but instead in terms of his own sense of self and his values. Marx, who thought he had the power as a soldier, a war hero, and an officer to abandon his Jewish identity, finds that both the expectations of others and his own history vigorously reassert themselves. He manages nonetheless to retain to some degree his ability to define himself, and to resist a fixed meaning or set of interests.

## B. Neglecting Multiple and Intersectional Memberships

The second, related difficulty is the tendency of identity politics to neglect "intersectionality."[116] This notion refers to the way in which any particular individual stands at the crossroads of multiple groups. All women also have a race; all whites also have a gender. The individuals stand in different places as gender and racial politics converge and diverge. Moreover, the meanings of gender are inflected and informed by race, and the meanings of racial identity are similarly influenced by images of gender.

Black women have confronted male violence and white domination in ways quite different from the experiences of either white women or black men.[117] Black women and black men have different experiences and interests, argues Kimberle Crenshaw. She provides vivid illustrations with black women's responses to the obscenity prosecution of the rap group 2 Live Crew and to the Senate's treatment of Anita Hill's sexual harassment claims during the confirmation hearings of Justice Clarence Thomas.[118] Men who are black may experience racial discrimination while also participating in harassment or discriminatory practices toward women. Women who are white may experience gender discrimination while simultaneously participating in exclusionary practices against nonwhites.[119] A Chinese American woman may object to a notion of culture that subordinates women; a Chinese American man may assert a "cultural defense" when he kills his wife after discovering her infidelity.[120] Neither gender nor racial identity groupings that ignore the intersections between them can fully describe common experiences, standpoints, and relationships with others.[121]

Individuals manifest not only race and gender, but also other bases for potential group membership, such as age, disability, religion, class, and sexual orientation. Political affiliation, music preferences, favored sports and other commitments further bisect and realign groups. The intersections seem to invite new "identity groupings," such as black women, Chicana lesbians, and male bikers. Noting some intersectional identities helps to expose the taken-for-granted presence of other intersectional groups, such as "white men," or "married women."[122] Recognizing intersectionality threatens to complicate identity politics by proliferating new, and old, identity groupings.

The idea of individual membership in multiple, intersecting groups implies a more profound challenge to identity politics. It implies ultimately that each person is alone at the unique crossroad of each intersecting group.[123] Each of us is a unique member of the sets of endless groupings that touch us, whether called racial, gender, disability, family, ethnicity, or nationality. Perhaps for strategic purposes we may choose to affiliate along one or a few lines of group membership, but these lines may shift as our strategies and goals change. Sociologist Mary Waters reports on many Americans who choose an ancestry from among options they find in their past and present; they can experience ethnicity as an option because they can lay claim to more than one type.[124] As Leon Wieseltier has asserted, "The American achievement is not the multicultural society, it is the multicultural individual."[125] Perhaps the very felt experience of multiple affiliations deepens people's desires to belong to one group, if only temporarily.[126] But being female and Asian and third-generation American are all mutually defining characteristics. Multiple traits inflect one another. Negative stereotyping tends to play on images that travel beyond one trait—to attribute poverty to all African Americans, or irresponsible sexuality to poor, nonwhite women.[127]

In a short story called "Blood Relations," Dorothy Bryant writes of the night that Frank took his grandmother to a play.[128] Frank is Italian American, gay, and living with his lover David. Both Frank and David are HIV positive; David has AIDS. So Frank is a gay man facing the prospect of death; he is also, though, his grandmother's only grandson. He knew she would come when he invited her; for once shameless about it, he "could count on her unjust preference" for a male descendant.[129] Picking his grandmother up on the way to the theater, Frank thinks about her life before he knew her: her life before she was widowed; her life tending for two years to a dying husband. As he sits beside her during the play, his thoughts compare their situations. During intermission, he asks, "'Did you ever get mad at my grandfather, I mean, when he was sick?'" He nods with recognition when she answers, without surprise, "'At the end, the last months, when he was leaving me.'"

They watch the second act of the play. It is a musical, *Sunday in the Park with George*, following generations through the puzzle of life. By the end, the baby in the first Act has become an elderly grandmother, singing about "children and art," the only things that matter when you die. Frank does not feel moved; he would never have children nor produce art. But he realizes that children are central to his grandmother; "the force that held them together was, in reality, a huge gap between them."[130] They squeezed hands. Although his sexual orientation is crucial to Frank's identity, so are his gender, his ethnicity, his race, his job, and his status as a grandson and his relationship with his grandmother. He identifies with his grandmother—as a caretaker for a dying loved one. But he also feels the tightness of a bond in which he is the child for his grandmother that he will never have for himself. No one identity category, sexual orientation, gender, ethnicity, class, family status captures his world. Instead, each facet forms the whole. These very differences afford chances for connection with his grandmother: as a male descendant, as a person who will never be a grandparent, as a unique being cherished by his parent's parent.

### C. Problems of Boundaries, Coherence, and Content

Yet, even these complications seem modest compared with the third difficulty. It stems from contemporary challenges to the basic coherence of group definitions. Consider the tensions among self-identification, assignment by self-claimed group members, and assignment by self-claimed group opponents.[131] You say you are a Choctaw, but do the Choctaws say so? The Catholics claim you, but do you claim them? The Apartheid government declared you to be colored, whether you did or not. The gaps and conflicts among self-identification, internal group membership practices, and external, oppressive assignments have given rise to poignant and persistent narratives of personal and political pain and struggle.[132] These gaps and conflicts also expose the inconsistent meanings of group membership. The persistent failure of group-based categories to yield consistent applications hints at the defects in their boundaries, their origins, their applications, and their ultimate meaningfulness.

Coherence is further challenged, though not automatically undermined, by historically shifting boundaries. Confusion about exactly where the border lies does not necessarily jeopardize clear instances, yet frequent border-crossing can render uncertain the distinctions between groups, communities, and identities. A "one-drop rule" defined nonwhiteness for purposes of much of United States history; but some parts of this country, and other countries at times, have instead recognized other degrees of ancestry, or multiple ancestry, or placement in a separate category of biracial or multiracial.[133] Certain groups, once defined as nonwhite, secured the status of whiteness over time.[134] Individuals who "crossover" from one racial identity to another expose the incoherence of the racial categories just as do others who insist on a racial identity that does not match the expectations of others.[135] Some people struggle to claim two cultures, based on complex ancestry and history, but feel alien or rejected in both.[136]

Similar boundary issues arise for the category of gender. Obvious boundary problems are posed by persons who claim to be in the wrongly gendered body and may secure transgender surgery, and others whose embodiment fails to match comfortably the expected bodies of females and males.[137] Women who seek breast amplification or breast reduction surgeries often seek to conform to an image of femininity; the very act of seeking surgery acknowledges the range of actual female bodies, many of which diverge from an image of ideal femininity. Efforts to define the boundaries between sexual orientations are stymied by the claims of bisexuality, claims that threaten the easy distinctions between homosexual and heterosexual.[138] Persons with disabilities controlled by medication or surgery challenge the boundary between ability and disability. So do people who by age and exposures to life's difficulties acquire disabilities gradually or late in life.

The charge of incoherence cuts ever more deeply into the concept of group identities. Ambiguous boundaries around racial, gender, and other identity categories expose their instability. For example, scholars have persistently questioned the coherence of "race" as a concept.[139] In so doing, they criticize any claims to its biological basis.[140] They also locate its precise origins as an historical idea.[141] Richard Ford suggests: "Because race is an unstable identity, its deployment depends on a symbolic connection between the characteristics that code as race but to which race cannot be reduced (skin color, facial features, etc.) and some stable referent."[142] When Ian Haney Lopez examined U. S. judicial opinions interpreting the meaning of "white person" used in the naturalization statute, he found no consistent meaning.[143] Skin color, national origin, facial features, language, public perceptions, social science, and ancestry each became candidates for defining whiteness, but no single factor nor combination of factors could maintain a consistent place in the judicial texts.[144]

Scientists dispute whether biological bases produce differences in the behavior of men and women, and whether genetics explains sexual desire for someone of the same sex.[145] Studies of gender emphasize that differences along a variety of physical and other attributes except reproduction range as broadly within groups of males and females as between those groups.[146] The significance of gender in explaining human differences lies with cultural practices that are subject to change rather than with inherent features of nature.[147] A compatible but somewhat different view stresses gender as a set of performances changing through time rather than a pre-existing nature.[148] Still another conception maintains that social practices, such as legal rules and institutions, layer upon women the image of people who are mothers, who are sexualized, and who are terrorized; these images are mutable and could come to encompass men, too, or might come to be moved away from the gender line altogether.[149] Many people attest to the contingent quality of their identities. Philosopher Akeel Bilgrami, while talking with a Hindu landlord in an Indian community hostile to Muslims, asserted almost to his own surprise his identity as a Muslim.[150] It seemed the only self-respecting response in the circumstances.

A distinguished philosopher notes that the very concepts of similarity or kind reflect more about human mental processes than logic, since sets include things that are not alike as well as alike, and cultural practices instruct people about how to categorize.[151] Scholars of cognitive development herald the human capacity to subsume objects within a general category based on a selected attribute—but also to shift readily from one attribute to another and to move freely among categories.[152] Moreover, people are able to use categories to reach objects by association and practical usage even if they exceed the familiar definition of the categories.[153] Thus, work on the nature of human knowledge seems itself to undermine the stability and naturalness of the kinds of categories used in identity politics. Indeed, some scholars of group identity emphasize fluidity and dynamism, and the processes of becoming, as crucial characteristics.[154]

Many works of fiction explore fluidity of identity. In a collection called *The Middleman and Other Stories*, Bharati Mukherjee includes a piece called "A Wife's Story."[155] It begins with the narrator criticizing, to herself, an ethnic joke in a play by David Mamet.[156] Quickly, the reader learns that the narrator is an Indian woman, at the play with a man from Budapest; reviewing an insulting line in the play about Indian women, the character speculates that perhaps the actors improvise and rotate ethnic insults depending on the day of the week, or whom they happen to spy in the audience on a given night.[157] The narrator thinks of protesting, or walking out, but recalls that after attending expensive girls' schools, "My manners are exquisite, my feelings are delicate, my gestures are refined, my moods undetectable."[158] Thus, from the start Mukherjee's story introduces a strong sense of ethnic identity both as a given and as a basis for the constant risk of ridicule. Yet, the story also suggests the suppression of real identity, desire, and feelings through external training and internal control. The self-conscious narrator knows that her sensitivity to insult is contingent and situational. She sees both sides, that of the old colonizer and that of the new pioneers.[159] "Postcolonialism has made me their referee. It's hate I long for; simple, brutish partisan hate."[160] But a simple and uncomplicated stance is not readily available in this world of shifting and negotiated relationships.[161]

One can feel both committed to the United States as a symbol of freedom and critical of apparently dominant values in the United States; one can feel both defensive of the United States as against critiques from other countries and at the same time experience life in the United States as an outsider, observer, or temporary resident. Simple fury against an opponent becomes unlikely amid such complex identifications, although the result need not be paralysis and quiescence. Instead, an analysis of the layered and competing sources of allegiance and justification can help individuals understand their mixed feelings and also devise principled stances for action.

Mukherjee's story includes many references to assimilation as a goal, a temptation, and an impossibility. The narrator's roommate is an Asian woman who recently had plastic surgery to have "her eyes fixed."[162] Her roommate's uncle once worked for the railways in Szechuan Province and was shot at, once, during the Wuchang Uprising. The narrator notes that when she is lonely for her husband and son, whom she left back in India, she thinks of this uncle. "If I hadn't left home, I'd never have heard of the Wuchang Uprising. I've broadened my horizons."[163] The narrator has traveled half the world to work for a Ph.D. in special education, and she compares herself with her mother, who sought to learn French despite the violent opposition of her own mother-in-law.[164]

The narrator's husband calls to say he is coming from India to visit her. Memories of her long-ago hopes for marriage mingle with her mixed feelings for the man she married by traditional arrangement—the man she still does not call by his first name.[165] She greets him at the airport, and he asks why she is not wearing his mother's ring. She answers that it is not safe in a city with muggers. She does not say that she thinks the ring is "showy, in ghastly taste anywhere but India."[166] She notes her husband's discomfort within a setting where she knows more than he does. He is "used to a different role."[167]

But her husband adjusts to his new role as tourist. He delights in American foods from Perdue chickens to McNuggets. They take a sightseeing tour. He shifts between excitement and disappointment in relation to images of America he had hoped to see. He says his wife, our narrator, should return to India because the men in America are not to be trusted, and he misses her. She refuses.[168] Later, he receives a cable calling him back to India. She prepares to make love with him, and "pretend with him that nothing has changed." But something has.

The narrator's identity has changed. It is not a given. She is different in America from the person she was at home. Her difference gives her a different vantage point on her husband; he is a tourist, she is not. When her husband wants to see Radio City Music Hall, he does not catch the sympathetic wink from her Hungarian friend. The narrator then feels "[g]uilt, shame, loyalty. I long to be ungracious, not ingratiate myself with both men."[169] She is already in a different relationship with her husband. She is both protective in a new way and distant enough from him to receive a private and condescending communication about him from another man. She sees herself as someone trained to comply and to give others, especially men, what they want and expect. Yet, she also has developed desires that resist her training.[170]

She soothes her husband as he complains about things, such as the cost of the sightseeing tour. She thinks, "He is not accusing me of infidelity. I feel dread all the same."[171] In order to believe that he is not accusing her of infidelity, she must first consider the possibility that perhaps her independence amounts to a rejection of him for more ambiguous loyalties. It is thus a coming-of-age story for the married woman immigrant, who leaves home to explore the possibilities for herself.

She experiences herself as someone with a beautiful body, waiting for her husband to come to bed that last night of his visit. She is "shameless, in ways he has never seen me." And she is "free, afloat, watching somebody else."[172] Her very bodily self is different in this different country where she is getting a degree in special education.[173] Her identity is neither constant through time nor fixed across relationships. Her own relationship with herself can and does change.

Crossing geographic, national, and social boundaries can give a character such as Mukherjee's protagonist occasions to shift her sense of self, and to change and multiply the meanings of her pre-existing identities, such as wife and Indian. A politics of identity risks treating such traits as "tightly scripted" and forcing individuals into particular roles, associated with particular viewpoints.[174] Critiques highlight the difficulties with coherence and boundaries, intersections, and reductionism of talk and political action focused on group identities. Yet, comparable difficulties arise from pretending that anyone can invent any self; the materials found, the world always already present, and the particular marks of power and oppression sharply restrict the available possibilities.

## II. But What About Power and Oppression?

Words like fluid and change, hybrid and multiple dot the fiction and essays by sympathetic yet critical observers of identity categorization.[175] The criticisms may even seem to add up to doubts about the reality of group-based identities. Yet even critics who emphasize that groups exist through labeling or language games also stress the real force and power that some people have, labeling their world with categories that enable them to regulate or dominate others while benefiting themselves.[176]

What else could explain a regime that, in historian Barbara Fields' words, "considers a white woman capable of giving birth to a black child but denies that a black woman can give birth to a white child"?[177] As another historian, David Hollinger, puts it in his recent book, *Post-Ethnic America,* "Racism is real, but races are not."[178] Demonstrated, historic power, held by some, to create groups and to oppress them is undeniable, but the rationales for those groups or for the assignment of members remain vulnerable to challenge.

Benedict Anderson's book, *Imagined Communities,* traces the creation of nations as official efforts by dynastic regimes to control workers and peasants; in the process, colonial powers created census categories that in turn stamped racial categories to replace previous religious, status, and anonymous identities.[179] Thomas Scheff argues that these cognitive maps of difference join with emotions of pride and shame to fuel prejudice and oppression.[180] Studies of stereotyping add that these maps can be passed on to children at an early age, before they are able to assess the validity or meaning of such attitudes. These attitudes become part of our regular methods for sorting the world.[181]

Thus, group-based differences need have no foundation in biology, or anything but historic oppressions, to make them real enough to warrant recognition and mobilization.[182] We do not need refined understandings of identities to acknowledge how much people in power have hurt others in producing the harsh reality of identities. The Nazis resolved the question of who is a Jew in the most definitive way.[183] "Black means being identified by a white racist society as black."[184]

Catharine MacKinnon locates gender difference not in biology but historic oppression when she asks "can you imagine elevating one half of a population and denigrating the other half and producing a population in which everyone is the same?"[185] Judith Butler argues that the meaning of anyone's gender is troubled and unfixed except by exercises of convention and authority.[186] Marilyn Frye and Peggy MacIntosh, among others, have detailed the ways in which part of the comforts enjoyed by those with more power is the distance from other people's pain and the seeming invisibility of their own privileges.[187]

Regardless of the theoretical arguments against essentialism and for intersectionality, many people believe and perceive that their identities are bound up with experiences of subordination along simplistic group lines.[188] Experiences of mistreatment along group lines influence how individuals view people from their own groups, and people in other groups. Empirical studies of individuals' self-understandings highlight the impact of societal views about groups, and the persisting effects of discrimination by more powerful groups.[189] Todd Gitlin's book, which is chiefly an attack—from the progressive left—on identity politics as a distraction from deeper issues of poverty and economic dislocation, nonetheless asserts confidently that "Blacks are more likely than whites to doubt the promise of America; women more likely than men to care about children and fear rape; Jews more likely than Buddhists to study the Holocaust."[190] The racial divide in public responses to the verdict in the murder trial of O.J. Simpson is only one recent confirmation of this perception.[191]

It is tempting, indeed, to wonder about the strange confluence of events that would lead to academic theorizing, hostile to notions of identity, just as identity groups with histories of oppression flex political and intellectual muscles in the culture. Reclaiming often despised traits of identity as sources of strength, memory, and insight, members of racial and ethnic minorities, women, persons with disabilities, and people asserting themselves as gay or lesbian could understandably react with fury or else risk a sense of sanity when apparently sympathetic academics respond that identities are fluid, uncertain, and unstable. It reminds me of the double bind constructed by a Zen master who told the student, "If you say this stick is real, I will hit you with it; if you say the stick is not real, I will hit you with it; and if you say nothing, I'll hit you with it."[192] The Zen pupil gains enlightenment by seeing yet another alternative—grabbing the stick. If this metaphor bears on the debate over the "reality" of identities, then perhaps participants in identity politics are right to grab hold of identities, through action; or perhaps, there are still other alternatives, not framed by the debate as usually structured.

One alternative starts with noting how group-based descriptions are approximate or probabilistic, not absolute and consistent. Students of power and oppression acknowledge—and want to celebrate—latitude for individual variation, resistance, change, and self-invention. Thinking in terms of group-based identities, forged through relationships of unequal power, does not illuminate these possibilities for individual freedom, yet historians and fiction writers testify to such possibilities.[193]

People vested with little or no power may nonetheless exercise some control over their identities. Even without total freedom to frame the options (a purely mythical possibility), individuals navigate among existing constraints, making choices about who and how to be.[194] Individuals often craft images for others to believe in while preserving a different inner self. Sherley Ann Williams introduces her story, "Meditations on History," with this comment about herself during the time she wrote it: "I sought during this time to conform, only to discover that even my attempts at conformity set me apart."[195] Paradox offers insights into experiences of belonging and exclusion.

In "Meditations on History,"[196] a white male writer in 1829 interviews a black female slave whom he describes as "a wild and timorous animal finally brought to bay."[197] The woman was involved in a slave uprising, but her execution is postponed so that her pregnancy can reach full term—and her child can become the possession of the master. She refuses to speak to the writer who is researching the facts of the uprising and the ensuing trial. It is through his eyes that we see her, or who he thinks she is. He describes her as an animal and as someone casting spells.[198] He notes that she moans and sings in ways he does not understand. Even when she responds to his questions, she remains incomprehensible to him.[199]

The writer is impatient with the slave woman's refusal, or inability, to answer his questions about the motivations behind the slave revolt.

That event led to the execution of nineteen people and punishment of ten others. To his great irritation, she does not look him in the eye, and she hums "an absurd, monotonous little tune in a minor key" over and over.[200] She tells of acts of resistance by the African slaves toward their masters. She is curious about his writing, and asks why he is recording what she says. He assumes she is set at ease when he responds that his book will be written "in the hope of helping others to be happy in the life that has been sent them to live."[201] But after talking a while, she asks if he really thinks that what she says will help people be happy in the life they are sent, and if so, then "'Why I not be happy when I live it? I don't wann talk no more.'"[202]

They meet again on Sunday. The writer asks her to stop humming while he reads from the Bible. She says the song is about righteousness and heaven; he asks her to sing it and she does, which pleases him. The next day he resumes questioning her. She responds initially, but returns to humming. He realizes she is capable of smiling and joking and even sees that she is pretty, but he still thinks her unintelligent and like an animal.

The writer's attention quickly shifts when a posse is formed to locate a settlement of escaped slaves. As he joins the posse, the writer hears the slave woman singing again. Before he departs, he chats with her, thinking he will yet discover the origins of the slave insurrection. She still offers no help, however, which angers him. The woman resumes her song, and he leaves with the posse. When he returns she has escaped with the help of three black men who participated in the uprising. No trace of her can be found.

Mary Helen Washington comments that in the story the white man conceives of the slave woman as "foreign, different, inferior, non-white, and non-male."[203] She continues, "We finish the story, however, convinced of her power, not his. She learns enough about his psychology to engineer his defeat."[204] She tricks him into thinking she is incompetent and crazy, when in fact she has been planning to escape and, through her songs, communicating the plan to her friends. She fashions an identity that plays into his prejudices in order to purchase time and space to secure her freedom. Williams imagines this brave, smart slave woman as a means to craft a new history and a renewed African American identity. Renaming and reclaiming experiences of resistance, Williams recasts images of contemporary black women in light of a reconstructed past.[205]

Williams suggests that people who lack power can nonetheless find space for free action by constructing identities that fulfill the expectations of others and thus distract them. She explores how people with little power may also find latitude for action by creating expectations in others or by remaking their own desires in line with the expectations of others.[206] Unlike the identity politics maneuver, in which people transform negative stereotypes into causes for celebration and pride, Washington's character uses the negative stereotypes to disadvantage those who hold them. Through this technique, people with the advantages of power may nonetheless find their purposes defeated, and their identities challenged and changed by the actions of those in their employ or below their social station.

This story about the nearly total oppression of slavery nonetheless highlights the degrees of freedom wrested by a slave woman in the very process of playing into a degrading stereotype. Power may seem total, yet resistance is possible. Some play in the joints might be found even under tightly controlled repressive regimes; resistance to assigned identities may be subtle or massively rebellious.[207] If some of the room for resistance and self-definition comes from playing into oppressive expectations, other space comes from defying or defeating such expectations. Room for resistance and self-definition can come from demonstrating how you cannot be reduced to a stereotype or to the essential elements presumed to accompany a particular trait, or how your intersectional membership in more than one group alters your horizon, or how you defy easy categorization or disrupt the coherence of the categories. In short, the precise defects in identity categories may afford latitude for freedom and resistance.

What if we understood identity as not a thing but a process, a process of negotiation? Proponents of identity categories and most critics of them provide little help in understanding the interaction, between people in specific historical settings, which shapes identities.[208] Yet, every person lives and operates within degrees of freedom and constraint. Yes, people who have relatively more power or enjoy its privileges can place others in oppressive conditions and even seem to define the identities of those so placed. Yet, the powerless people have more control than observers may think, because they have power to shape their identities, and to take advantage of the space between their assigned identities and their own aspirations and alternate conceptions for themselves.[209] People with apparently greater power in these areas nonetheless encounter sharp limits because of the presence and influence of others, even those who have less status and authority. Through an ongoing process of negotiation, identities, even group identities, constantly change.[210]

Flannery O'Connor's story "The Displaced Person"[211] explores what happens when the white widow of a prominent judge hires refugees from Poland to work on her farm; she faces realignments in her relations with her existing Negro and white employees. At first delighted with the efficient and hard-working refugees, the widow plans to discharge her prior white employees, who catch wind of the plan and bolt from the farm. Then the widow learns that one of the refugees plans to arrange a marriage between his cousin and one of the Negro employees. Offended by this violation of her racial code, the widow decides she cannot keep the refugee workers and wants her prior white workers back. One does return. Yet the widow postpones the actual discharge of the refugee who planned to marry a Negro, apparently because the refugee had been such a productive worker. Then, suddenly, the widow witnesses a tractor accident, killing the refugee. Her eyes freeze in collusion with the other employees who passively watch, and most probably caused, the accident. Shocked and confused, the widow feels herself like a foreigner or stranger. One by one, the other employees leave, and the widow sells the farm. Each person on the farm—including the owner-mistress—is displaced by the anxieties, hopes, and fears of the others.

In this story, and so often in life, shifts in identity seem accidental. Yet, individuals can also make concerted efforts to act or to make claims in ways that defy assigned status or position. Noting where there are restrictions, where there is room for movement, including room permitted by restrictions themselves—these are the conscious and unconscious activities of forging identity, giving voice to self-expression, making claims on others, and making a life.

People negotiate over time between one another and in specific contexts. When Harriet Jacobs published *Incidents in the Life of a Slave*

*Girl, Written by Herself* in 1861, she addressed Northern whites, especially white women, to appeal to their compassion but also to try to alert her audience to their own possible misunderstandings. She tried to teach them about the moral agency as well as victimization of slaves, and to encourage them to respond to slavery with outrage, and not just with compassion.[212] In so doing, she contributed to the cause of abolition but she also helped to invent her own identity as a free woman.

To view identities as negotiated—held through communication, managed, arranged in conference[213]—is to borrow from theories about how we make meaning. For example, this book can be understood as an exchange of meaning between author and reader.[214] We notice the inevitable mutability of meaning. You may not get what I meant; you may supply meaning I had not anticipated but would find persuasive, or irritating. Readers thus are crucial to the meanings of texts; and authors do not retain exclusive or even major control over those meanings. Yet readers do engage with something set forth, already, by authors, just as authors encounter something already there in readers.

This flow of possibilities does not occur, however, just between two people, whether author and reader, or two people sharing a bus ride or a college classroom or a court hearing, but instead it is nested within patterns of social, political, economic, and cultural practices through which people relate. These patterns create constraints against which individuals may push, but each person is situated differently, by birth and experience, in relation to constraints. Identities are not stable, fixed, innate, essential, singular, or clearly bounded. Neither are they entirely mutable at the wishes of anyone. The weight of one's own experiences and social positions, and the press of others' expectations and practices, stack all struggles over identities.[215]

Over time, some of the seemingly fixed points do move. Slavery did end in the United States; some forms of racism have moderated and other's have developed. Assumptions about what women can do and be have changed, as have views about at least some kinds of disabilities. Of course these alterations have not just "happened"; they reflect complex cultural and social responses to social movements, wars, economic shifts, academic research, and "exceptions" that challenged prior, established views. No small part was played by the mobilizations against group-based harms that inspire identity politics. Even the seemingly fixed points, the givens of social relationships, can be changed through struggle.

## III. How Not to Become the Thing You Hate

*Mona in the Promised Land,* Gish Jen's recent novel about a Chinese American teen growing up in the 1970s in a New York suburb, wrestles with what seems given and what seems mutable in group identities.[216] Mona tries to learn from her Jewish classmates how to be a minority member in America. In the process, she decides to be Jewish, which means not only a religious conversion but also an embrace of social justice ideals and a commitment to action. Her parents find these developments appalling, especially because they lead Mona to reject the role of obedient daughter.[217] Mona also befriends an African American employee in her parents' pancake restaurant, and meets his friends, including one who warns that "'Separatism is just a mimicking of Jim Crow.'" He quotes Gandhi: "'One becomes the thing he hates.'"[218]

How can resistance to oppression avoid mimicking oppression? How can people seek equality and justice without becoming what they hate? Reclaiming a stigmatized identity as something of value can be one way to resist oppression. Reclaiming a stigmatized identity can also stabilize symbols of the stigma and the conceptions it unleashes. Resisting officials and those with private power who exclude and degrade people along group lines can move the seemingly fixed points of degradation, but doing so in the name of some new, exclusive group can create a new version of an old problem. Mobilizing African American males, as, for example, in the Million Man March, can stimulate pride, therapeutic connection, and energy for responsible action, but that very strategy risks splintering men and women who could be working together.[219]

Privilege and oppression together can mark a person's experience, even simultaneously. Simply validating an experience of oppression affords no guarantee of ending a person's own role in dominating others. Research suggests that some African American males develop an exaggerated conception of male power and devalue females, apparently as a coping response to racial and economic disadvantage.[220] Here is a place where the errors of essentialism, the insights of intersectionality, and the basic incoherence of group identities run up against the ease of adopting categories that were never designed to help those assigned to them.

As one observer recently put it, "This politics of being, essentializing or fixing who we are, is in actuality often an inversion or continuation of ascribed colonial identities, though stated as 'difference.' The stereotypical contents of Africanness or Indianness, for example, are in the end colonial constructs, harbouring the colonizer's gaze. We look at ourselves with his eyes and find ourselves both adorned and wanting."[221] The internalized sense of inferiority and the assumption that human relationships must be marked by hierarchy and domination are legacies of oppression. A piece of the oppressor, then, lies within each person, as Franz Fanon, Albert Memmi, George W. Hegel, and many others observe.[222] Paulo Freire has argued that the true focus of revolutionary change is never merely the oppressive situation, but also the piece of the oppressor, which is implanted within each person, and which knows only the oppressor's tactics and relationships.[223] This insight undergirds Jacques Ranciere's observation that emancipation is never the simple assertion of an identity; it is always, at the same time, the denial of an identity given by the ruling order.[224] The identity itself does not have to be framed by pain and damage, but disentangling it from the oppressors' way of thinking is difficult, if not impossible. For even though the category, and the people in it, are not the problem, the process of categorization and degradation by category, reasserting strength and value while retaining the category, risks invigorating the oppressors' own framework.

Besides strengthening the categories and methods of oppression, identity politics may freeze people in pain and also fuel their dependence on their own victim status as a source of meaning. Wendy Brown has written powerfully about these dangers. She argues that identity-based claims reenact subordination along the same lines as historical subjugation.[225] This danger arises, in her view, because of the ready acceptance of those very lines of distinction and oppression in a society that has used them. People become invested in their pain and suffering, or in her terms, their "wounded attachments."[226] She writes:

> Politicized identity, premised on exclusion and fueled by
> the humiliation and suffering imposed by its historically

structured impotence in the context of a discourse of sovereign individuals, is as likely to seek generalized political paralysis, to feast on generalized political impotence, as it is to seek its own collective liberation through empowerment. Indeed, it is more likely to punish and reproach . . . than to find venues of self-affirming action.[227]

Brown calls for shaping a democratic political culture that would actually hear the stories of victimization while inviting victims to triumph over their experiences through political action.[228] Toward this end, she proposes shifting the focus from identity toward a focus on desires and wants, from the language of "I am" to the language of "I want."[229] In this way, politics could move beyond artificially fixed and frozen identity positions and blame-games toward expressive and engaged political action. Beyond this instructive suggestion, I think that political discussions should invite each person to move from the "I" to the "we," even while putting up for debate how wide will be the "we." To shift from a focus on what we lack (or need) to attend instead to what we want is to engage with purposes, visions, causes, connecting across individual's felt wants. The aim, and the method, is collective action, not just individual claiming.

Therapeutic understandings of trauma and recovery support this call to shift from what an individual lacks to what an individual, with others, can envision and seek. Judith Herman's work on child abuse, incest, rape, and wartime trauma emphasizes the crucial importance to individual psychological health of recovering memories and learning to speak about atrocity.[230] She also stresses the significance of moving through stages of mourning, taking action and fighting back, and reconnecting with others.[231] Identity politics, at least the contemporary kind that emphasizes victimization experiences, risks directing all energy and time to pain without moving through recovery, action, and reconnection with larger communities. When identity politics takes the form of using excuses based on past victimization, it may actually make it difficult for others to remember and acknowledge past wrongdoings and harms.[232] Invoking racial, gender, sexual, or other identities does not automatically develop a rich sense of who you are; nor does it do much to explain your life circumstances.[233]

Philosopher Kwame Anthony Appiah writes,

> Demanding respect for people as blacks and as gays
> requires that there are some scripts that go with being an
> African-American or having same-sex desires. There will be
> proper ways of being black and gay, there will be expecta-
> tions to be met, demands will be made. It is at this point that
> someone who takes autonomy seriously will ask whether we
> have not replaced one kind of tyranny with another.[234]

Identity politics tends to locate the problem in the identity group
rather than the social relations that produce identity groupings.[235]
Personal testimony about oppression risks replacing analysis of social
structures that produce and maintain it.[236] Personal testimony is crucial to articulating and maintaining memories, but incapable of providing either analysis of the past or constructive programs for the
future. Cornel West observes: "we confine discussions about race in
America to the 'problems' black people pose for whites rather than
consider what this way of viewing black people reveals about us as a
nation."[237] Serious discussion of race in America, he argues, "must
begin not with the problems of black people but with the flaws in
American society—flaws rooted in historic inequalities and long-
standing cultural stereotypes."[238]

Identity politics is likely to reinforce white people's conception of
blacks as "them" rather than bringing home people's mutual dependence and relationships.[239] Identity politics tends to produce not only
defensiveness among white men, but also makes it easier for white
men to abandon and even blame people of color and women of all
sorts for their circumstances. More basically, identity politics seems to
breed more identity politics.[240]

Judith Butler put the limitations of identity politics bluntly: "You
can articulate your identity all you want; you need the damn resources
in order to respond to the concrete problems of bodies in pain."[241] To
get the resources, you need to work with others; to care about other
bodies in pain, you need to move beyond your own circumstances.
Racial patterns of inequality persist and expand.[242] Yet, there remain
twice as many whites as blacks below the poverty line.[243] Something

more than identity politics is needed to get a grip on these developments and to engage in resistance to them.[244] A politics not of identities but of envisioned alternatives could bridge identity cleavages without demanding that people dissolve their differences in a pot of assimilation that does not absorb all.

I do not want to understate the positive aspects of identity politics:
valuable conceptions and occasions for being for oneself and forging
solidarity with others based on a perception of a shared trait; important challenges to exclusionary practices; and effective questions
about exclusionary practices that claim to be inclusive, such as color-
blind policies that nonetheless produce virtually all-white beneficiaries. Identity politics also disturbs the repression of historic and
continuing group-based injuries. Yet, ironically, identity politics
responds to group-based exclusions by reiterating the very same
group boundaries. The problem is not only that responses to oppression reiterate the oppressive strategy of treating identity as fixed. The
potentially multiple, fluid qualities of any person's identity seem to
evaporate in the assertion of a single trait. Considerable power must
be marshalled to accomplish this disappearing act, given the complexity of anyone's identity. And this magical result does not, at the
same time, produce purposes or causes that effectively mobilize people against oppression.

Identity politics exhibits, but does not begin to resolve, a series of
dilemmas.[245] To resist group-based harms, to move the seemingly
fixed points of power, and to permit individual self-definition, people
could mobilize and struggle, reclaim aspects of their identities that
others despise, and discover the power of memory and resistance. To
do so along group-based lines, however, may refuel prejudices and
force individuals to subordinate their own multiplicity. People need a
sense of history and memory of oppression, but dwelling on historic
harm saps energy for new living. Individuals can resist confinement by
embracing or playing into negative stereotypes, but they thereby risk
reinvigorating them. People can invent new lives, but they cannot
erase their prior experiences. Mona, the fictional Chinese-American
teen, wants her parents to get over the Chinese revolution and live
with less cautiousness, "but in another way she understands it's like
asking the Jews to get over the Holocaust, or like asking the blacks to

get over slavery. Once you've lost your house and your family and your country, your devil-may-care is pretty much gone too."[246]

Instead of debating whether identity politics is threatening American unity, or diverting us from other important issues, or freezing otherwise fluid and free-floating identities, I wonder whether we can proceed freshly with these as working (though refutable) hypotheses: the materials for negotiating identity can be more than the legacies of mistreatment; people of all backgrounds can find room in the joints for freedom and dignity—or else move, through collective political action, the seemingly fixed barriers; and even diverse and divided people can come to understand that we each are mutable but not completely, even though generation after generation forgets this. Law contributes substantially to all these matters, as the next chapter explores.

# CHAPTER 3
## *Laws*

<>

Law plays a substantial role in making identities seem fixed, innate, and clearly bounded.[247] American legal treatments of race, family status, and Indian tribal identity provide illustrations. In these areas, legal institutions have sometimes tried to make their own decisions seem natural, inevitable, or indisputable. Yet it is quite possible to demonstrate the human choices and contests surrounding legal decisions about identities.[248] Legal methods more candid on these scores offer their own promise, and difficulties.

### I. RACE BY LAW[249]

From the first, the U. S. Congress decreed that only "white persons" could become U. S. citizens through the "naturalization" process.[250] The term survived all other changes in the law until 1952.[251] In an important recent book, Professor Ian Haney Lopez has analyzed the relatively few but nonetheless significant judicial treatments of "white persons" that responded to claims by applicants rejected for naturalization. The meaning of "white" was disputed, and changed over time in these judicial opinions. The courts rejected applicants from Burma, China, Hawaii, Japan, and the Philippines; some courts rejected while others accepted as "white" petitioners from Syria, India, and Arabia.[252]

The legal justifications varied and shifted. Some courts sought scientific evidence, others relied on dictionary definitions, or "common sense" perceptions of physical appearance; still others turned to what "the average well-informed white American" would know to be "white."[253] In one case, the Supreme Court was especially attentive to how unclear and manipulable each of these sources could be. The district court had approved the citizenship application of Bhagat Singh Thind, who was born in India and graduated from Punjab University. The Supreme Court had already ruled that "Caucasian" meant "white," in a decision rejecting an applicant from Japan.[254] Thind argued that he was Caucasian, according to anthropological categorization, and that he had already served six months in the U.S. Army, and should be benefited by a congressional decision to extend citizenship to veterans who served three years.

The Court agreed that Thind was Caucasian, but stressed the "average man" knows the difference between "the blonde Scandinavian and the brown Hindu."[255] Anthropologists, biologists, and other scientists had failed to devise definitions of race that would be both clear and compatible with the assumptions or prejudices of ordinary American white people. Rejecting any claim of science to define who is "white," the Court also abandoned "Caucasian," or facility in English, or any test beyond the views of the average person. In the wake of the decision rejecting Thind's application, the federal government stripped at least sixty-five other Asian Indians of citizenship granted by lower courts.[256]

This history illustrates not only the uncertainty and mutability of the racial category, but also the law's apparent need for clear, bounded categories. In the midst of defining who was "white," and thus eligible for citizenship, the courts treated the question as one of discovery rather than invention. Haney Lopez concludes that legal rules actually help to create and then maintain racial differences.[257] Judges treated race as something real that can be discovered; they made it difficult to imagine people without a race. Across time and place, they accepted the link between race and belonging. And they elevated popular racial beliefs over any other classification rationale.[258]

When lawyers and judges neglect the dynamic negotiations over questions of identity, and treat identity as simply something that exists innately, and ready for discovery, they risk producing not only unfortunate results but also unconvincing reasons. If lawyers and judges treat identity as something discoverable rather than forged or invented, they hide the latitude for choice and the ongoing struggle over identity. At the same time, they exercise their own power to make those choices. The use of a specific notion of identity to resolve a legal dispute can obscure the complexity of lived experiences while imposing the force of the state behind the selected notion of identity.

One person committed suicide after the government took away his citizenship in the wake of the decision in *Thind*.[259] He wrote in his suicide note, "What have I made of myself and my children? We cannot exercise our rights, we cannot leave this country. Humility and insults, who are responsible for all of this?"[260] As this painful plea makes clear, official decisions about identity can have enormous, and potentially devastating, consequences. The courts enforced and monitored the link between race and citizenship—and thus between race and equality—with no regard for the actions, expectations, or self-understandings of individuals.

Law has fixed racial identities in other contexts, and helped to maintain privileges for those defined as "white." The "one-drop rule" used in many state statutes defined any person with any known African ancestry as Negro.[261] Under slavery, any child of a female slave was a slave. As of 1996, the U.S. Census requires the assignment of individuals to one race, even if their parents are of different races.[262] With the rates of interracial marriages doubling between 1960 and 1970, and tripling from 1970 to 1980, the numbers of people affected by this rule is growing rapidly.[263] Alternating between ruling that a child should take the race of the mother and that a child should take the race of the father, Census officials are under pressure from some quarters to add the category of "multiracial."[264] Others worry that such a category would dilute the electoral power of long-recognized racial minorities and also obstruct enforcement of civil rights laws.[265] Meantime, more people eligible for the "multiracial category" may be claiming the category "white" despite Asian and Hispanic ancestry.[266]

Claiming to be "white" is one way of negotiating around the seemingly fixed racial hierarchy in the United States. Noel Ignatiev argues in his book, *How the Irish Became White*,[267] that Irish Catholic immigrants to the United States in the nineteenth century came from a world that assigned them to the lowest caste, and encountered a world in the United States offering them pitiful wages and onerous working conditions.[268] Popular culture and sayings in the nineteenth century connected the Irish with Negroes; in one quip, a Negro is reputed to say, "He treats me as badly as if I was a *common Irishman.*"[269] In another from 1881, an Oxford University professor told an American audience, "The best remedy for whatever is amiss in America would be if every Irishman should kill a [N]egro and be hanged for it."[270]

Ignatiev traces the growing efforts by Irish immigrants to affiliate with political parties and labor groups to distance themselves from Negroes and to side with white supremacy.[271] "To learn to become white they had to learn to subordinate county, religious, or national animosities, not to mention any natural sympathies they may have felt for their fellow creatures, to a new solidarity based on color—a bond which, it must be remembered, was contradicted by their experience in Ireland."[272]

A different kind of negotiation and struggle could target the idea of racial classification itself, or the uses to which it is put. Because many uses of racial categories now involve enforcement of remedial civil rights laws, those categories are defended by civil rights advocates. For them, maintaining the categories is crucial to ensuring enforcement of laws against discrimination on the basis of race in employment, voting, housing, and schooling—and implementation of affirmative action and desegregation programs. White supremacy, in this view, should be attacked by exposing its continuation, claiming the merits of members of previously degraded groups, and ensuring integration and distribution of benefits and opportunities with full participation of members of all races in mind. From this perspective, racial classifications should be defended explicitly in pragmatic terms, and tested accordingly: are they benefiting those who had been disadvantaged in the past? Identities, some suggest, can be invoked provisionally, for strategic purposes.[273] Yet, the use of legal categories and governmental power tends to imply a reality or truth about racial categories that stretches beyond such remedial and political purposes.[274] The categories, once used in law and government, take on lives of their own, despite the provisional context of their deployment.

Even more promising are efforts to generate a public and legal discourse about the constructed, social features of group-based identities. The most important federal civil rights law addressing disabilities includes as one of its three definitions of an individual's disability "being regarded as having" a physical or mental impairment that substantially limits one or more of the individual's life activities.[275] Under the statute, individuals may seek protections against discrimination in employment, public accommodations, or other contexts covered by the law, when those individuals have a virus like HIV or hepatitis, even without symptoms or prior drug use.[276] This means part of the inquiry into who deserves protections involves an investigation of the prejudices of other people. It also means that the claimant need not always assert an immutable or coherent, bounded trait, even while exposing others' beliefs precisely in those conceptions of disability.

Taking a related tack, Professor Janet E. Halley argues against claims of immutability in civil rights efforts for gays and lesbians.[277] She thus warns against the temptation for law reformers to use recent scientific reports claiming to show a biological basis for same-sex sexual preferences. Not only are those studies flawed, she indicates, but also the argument that sexual preference is biologically based itself divides supporters of gay rights. It excludes bisexuals, for example. Moreover, it does not necessarily help gays because many people, including judges, that restrict rights of gays also think homosexuality is immutable—and sick or bad. Thus, gay rights claims can lose both under claims that sexual preference is innate and claims that it is not. Halley argues for an alternative to both claims.[278] "In most cases, the focus should fall not on the nature of the people discriminated against, but on the *idea* of them formed in the policies and programs that disadvantage them, and on the implicit premise of all anti-gay legal policy, that the state should serve as a facility for constructing those ideas into social reality."[279] This is a way of urging attention to the arrangement of power and disadvantage at stake rather than an inquiry into the allegedly immutable nature of some people injured by that arrangement of power and disadvantage. Perception and mistreatment are and should be the focus of attention, not the naturalness of the categories.

Legal protections for people "regarded as disabled" or for people harmed by stereotypic ideas about homosexuality do not solidify or freeze the categories of disability or homosexuality. They focus instead on the legal inquiry about the social processes that exclude or degrade some people. Would this approach be effective in dealing with questions of gender, race, ethnicity, a combination of gender and race, or other variants of identities used in civil rights struggles? This is not clear. Yet this approach is worth a try. Its very presence in the array of civil rights strategies calls attention to the social and cultural dynamics of oppression rather than forcing people into fixed categories of victimhood. Pressing this approach could be one way out of the dilemma posed by asserting group status to rectify group-based mistreatment.[280]

In contrast, when governmental power is mobilized to invest group categories with significance and to assign individuals to those categories, the use of identity groupings can injure at the same time as it can help. Governments enjoy a monopoly on lawful violence. Holding this most basic power, governmental authorities can work with the more subtle devices of words and texts.[281] Governmental force can convert personal and political preoccupations with group identity into an appearance of natural and immutable fact. Reinforced by consumer marketing strategies that produce and sell identities,[282] legal institutions tend to prefer simple, mechanical notions, despite more complex lived experiences. When institutions, like courts and agencies, do our thinking for us, it is easy to forget the human authors of entrenched categories.[283] Legal uses of identity categories make it easy to forget how fluid and contestable identities can be, and also, perhaps paradoxically, how often identities are not changeable at the will or whim of an individual.

## II. Family by Law[284]

Some legal contests over identity seem amenable to scientific or empirical answers. Who is this woman's husband? Who is the owner of this property? Who is the father of that child? Yet, even these questions often yield genuine debate. Such contests reflect the complex, negotiated practices and power relationships within which even simple matters of identity take hold. Judicial practice often seeks to suppress such complexity and to hide this suppression.

Societal rules, a woman's desires, and a man's own efforts to take on the identity of another, can create a setting for enormous disagreement over who is a husband, as Natalie Zemon Davis explored in her historical study, *The Return of Martin Guerre*.[285] Even after the advent of

Social Security cards, fingerprints, and other techniques of identification, disputes over identity quickly become complicated when an individual takes on more than one identity, with relationships to different people who will vouch for him or her.[286] So basic a legal question as who is the owner of property can be deeply contested not only by people claiming the same ownership rights, but also by people in relationships of reliance or mutuality.[287]

Much litigation swirls around the question: who is the father of a particular child? Often pursued for child support and sometimes propelled by the man's own desire for affiliation, paternity actions are familiar in any family or probate court. Public assistance laws routinely require a mother to name the father of any child considered for aid; the mother must also name a father to seek private child support outside the welfare system. If the man who is named contests the identification, courts use blood and genetic typing to establish paternity of a child. But the question of who is a child's "father" is not always, or only, a biological one.[288] Cultural practices surrounding marriage and parenthood, the man's own acceptance of or resistance toward the parental role, the child's perceptions and feelings—each, or all, may be crucial.[289] Proponents of psychological notions about the bonds between parents and children have introduced a concept of "psychological parenthood," which looks to the child's own perceptions and feelings about who is the parent.[290] Translating this psychological understanding into a tool that courts can administer can wrench subtle understandings into a crude tool. Courts look for *one* psychological parent when the child may be attached to more than one.

Legal rules are often designed to close off discussion—to cut off some inquiries based on the view that certainty may be more important than truth or even more important than fairness. For example, legal presumptions, especially those that are irrebuttable,[291] work by a legal rule that states that proof of $x$ shall be deemed to be proof of $y$. If the presumption is irrebuttable, no amount of contrary evidence about not-$y$ can make a difference to the legal conclusion.[292] An irrebuttable presumption that a girl under the age of eighteen cannot give meaningful consent to sexual intercourse requires only evidence of her age to conclude the question of consent in the context of a rape prosecution.

Questions of identity—for legal purposes—have often historically been handled through an irrebuttable presumption. For example, many states have a rule that a child born to a married woman who lives with her husband is presumed to be the child of the husband.[293] Such a rule may reflect a goal of eliminating uncertainty about the parentage of children born to married people. It also may aim to reduce the chances that husbands may refuse to accept paternity, including support obligations, when their wives have children. It may also stem from a time when paternity was difficult to establish and when illegitimacy stigmatized children and deprived them of inheritance rights.[294] Each set of goals could be reexamined in light of changing cultural and technological developments affecting parentage. For example, advances in the technology of blood tests to establish paternity could render obsolete the premise that the presumption solves an otherwise protracted question.[295] A conclusive presumption forecloses any such reconsideration.[296]

The Supreme Court faced a challenge to a presumption of legitimacy in *Michael H. v. Gerald D.*[297] There, Carole gave birth to Victoria while married to Gerald; Carole told Michael she thought he was the father and blood tests showed a 98.07 percent probability of that fact, which Carole never contested. Carole separated from her husband and spent time with Michael. Michael treated the child as his own during some periods; during some spans of time they lived together as a family. Carole ultimately returned to Gerald, and Michael sought visitation rights. Based on the arguments of an attorney and guardian appointed by the court to protect the child's interests during the litigation, and also on the evaluation of a psychologist, a California court ordered limited visitation rights for Michael during the litigation. Meanwhile, Gerald, the husband, successfully sought to terminate the litigation on the basis of the conclusive presumption in California law that the child born to a cohabiting married couple is the offspring of the marriage.

On appeal, Michael pursued a constitutional challenge to the presumption as a violation of both his right to procedural due process and his protected liberty interest in his relationship with the child. In a plurality opinion for the Supreme Court, Justice Scalia wrote, "California law, like nature itself, makes no provision for dual fatherhood."[298] By invoking nature, Justice Scalia treated the presumption as inevitable and immutable—as beyond reconsideration. He used the analogy between law and nature to conceal the fact that the Court's plurality opinion was precisely rejecting another competing claim of nature—that Michael is the natural, biological father of the child. The plurality opinion also rejected Michael's arguments more specifically[299] but this introductory remark sets the tone for the analysis. Identity is treated in the opinion as natural, discoverable, and unable to be changed. Even when acknowledging that alternative understandings of family identities are possible, the plurality converts the issue into one that can be answered by reference to an unchanging source of evidence: "the historic practices of our society" that recognize a protected family unit.[300] The plurality's approach is intended to reduce disputes. It treats the judicial inquiry as one readily answered by pre-existing traditions. It declines to consider whether changing social practices could justify modifications in the law or whether the particular parties involved make compelling arguments for departing from traditions.[301]

The plurality's approach exemplifies the faulty view that identities are fixed and knowable, rather than contingent and capable of change. Perhaps Justice Scalia's opinion never intended to speak to the nature of identities, and meant only to preserve the time-saving device of a presumption. The plausibility of the presumption in question depends, however, on popular as well as legal conceptions of the identity of a father. By referring to tradition and nature, Justice Scalia turns to particular, cultural notions of fatherhood. The plurality opinion neglects the varied sources of a father's identity. Besides, or even instead of biological connection to the child, the father may have an emotional relationship, a financial responsibility, or a set of caretaking functions. Treating as conclusive the presumption that the husband of the mother is the father of the child allows the plurality to reinforce structures of social and institutional power that have selected some family forms as preferable. Most importantly, the plurality seeks to cover its own tracks of choice despite its critical power to choose what kinds of family roles to permit, and even what kinds of debates over family roles to countenance.

The plurality thus hides behind a historical test for identifying traditional family forms while determining who should receive constitutional protection.[302] This test for answering questions about family is faulty in part because it disguises the exercise of legal power enfolded with the fiction of a discoverable past. Histories of many communities' experiences with extended families, households, and subgroups at least cast doubt on Justice Scalia's basic notion that "family" has had a stable meaning even within Anglo-American culture over time.[303] Changing patterns of divorce and remarriage and increasing births of children outside of marriage make Justice Scalia's emphasis on a nuclear family with one father and one mother less and less germane to the lives of most people today.[304]

Within any given period of time, family roles have acquired meaning through a complex process of interpretation by the people who fill them.[305] Family identities unavoidably are relational. An immigrant woman develops a new identity while living apart from her husband, and shapes still another while spending time with him in a world she knows better than he does.[306] The very meaning of her status as "wife" changes in the course of these experiences in relation to her husband and to other people. Similarly, a woman is a mother in relation to a child; a boy is a brother in relation to a sibling; they are a family in relation to one another. None of these relationships is intrinsic to a single person; each depends on the patterns of connection between individuals, and between those people and the larger society's institutions and culture within which they live and make meaning of their lives. A new person entering a workplace or a family requires others to remake their relationships to one another as well as to the new arrival.

These relationships are not reducible solely to biological or officially sanctioned connection. Even historically, the fact of a biological connection could be supplanted by people's refusal to recognize a biological basis for a family tie or to act in accordance with it.[307] In this era of new reproductive technologies,[308] growing numbers of households with gay or lesbian parents, high divorce and remarriage rates, and high levels of cohabitation outside of marriage for both heterosexual and homosexual partners,[309] a child may have relationships with more than two adults who can each claim a parental bond. The actual social and psychological relationship forged through time, care, and experiences that build trust exemplifies what our culture means by "parent" at least as well as the sheer genetic fact of parenthood.[310] Family identities are contingent and mutable, not fixed. There are multiple contributions to family identities. These include biological facts, individual choices by adults to be together, community support or hostility, and legal recognition.

Legal recognition is but one aspect of family identity. Legal traditions can be in conflict with other sources. Predictably, people have begun to assert legal claims to protect social relationships in addition or in contrast to biological relationships and relationships assigned by legal presumptions.[311] A legal response that treats such claims as irrelevant and undeserving of attention expresses an act of state power to supplant identities that people develop and assert. Of course, courts might question and evaluate whether those relationships should be recognized and protected, but the refusal even to discuss them is a sheer imposition of judicial power in framing the question so it cannot be discussed.

One need not explore all the complex layers contributing to family identities to recognize that the use of heavy presumption in *Michael H. v. Gerald D.* prevents any legal inquiry into the "demonstrable fiction that Gerald is Victoria's father."[312] Consequently, the dissenters maintained that the use of a conclusive presumption operated to deny Michael's chance to be heard, and thereby violated requirements of constitutional due process.[313] Even before asking whether an individual claimant, such as Michael, should obtain legal recognition for his identity as father along with any associated rights, such as the right to visit the child,[314] the law governs whether the claimant has a right to raise the question of identity and make an argument about it. The conclusive presumption works to avoid even that initial stage.

Such a presumption may itself be warranted. It may be a good way to ensure financial protection for children. What seems strange and indefensible in the Supreme Court's plurality opinion in *Michael H.*, however, is the refusal even to permit debate over its warrant. By refusing to consider the possibility that Michael H. has a protected liberty interest in his relationship to the child, the plurality bypassed the inquiry into justifications for a presumption, cutting off his legal claims.[315] Not only does this approach redefine the shape of liberty interests protected by the Court, it also treats the very issue of what cannot be questioned as beyond debate. Especially when the potential question concerns a matter of personal identity, this refusal to entertain basic questions represents an extreme exercise of power beyond the checks usually available through adversarial challenge and appellate review. Presumptions often serve useful and efficient purposes, but there should be some avenue, at least occasionally, for testing whether an old presumption continues to advance worthy goals. The extraordinary circumstance of review of a family law matter in the U. S. Supreme Court could have provided such a testing opportunity, but the justices in the plurality preferred to duck the chance and then announce that they had to do so.

The case of *Michael H.* is an example of the legal actors trying to pretend there is only a wall, not a locked door, between the unmarried father and the child, in hopes that disputes will go away. In this case, the democratic process produced an epilogue. After the Court's decision in *Michael H.*, the California legislature amended its statute to accord the status of a presumed father to the biological father if he receives the child in his home and openly holds out the child as his natural child.[316] This amendment was possible because the Court's decision merely rejected a constitutional challenge to the previous version of California's law. It did not install that law as a constitutional matter. The amendment was also possible because a democratic process kept the issue of the definition of a father alive and open for debate, and remained opened to interested parties. Not all matters of identities treated by courts have the chance for this kind of postscript.

III. Tribe by Law
The contrast between courts and legislatures does not sort into bad versus good uses of identity categories, nor does it readily translate into rigid versus flexible ones. Sometimes, a court can shape a particular judgment to respond to complexities. For example, a trial judge concluded that the parental rights of one set of parents—who had placed their disabled child in an institution—did not need to be terminated for another set of parents to assume decision making and day-to-day caretaking.[317] Sometimes, it is the legislature rather than the court that announces rigid categories as the critical element of a protection or entitlement. Such statutes launch legal inquiries in the form of "is this a that?" Questions of characterization, often involving

the identity of an individual or a group, can turn to purposes, or historical narratives, or formal definitions, or community conceptions.[318]

Consider what happened when a group of people from Mashpee, Massachusetts filed a lawsuit claiming that they possessed about 16,000 acres of land in the area called Mashpee on Cape Cod.[319] Following the lead of other suits, the plaintiffs claimed that they were an Indian tribe entitled by the Non-Intercourse Act of 1790 to protection from exploitation in land purchases.[320] The defendants, including a large land development company and more than 100 individual landowners, insurance companies, and other businesses, did not dispute that the plaintiffs had Indian ancestry. Mashpee historically was known as the Indian town on the Cape. Nonetheless, the defendants argued that the plaintiffs were descendants of Indians who had intermarried with whites and blacks and thereby lost any possible identity as a distinctive tribe, if indeed such an identity ever existed.[321]

James Clifford, an anthropologist observing the trial, later described two versions of the history of Mashpee trial status that emerged in the lawsuit.[322] According to one view, there never was a tribe. People from varied Indian tribes and other minority groups settled in the area and intermarried with whites. They sought full citizenship both in Massachusetts and in the United States; they pursued assimilation into American culture. Most of the residents converted to Christianity during the course of the eighteenth century. Eventually, Mashpee became a town. Its early legal form as a collective plantation prevented sales and purchases of individual plots of land. During the nineteenth century, local residents joined a reform movement against these initial restraints on alienating land. By 1870, the state legislature abolished the special restrictions. Transfers of land to outsiders began and continued for 100 years. An ethnic heritage continued to provide some residents with a sense of affiliation, but no tribe existed. Instead, some individuals in the community were descendants of an eclectic group of Native American, black, and white people who had lived in the Mashpee area.[323]

The alternative story presented by the plaintiffs at trial questioned the very idea of a "tribe." Seen as an invention by whites that reflected regulations of Indians in the nineteenth century, the notion of "tribe" invoked elements of organization, religious identity, kinship, and culture that held significance for whites who classify Indians, not to Indians themselves. Even the images of Indians captured in nineteenth-century photographs depended on clothing and poses contrived by white photographers.[324] Outsiders saw the retention of collective land ownership in Mashpee, long after other Cape Cod towns had abandoned it, as a sign of backwardness. Insiders considered collective land ownership an important device for preserving traditions in the midst of change.[325]

The plaintiffs emphasized that evidence of assimilation by their ancestors and themselves did not mean the demise of their Indian identities. Conversion to Christianity did not mean abandonment of Indian identity. Native Americans view religion inclusively and pragmatically. Christian ministers in Mashpee for the most part identified themselves as Indians. The churches helped to maintain a distinctive cultural heritage in Mashpee. Similarly, marriage between Indians and non-Indians signaled the capacity of the Mashpee to absorb outsiders, not assimilation to the surrounding dominant culture. Centrally, the plaintiffs cited their self-conception as Indians, as a group apart, with a continuous presence over several hundred years and commitments to pass on their traditions to succeeding generations. Appearing to assimilate to white culture was simply self-protection. Reviving aspects of traditional culture after periods of apparent assimilation demonstrated reaffirmation of identity.[326]

The competing arguments at trial produced sharply contrasting interpretations of particular evidence. For example, no one disputed town records of an 1868 debate over whether to end all restrictions on land sales. A minority favored a quick change; a majority favored a slow change, and voted for no change that year. But all agreed with the long-term goal of ending the restrictions. On the defendants' view, this agreement marked a collective desire to assimilate into the dominant culture and abandon remnants of tribal identity and practice.[327]

The plaintiffs countered that the public arguments of 1869 should be understood as self-consciously framed for the outside audience of the Massachusetts General Court, which still thought of the Mashpee plantation as a ward of the state and had already decided, and would again decide, its fate. In Clifford's words, "It would be impolitic in addressing this body to say that Mashpee rejected full township status in the name of a distinctive vision of Indian community and citizenship. An argument for delay couched in paternalist rhetoric was more likely to succeed."[328] If the Mashpee leaders bought some time for their distinctive community by appealing to the legislators' paternalism, the legislature's decision in 1870 to remove restrictions on the sale of Mashpee land gives no particular evidence of tribal status.

With their identity as a tribe at issue, the plaintiffs faced a modern iteration of that same power dynamic. A majority group in power would decide its status. Asked to decide whether the Mashpee were a tribe,[329] a jury of non-Indians sat in a position of power over the plaintiffs in the lawsuit but also thereby wielded power in the broader society. The jury rejected the plaintiffs' claim that a tribe, under federal law, existed continuously from the period before the colonies through 1976. But the jury also rejected the defendants' claim that there had never been a tribe.[330] Perhaps the jury found persuasive the plaintiffs' challenge to the very notion of "tribe" or to the process that put nontribal members in the position of defining a tribe.[331] Perhaps the jury resisted the "yes or no" question of tribal status, given the complex and shifting evidence they had heard. By refusing to define the tribe in one way, the jury thus may have acknowledged what its members probably knew from their own lives: identities can change and still represent important continuities with the past.

After surveying the jury's ambivalent response, the judge concluded that tribal status had been abandoned by the plaintiffs' ancestors and therefore could not be resumed for the purposes of the lawsuit. The appellate court affirmed. The case decided not only that the Mashpee were not a tribe, but also that the defendants had properly purchased, and could pursue their plans for converting, the disputed area into resorts and other developments. Perhaps the problem came from imagining that these significant questions of land ownership, compensation, and land development could or should be resolved by characterizing the plaintiffs as within or outside of the identity as a "tribe." If the purpose of asking about the tribal status of the Mashpee was to determine whether the plaintiffs should obtain compensation for past land sales or protection against future land sales, that purpose is shielded from discussion by the intervening question: are the Mashpee a tribe? Considering the underlying issues directly exposes questions of power, politics, justice, and distribution of wealth. These are, in fact, the very questions embedded in characterizations of identity.

A judge or jury could frame the legal question—are the Mashpee people a tribe—in terms of purposes. For the purpose of protection against unscrupulous property transactions, should they be a tribe? Alternatively, for the purpose of receiving federal benefits for education and training, should they be a tribe? Once purposes named and described they become debatable, and subject to competing arguments from varied perspectives. The result could be more honest and potentially difficult to debate. Perhaps for this reason courts and legislatures often substitute for inquiries into purposes tests that ask, "is this a that"; as in, "are the Mashpee a tribe?" or "is the governmental regulation of property a 'taking' requiring just compensation?" Deploying definitions and sorting historical evidence, such inquiries foreclose attention to purposes and to the shifting influence of contexts on meanings. Judges thereby contain debates and move politics, choice, and power off stage. In a case like the Mashpees', this approach makes identities seem like simple yes or no propositions rather than complex, negotiated interactions. Not only are future purposes cordoned off from discussion, but historical complexity is also pushed aside.[332]

Even when a tribe is recognized, the scope of tribal sovereignty has triggered peremptory judicial treatment—with confused results. Sometimes tribal sovereignty is based on geography: the tribal government has authority over all persons within its geographic territory. On other occasions, the federal courts have ruled that tribal governments have authority only over tribal members, and not over others who come or stay within tribal territory.[333] The mixed decisions pointing in these diverging directions increasingly put any tribal sovereignty in jeopardy, despite treaties and constitutional guarantees.[334] Federal agencies also define Indian identity for purposes of receiving educational, employment, and other benefits, and for purposes of assigning people inside or outside of tribal jurisdiction over criminal law and family law. These governmental assignments, and people's perceptions of their past and present experiences, often clash.

IV. COMING TOGETHER AND FALLING APART

Legal assignments of race, family status, and tribal membership converge in custody determinations involving children with Indian heritage. Congress adopted the Indian Child Welfare Act of 1978 as an effort to remedy abusive child welfare practices that resulted in removing as many as 25 to 35 percent of all Indian children from their families and tribes through adoption and foster-care placements, almost always in the homes of non-Indians.[335] Congress concluded that state administrative and judicial institutions failed too often to respect Indian families, to understand cultural and social standards in Indian communities, and to recognize tribal relations among Indian peoples. Therefore, Congress established exclusive jurisdiction in tribal courts for proceedings concerning an Indian child who resides within the tribe's reservation or who is a ward of the tribe. The law also provided for concurrent tribal and state court jurisdiction for other Indian children, while allowing the transfer of any such cases from state to tribal court if parents or tribes so requested. Congress also specified that absent "good cause" to the contrary, adoptive placements should be made preferentially with first, members of the child's extended family, second, other members of the same tribe, and third, other Indian families.[336]

Recent debates in Congress have challenged the use in adoption practices of racial or ethnic identity for any but Indian children.[337] Critics attacked long-standing practices by child welfare agencies and state laws calling for racial matching of adoptive parents and children. Under these practices, nonwhite children have been more likely to spend much more time in foster care, awaiting adoptions that often never happen.[338] Critics also assaulted the role of the state in assigning children to races in order to match them with adults. Despite arguments from some quarters that adoption of nonwhite children by white parents jeopardizes the African American, Latino, and Asian communities, the commitment to racial neutrality prevailed in recent reforms banning race matching in adoption; excepted, however, are Indian children. The Indian Child Welfare Act is vulnerable to the same kinds of criticisms as race matching in adoption, but the legislative findings of such extraordinarily frequent wrenching of Indian children from Indian parents, and the cultural insensitivity of child welfare agencies removing those children, made this a special case, in Congress's view.

Judges in state courts often strain to avoid the Indian Child Welfare Act's directives. They seem uncomfortable with the provisions deferring to Indian courts and the provisions elevating tribal membership over other factors affecting the children's interests. The leading Supreme Court decision interpreting the Act mandated that a tribal court decide the custody of twins who had never themselves lived on the reservation, and whose parents had deliberately left the reservation so the children would be born outside of it.[339] Indeed, the children's unmarried parents voluntarily surrendered the children for adoption, and apparently sought nontribal adoptive parents in order to improve their children's chances for middle-class lives. The Court nonetheless concluded that since the mother officially resided on the reservation, her children did as well, even though they had never even been there.[340] Individual tribal members could not by their own acts or choices defeat the tribal power over custody decisions affecting Indian children.

By the time the Supreme Court acted, the children had lived the first three years of their lives in the home of an adoptive white family. In sending the case to the tribal court, the Supreme Court Justices reasoned, "It is not ours to say whether the trauma that might result from removing these children from their adoptive family should outweigh the interests of the Tribe—and perhaps the children themselves—in having them raised as part of the Choctaw community.[341] Marked here by dashes is the central dilemma posed by the Indian Child Welfare Act; do the children have the same interests as the tribe, and if not, should the group's interests prevail? In this case, the tribal court heard evidence about the best interests of the children, and ultimately decided to let them stay with the adoptive family. Does the case—from Supreme Court to tribal court—stand as a victory for group identity as a principle but a victory for individualized judgments in practice? A hypocritical pretense of respect for group identity? A signal to lower courts to enforce more vigorously the group identity dimensions of the Indian Child Welfare Act? The case is arguably all of these, and also manifests the grave difficulties involved in assigning race, family, and tribal status by law. At the end of a legal dispute, courts know there must be an answer; clarity and closure are more important to the judiciary even than correctness and attentiveness to messy dilemmas.

The difficulty for law and politics is in devising rules and practices responsive to and not merely reflective of both the experiences of unique individuals and meaningful group membership. Legal decisions are more likely to exhibit than resolve the tension between betrayal and connection. Discomfort with uncertainty and a persistent thirst for fixed answers compounds the problem. So does the practical need for simple, easily explained and easily administered rules and practices. Perhaps, these reasons explain in part why groups, and legal rules, so often adopt rigid notions of group identity.

Novelist Barbara Kingsolver tried her hand at an artistic treatment of these dilemmas. In *Pigs in Heaven*, Kingsolver offers sympathetic portraits of Taylor Greer, the unmarried white woman who adopted an abandoned child; Turtle, the six-year-old child who is recognized after a television appearance as a missing grandchild of a Cherokee man; Taylor's mother Alice, who leaves her silent, unfeeling husband; Annawake Fourkiller, a Cherokee lawyer who presses for strict application of the Indian Child Welfare Act; and Cash Stillwater, the child's grandfather who aches for his missing grandchild.[342] Turtle's own mother died in a car crash; Turtle was left in the care of an alcoholic aunt who abandoned her. Not knowing anything of Turtle's origins, Taylor found and cared for the child for nearly three years and formally adopted her. The novelist powerfully crafts a circumstance with equities and feelings on all sides.

The novel culminates with a tribal court decision about whether Turtle should go back to her grandfather or remain with her adoptive mother. The idealistic Cherokee lawyer, Annawake, consults her uncle, a tribal elder, before reaching a recommendation for the tribunal. He tells her a story of a child claimed by two clan mothers, and a threat by the "Above Ones" to send a snake to divide the child in half. The threat of dividing the child leads one mother to protest while the other seems satisfied, and the protesting mother is thus revealed as the "true" mother who deserves the child.[343] The uncle is undisturbed when Annawake exposes his "old Cherokee story" as the biblical story of King Solomon. Here the novel evokes a comfortable intermingling of traditions in contrast to its central dilemma of picking between worlds for the child. Indeed, retelling of the Solomon story as a tribal story prefigures the novel's ending: joint custody between grandfather and adopted mother.[344] And then, a real *deus ex machina*: on the spot, the grandfather proposes marriage to Alice, the adopted mother's own mother, after brief hints of romance between these two, the biological and adoptive grandparents. This happy ending wraps up all the loose ends, too neatly. The novel's tensions remain more memorable than its tidy ending. What lingers are the shifting connections and betrayals, within and across group identities.

## V. WHAT CAN LAW DO?

Failure to acknowledge the messiness of the past—and nonetheless the harms done—can make people feel hollow, or furious. Can law ever afford chances for people to work emotionally through pain about the past, so they will not be trapped by the past in inventing the future?

Legal assessments of identity run two basic risks. The legal treatments of identity may trap people in categories that deprive them of latitude for choice and self-invention; legal assignments of identity may also fail to recognize affiliations that are meaningful or weighty in the lives of individuals.[345] This tension between freedom and constraint is mirrored in the judicial process itself. Judges may reason in a way that obscures their own range of choices; they may also think they have room to reinvent a world that instead resists their pronouncements.

Court decisions defining who was white for purposes of citizenship pretended to discover while actually inventing the category of whiteness. They actually created the mechanism for sorting people who sought full political membership. Similarly, when the Supreme Court approved of a conclusive presumption that a married man is the father of his wife's child, it hid its own exercise of power over so fundamental an identity as parenthood. When the Mashpee lost their claim to tribal status, the judiciary neglected options such as looking to the purpose of the inquiry, finding resilience rather than assimilation, or exposing the very criteria for "tribe" as a colonial imposition on the claimants. Over the objection of the parents, the Supreme Court applied the Indian Child Welfare Act to assign a tribal reservation as the residence of children who had never stepped foot on it.

Simultaneously, legal efforts to affirm identities sought by individuals cannot always, or even often, overcome societal harms. Sometimes, legal responses make some things worse. Laws according special education for children with disabilities repeatedly remove nonwhite children from mainstream classrooms in disproportionate numbers.[346] Rules establishing different admission criteria for students of different races may end up stigmatizing African American and Latino students and mobilizing the Asian American community against them.[347] More basically, the shift from judicial power to define who is white to judicial power to define who is black maintains structure of racial categories and the coercive state control of personal and social meanings.

Part of the difficulty stems from a tension central to the ideals of law. On the one hand, this ideal seeks to govern by rules, not people. Predictability and notice to all who are affected are crucial. Fixed and specific terms and categories, restricting the discretion of judges and administrators, become the preferred form for legal rules. Given a commitment to correct racial discrimination and sex discrimination, the rule of law seeks clear, predictable guidelines. Many businesses whose executives might otherwise dislike affirmative action actually indicate they have settled into it and want to avoid the disruption of change and uncertainty. They also find it good for competitiveness and job growth.[348] The ideal of predictability would favor a ruling that treats racial categories as clear and that requires employers to report on their recruitment, hiring, and promotion practices by racial categories. The results may drag some people into categories who do not belong, or leave some out, all the while enshrining the categories as permanent and immovable.

On the other hand, the ideals of law also involve fairness and justice, individualized treatment and equitable adaptations—which require flexible responses to particular situations. Critics of rigid legal categories have argued for nearly a century against legal categories that seem to deny human authorship and choice.[349] Instead, law should highlight purposes and should test proposed judgments and rules in their light. Different judges can easily interpret purposes differently, however, and there goes predictability. If the stated purpose is to overcome racial oppression, some would want affirmative action plans, and some would reject them. Some would want to identify each person by race and others would oppose any effort to do so. Explicitly exposing this kind of debate to the public has the further risk of jeopardizing respect for, or compliance with, judicial decisions.

When the underlying legal question is whether an individual deserves protection or a remedy against being badly treated because of group membership, there is an alternative, as I have already noted.[350] Legislatures and courts could use legal concepts that explicitly focus on the negative attitudes that hurt individuals, such as the perception of disability, or the disapproval of gays. Disabilities laws already proceed with protections for persons regarded as disabled. This turns the inquiry directly to the social origins of the category and its use by some to harm others. Efforts in this direction could also successfully reveal the interaction between two traits, such as race and sex, in the mind, for example, of the sexual harasser using specifically ethnic or racial epithets against women.[351]

Of course, the issues of proof and proper remedy remain. Can a complainant show she is the kind of person subjected to negative views, without claiming membership in the group defined by the negative views? Can a claimant show she has been harassed not just on a faulty view of race or a demeaning view of sex but on a harmful view conjoining the two? If relief other than compensatory damages can be considered, can or should the court or some other decision maker use the group definition, for example, to call for diversity in the job selection criteria? And what if the individual wants accommodation, such as a voice-activated computer, or insurance coverage for an unmarried partner, that recognizes a difference, based on disability, or sexual partnership? Group categories will still play important roles in the legal solution.

Another alternative legal treatment of groups comes from the constitutional treatment of religion; it could provide a rich analogy for treatment of a range of individual identities. The First Amendment to the Constitution contains two clauses addressing religion; one guarantees the "free exercise" of religion while the other forbids governmental "establishment of religion."[352] Individuals thus are assured the chance to practice their own religions and the government is precluded from endorsing or preferring one religion over others.[353] Perhaps it would be possible to pursue a similar governmental stance toward identities. Individuals should be free to claim their own identity and shape or express it as they wish; the government, however, should not be able to install a regime preferring one over others.[354]

To be sure, this would require expansion and reinterpretation of current legal doctrine. Neither the equality nor due process clauses of the Fourteenth Amendment explicitly include "free exercise" or "establishment" language. Some people might be deeply disturbed by the idea that individuals could choose their own race, or gender, or by the idea that the state could not prefer one ethnicity over another, or one sexual orientation over another. Yet, there are some precursors of this position even in existing legal decisions interpreting the Constitution and civil rights statutes. For example, the Supreme Court has rejected a state law forbidding interracial marriage on the ground that it implemented white supremacy.[355] In addition, regarding racial or sexual harassment as unacceptable discrimination in the employment context, courts have announced that employers cannot lawfully maintain workplaces that make it more difficult for one group of people to do their work.[356]

American law can also respond indirectly to the risks of legal assessments about identity. The U. S. legal system maintains what might seem like inefficient redundancy in the legal system. Different branches of government engage in checks and balances. This sometimes permits legislative corrections of judicial mistakes, judicial rejection of legislative approaches, and executive actions as well.[357] The two tiers of government—state and federal—often permit second chances. The states may explore alternatives that the federal government has foreclosed for itself; the federal government may scrutinize and learn from or reject state laws and decisions. Of course, these multiple settings give room to maneuver for not only those who seek to advance equality and tolerance but also those who seek to obstruct (or define these values differently). Yet, the very possibility of another forum, another legal setting, keeps open what otherwise might be irrebuttable identities or conclusive refusals to recognize a group. The California legislature did have the chance to reject the Supreme Court's crude assertion that children cannot have two fathers.

If law plays a substantial role in making identities seem fixed, innate, and clearly bounded, these multiple settings make it possible to keep open or reopen some of these legal determinations of identities. Similarly, within the judicial process, dissenting opinions keep countervailing views alive, and add plural voices to what otherwise could seem monolithic legal responses to identity claims. Adversarial arguments in briefs and in court permit competing narratives to be heard, and retold, if only by representatives. The Mashpees lost their lawsuit, but won pages in the works of historians and anthropologists, and a chance at reviving and recasting memories.

On sunny days, I am hopeful about possibilities for using law to redress historic oppression and mistreatment of disempowered groups. A world that forbids Jim Crow segregation is better than one that enforced it. A long struggle through the courts played a big part in the end of Jim Crow laws.[358] A country that affords political asylum to a woman who otherwise would face genital mutilation at home is better than one that does not, and legal advocacy in a public setting secured the asylum.[359] Many more persons with disabilities have opportunities of decent treatment, education, and paid employment because of law reform initiatives. Gays and lesbians cannot be excluded from the political process, because of a successful constitutional struggle.[360] More basically, courts have provided arenas for evidence of harms against groups or against individuals on the basis of a trait that draws them into a despised group. Histories and current abuses can be exposed. And sometimes, justice can be done.

On rainy days, I see retrenchment in civil rights, rising antigay legal and political activities, and defunding of services for people with disabilities, and of legal services generally. I see the real problems in legal remedies that were supposed to be successes. School desegregation orders seem to spur white flight from cities and leave crumbling, dismal education. Bilingual education classes in some schools produce children illiterate in two languages. A court orders a fire department to recruit, hire, and promote African Americans, and then the white firefighters successfully object that this undermines their rights.[361] A landlady invokes religious freedom to justify her refusal to rent to unmarried couples.[362] People opposed to civil rights can use group-based categories for their own ends. How can these be compared with the dangers of pretending that discrimination and mistreatment along group lines do not exist or do not deserve redress?

Like days with rain and days with sun (not to mention days with both), legal decisions and institutions have varied faces and effects. Law can help and law can fail to respond to oppression and mistreatment along group lines. At its best, the response is only partial; law can only do so much. At its worst, it reinvigorates group cleavages. Perhaps people who seek equality and justice for oppressed groups can capitalize on the tensions within law. Enforcing civil rights laws that specify protected groups remains a potentially fruitful strategy for remedies, and for exposing objectionable practices to view. This may make identities seem fixed, immutable, and clearly bounded; but adversarial arguments, dissents, and debates between the branches and levels of government can reopen the questions of identity, history, and justice, and expose the room for negotiation and human choices in the definitions of who we, and others, are.

The condition of group identities in the late-twentieth-century United States is a problem with two sides. On the one side remains ignorance of the history and ongoing ways in which individuals have been unfairly trapped or burdened by status assigned on the perception of group membership. On the other side is constant categorization by racial, ethnic, gender groups. The U.S. Census, schools, and employers sort by category; so do the eyes of bystanders on the street or subway. Laws help to sustain the illusion that these categories are natural. Laws can also provide avenues for objecting to harms based on these categories. In so doing, however, laws reinvest these categories with meaning. If that reinvestment exacerbates rather than heals "wounded attachments" to identities, law can only offer part of the way out of the knots created by group-based harms.[363]

Law, at its best, cannot resolve tensions between connection and betrayal, individuality and group affiliation. Law can only manage them, temporarily. Art often affords insight that can helpfully disturb apparent resolutions. *M. Butterfly*, a contemporary play, far from child custody but quite close to family intimacy and racial (and gender) categorization, reminds audiences of the mutability of identities while also exposing the weight of group-based oppressions in the lives and imaginations of characters and audiences.[364] Playwright David Henry Hwang read a *New York Times* account about an actual affair between a male French diplomat and a Chinese opera singer who appeared to be a woman but who was actually a man. According to the *New York Times* story, the actual gender identity of the opera singer remained unknown to the diplomat, and Hwang brilliantly asked, how could this be?[365] In the news story, the diplomat said he had never seen his Chinese lover naked and thought "her" modesty reflected Chinese custom. Hwang explained his own chain of thought:

> I thought, wait a minute here, that's not a Chinese custom? I begin to think, maybe the guy had not fallen in love with an actual person but with this sort of fantasy stereotype of the Orient. I was driving along one day, somewhere, thinking, hey, the diplomat thought he had found Madame Butterfly! I pulled into a record store, bought Puccini's opera, looked at the libretto, and, right there, in the store, I began to structure the beginning of the play where the diplomat fantasizes that he's Pinkerton and has found Butterfly. He realizes—by the end—that he, himself, is, in fact, Butterfly. He's the one who has been sacrificed for love, exploited by his lover, who turns out to be a spy.[366]

*M. Butterfly* teases the audience about the identity of the opera singer. The playbill lists only the actor's last name and first initial to keep the real person's "real" sex a mystery. The play gradually, methodically, and fantastically explores the projection of fantasy on what we think is different. The diplomat, and the audience, project gender difference on top of racial and national differences. The stereotype of Chinese femininity allows the diplomat to dupe himself in searching for human connection, and in the midst of the jeopardy of betrayal. It is critical to the play that the audience suspend disbelief about who is the opera singer, who is the diplomat, and ultimately, who we all are, struggling to know and be known. Rather than entrenching fixed and cramped views of identity, the play opens possibilities for new understandings, it re-presents human experiences, present and absent from consciousness. Can any combination of legal and political strategies do this, while seeking to remedy historic harms?

# CHAPTER 4
## *Remedies*

<>

What needs to be remedied: an identity politics that seals people in their dependence on victim status as a source of meaning? Or widespread ignorance of the mistreatment of people because they are black, Hispanic, Japanese, Korean, Irish, disabled, women, Moslem, gay, lesbian, or otherwise "different"? I think both. But is it possible to attain sustained public acknowledgment of past and continuing oppressions along group lines *and* to promote individual self-definition and fulfillment, while somehow avoiding the truncated effects of assigned group identity or victim status? Can the broader society acknowledge the meanings that group affiliation affords to individuals without forcing individuals into groups? Can the broader society recognize the value of pluralist group experiences without turning them into objects of curiosity or advertising marketing strategies?

To respond to group-based mistreatment and to promote individual freedom means at times to pursue divergent or even conflicting paths. Yet, to do one alone is to risk deepening the other problem. To attack the wide-scale removal of Indian children from Indian families, the Indian Child Welfare Act gives tribal courts and tribal court members authority in custody decisions—thereby elevating tribal status over parental freedom or exclusive concern with the individual child.[367] Similar arguments for matching children available for adoption with parents of the same race could promote a sense of pride and community for blacks—or could perpetuate stereotypes about racial differences in values, tastes, and individual worth.[368]

Yet, to promote individual self-definition and fulfillment without pursuing acknowledgment and redress for group-based injuries preserves those injuries, unhealed. College admission policies that ignore historic exclusions of blacks, Hispanics, and Native Americans produce classes without many individuals with those backgrounds. Workplace practices that ignore the exclusion of persons with disabilities render it difficult or impossible for many people with disabilities to get and maintain employment.

Rather than picking strategies, I suggest pursuing both. We should seek both sustained public acknowledgment and response to past and continuing burdens along the lines of group membership, and we also should promote opportunities for individual self-invention and individual decisions to embrace or de-emphasize particular aspects of themselves. This double mission requires settings for telling and knowing truths about exclusions and degradations because of group status *and* structures that permit people to experiment with and negotiate through the groups, interests, and practices that can afford them personal meaning. Both approaches are needed to respond to real injustices. Both also could help individuals, and groups, gain more trust in the polity, more acknowledgment by others, and more hope for a better future. Both approaches, taken together, are necessary if the paradoxes of identity and diversity are to be acknowledged rather than enacted: the universality of our uniqueness, and the rich variety of our beings.

Seeking truths about exclusions and settings for self-invention calls for language and politics that make it safe to be for oneself and for others. It also calls for analysis of the ways that identities and group differences appear and seem to become inevitable. That semblance of inevitability mistakenly locates the causes of disadvantage within disadvantaged groups.[369] Resisting the imposition of group identities does not mean forever abandoning the categories, but it does mean promoting avenues for individuals to select, shift, reclaim, and mix their affiliations.

To fight against ignorance about the sources of disadvantage AND against rigid group assignment will inevitably involve different, and at times inconsistent, strategies. I mean to encourage a view of tensions among strategies not as a defect but instead as opportunities for creativity; paradoxes about identity do not need resolution as much as recognition.

To change the broken record of debates surrounding identity politics, many competing strategies could be tried. Some could specify roles for the government; some could urge governmental restraint. Some would be well advanced through collective but private means: social movements, philanthropy, grassroots activities. Some will resist any use of group names: others will revel in them. I mean here to incite debate and promote a proliferation of strategies rather than to pronounce any one of them the answer. To start, consider three each for the goals of (1) remembering and remedying group-based harms, and (2) encouraging more avenues for individual self-invention.

## I. Remembering and Remedying Group-Based Harms

Three suggestions here are: intensive and aggressive enforcement of antidiscrimination laws; exploration of public compensation and reparations for past and continuing group-based harms; and framing better settings for eliciting facts and narratives about group-based harms.

### A. Enforcing Antidiscrimination Laws

Laws already adopted at the federal, state, and local levels forbid discrimination in employment, housing, public accommodations, and school admissions in institutions receiving public funds; discrimination requires some proof of intent or, in some circumstances, disparate effects and demonstration that the claimant is otherwise qualified and also fits one of the categories of groups receiving protection.[370] Vigorous enforcement of such laws could strengthen a sense of trust in the larger community, especially for people who identify with the protected categories.

Such enforcement could, of course, fuel resentment by others, especially if the remedies pose losses to them in what may seem like a zero-sum game. Hence, the ongoing debate over affirmative action and "reverse discrimination."[371] Enforcement of civil rights laws also can invite demands for expanding the covered Mexican American categories. These expansions may trivialize the effort. Wendy Brown, for this reason, objects to a city ordinance that prohibits discrimination not only on the basis of race, ethnicity, gender, sexual orientation, and disability, but also appearance.[372] She worries about treating as equivalents the risks faced by African Americans and by white teens who dye and spike their hair; she cautions against a regulation that obscures the effects of social power.[373] She also warns that identity categories, even when used in a remedial mode, become complicit with the regulatory regimes that produce them.[374] Similarly, Kristen Bumiller observes that civil rights laws require individuals to claim the status of victims in a way that recapitulates their group-based exclusions. Refusing to assert such a claim then becomes a way to reassert dignity.[375]

These cautions warrant attention. They neglect, however, the possibility that I have already described that refines the antidiscrimination effort to focus specifically on the faulty and harmful use of group stereotypes rather than on group membership as a privileged position. This possibility, already pursued in disability law, stresses the harm of "being regarded as" a member of the group and redirects attention to the process of being labeled and mistreated by others.[376] Enforcing civil rights laws with this conception invites an examination of the ways that people form attitudes and misapprehensions about people who seem different from themselves. The challenge is to make it clear in the very actions of invoking and applying civil rights protections that the groups are not so much essential, singular, or real as they are expressions of social power.[377] This analysis applies no less to race, gender, ethnicity, and sexual orientation than to disability.[378]

Civil rights laws should be preserved and vigorously enforced even if the "being regarded as" approach does not prevail. Such enforcement permits exposure of group harms, and public debates over what should count as a group harm. Efforts to dislodge the seeming naturalness of group identities can be pursued in other arenas without sacrificing the important principles the civil rights laws embrace. Those principles include equality and fairness but also acknowledgment: acknowledgment of past and present oppression and acknowledgment of hard-fought struggles for acknowledgment.

In an era when black churches are torched, when reported hate crimes have escalated, when sexual harassment has not diminished, the need for civil rights laws has hardly abated. Apparently profound racial divisions in perceptions of fairness in operations of the criminal justice system[379] indicate at minimum an urgent need for that system to demonstrate its compliance with fair, unbiased procedures. What we need is not less but more vigorous enforcement of the civil rights laws, and more inventive uses to educate journalists, employers, and other influential parties.

In this spirit, I think that legislatures, police departments, prosecutors, governors, and mayors should examine massive group disparities in their purview as clues to underlying problems deserving remedy, rather than accurate reflections of real differences among people. For example, if one out of three African American males in their twenties are supervised by the criminal justice system, this should be a clue that something is terribly wrong in that system and in the larger society—and not instead serve as a confirmation of stereotypic notions of African American male criminality. Investigation into these practices might not justify compensation or relief to particular individuals, the sort of remedies a court normally would consider. Structural changes in the operations of police and prosecutors might be called for, but they would be more effective if designed by those personnel than if ordered by courts. The adoption of community police approaches that try to ensure access to sports and constructive out-of-school activities especially for young black and Hispanic males is an example of the view that their overrepresentation in the criminal justice system reflects failures in the broader environment rather than defects in themselves. Governmental practices that yield massive racial, gender, or ethnic disparities should raise questions for those in charge about those practices and challenge assumptions that the problem lies in "those people."[380]

Genuine leadership of cities, states, and the nation should welcome critics of the gaps between our ideals of equality and freedom, and realities. A focus on those gaps offers the best hope for pulling this country together. From the beginning, the ideals of equality and freedom were not manifest in practice.[381] Nor are they fully now. What makes politics and law capable of drawing us together is the readiness of individuals brash enough to say, "but you said . . ." and courageous enough to hold people accountable to the ideals so often stated. Vigorous enforcement of civil rights—from inside and from outside of the operations of both public and private organizations—can exemplify this process of accountability.

## B. Facilitate Public Compensation and Reparations for Past and Continuing Group-Based Harms

Compensation involves payments for specific losses or damages identified and measured through a legal procedure; reparation involves payments to amend for more general wrongs and injuries through a political process.[382] Greater use of public fora for debating compensation and reparations for group harm could air enduring grievances, educate a broader public, and produce some sense of closure. The very same practices could trivialize atrocities, encourage unmanageable numbers of claims and "wounded attachments," invite trivial claims, and feed resentment by those who do not personally benefit.

Although these negative consequences deserve attention, I think the positive possibilities are more powerful. Consider the following two examples. In May, 1994, the governor of Florida signed into law a claims bill, passed by the legislature, for the destruction in 1923 of the town of Rosewood, Florida.[383] A group of whites burned down the town, which was inhabited entirely by African Americans (except for the sole white store owner), and also killed at least eight people. The precipitating event was the claim by a white woman in a neighboring town that she had been raped by a black man, although no such man was ever found. Law enforcement officials did not intervene during the week-long period of destruction. After an investigation, an adversarial hearing, and a public debate, the state Senate approved a bill to compensate survivors, to compensate families of residents who lost property, and to create a minority college scholarship fund with preferences for descendants of Rosewood residents. The state law enforcement department was also directed to conduct a criminal investigation.[384]

The incident is distinguishable from others, such as the massive Southern lynchings, because of the extended time during which the public officials could have acted but did not. In addition, good evidence, including considerable contemporaneous press coverage, substantiated the claim. Thus worries about inspiring massive additional claims were somewhat moderated.[385] The allocation of money did produce tension and conflict, first by whites opposed to the bill and then by claimants for the compensation itself.[386] The ultimate amount of the compensation was small when divided among the claimants, and many found the experience incomplete if not anticlimactic.[387] But the experience unearthed a history that had been suppressed, permitted many individuals to work through trauma they and their families had experienced, and taught a watching nation about prejudice, violence, and official complicity.[388]

A second example is reparations for the internment of Japanese Americans and Japanese residents in the United States during World War II.[389] Again, there were risks of trivializing the harms and also the risks of provoking majority resentment and hostility. Yet, the process of seeking and substantiating the basis for reparations afforded a constructive method for recalling history and acknowledging group harms.[390]

Serious scholarly arguments for reparations to African Americans for slavery have hardly sparked political success, and the topic may raise special difficulties, not least of which involve identifying the right beneficiaries and risking partial and therefore unfair results.[391] Nonetheless, sustained political debate on this issue might permit people to express long-standing perceptions about the scope and consequences of group-based injuries. At the least, reparations would offer a different frame for the debate over affirmative action than the debate that assumes comparison with a frame of neutrality.

Remedies besides money could be part of the inquiry into reparations. Apologies, changes in government or corporate practices, or creation of scholarship funds or other investments in the harmed community could be powerful ways to express acknowledgment of wrongs without pretending to erase them.

*C. Devise Settings for Eliciting Facts and Narratives of Group-based Harms.*
The government of South Africa has recently established a Truth and Reconciliation Commission. It will have no law enforcement duties nor any power to hear compensation or reparations claims. Instead, this official body will seek testimony and evidence about what happened under Apartheid in order to get a truthful record, acknowledgment of suffering, and a basis to permit the entire society to move ahead in forging a new future. To achieve these ends, the Commission plans to grant immunity from prosecution or liability to participants in Apartheid policies

and to African National Congress (ANC) participants for violent or other criminal conduct, but only if they voluntarily come forward to speak. Although many sophisticated discussions may be had about the elusiveness of truth in history, the Commission seeks the kind of information that even such discussions do not disturb: how many people were killed, who gave the orders to kill; where are the missing bodies. Opportunities for debate over interpretations and moral judgments readily follow the gathering of such basic information.

There may be no direct analogue for this device in an ongoing governmental regime such as we have in the contemporary United States.[392] Nonetheless, the idea of a procedure designed to elicit narratives, freeing the participants from legal consequences holds promise here.[393] Experiments in producing public histories, integrating oral histories with documents, engage a range of people in the project of reclaiming richer and more inclusive versions of the past.[394] How did generations of African-Americans make a world of work, clubs, church, and families in Worcester, Massachusetts? How did women exercise choices as homesteaders and early factory workers? What courageous leaders have been forgotten, and why?[395] Stories in the past now told only inside family homes can inform a broader public; missing pieces do not only fill in gaps but also remake the picture of the whole.

In his recent book, *Racial Healing*, Harlon Dalton calls for attention to the contemporary consequences of slavery rather than emphasizing concern with slavery as history.[396] Quite beyond the monstrous but transitory harms to the enchained, slavery "served to indelibly link blackness and subservience in the American subconscious. At a deep level, slavery stamped black people as inferior, as lacking in virtue, as lacking the capacity to order their own lives."[397] Creating public settings in which interracial groups could examine such claims would instruct all involved and trigger a probing exploration of the processes producing group identity and prejudices against groups.[398]

Dalton also suggests that attention to the consequences of slavery would require considering the paradoxical benefits of racial separation in strengthening a sense of community and actual independent institutions.[399] This kind of insight would also highlight the processes producing group identities and attachments to them while inviting comparisons with other ways to build and sustain community responsibility and vibrant institutions. To learn from the still-new model of South Africa's Truth and Reconciliation Commission, a parallel activity here would need to consider ways to air internal criticisms of oppressed groups themselves.

Private and public support can launch electronic discussion groups, interfaith gatherings, and therapeutic support groups that take as a central purpose promoting investigation of intergroup misunderstandings, resentments, and grievances. The point would be to convene people to talk and listen about why group statuses have taken the shapes they have, complete with paradoxes and complexities, rather than simplistic and blaming claims. Opportunities for individuals to construct and present their stories could be instructive to others and deeply healing for themselves. Trauma and recovery require recollection and remembrance if they are not to halt productive daily life; this is the insight behind the South African Truth And Reconciliation Commission as well as trauma recovery groups elsewhere.[400]

Many settings for truth telling and support should be framed to feel safe, and therefore less than fully diverse across groups that do not trust one another. But constructing settings precisely for mutually mistrusting individuals and groups would be a crucial, complementary part of this strategy; so would devising settings for people to rub elbows or collaborate on issues unrelated to past and present group conflicts. Such settings could be privately sponsored and confidential, or privately sponsored but open, or even broadcast. Robert Cover explored the dramatic efforts to use trial-like formats outside of any claim of official power, such as a war crimes inquiry with no pretense of authority.[401]

Perhaps the idea of more settings for grievance telling—on top of the current media talk shows—seems redundant or repellent. I do think settings with better ground rules and incentives than talk shows could improve the conversation. At the same time, if a proliferation of settings makes more people feel oversaturated with conversations of group identities, injuries, and sources of pride, that might be a productive way to help more people move on to other topics of conversation with knowledge rather than fear as the reason for the shift.

## II. Expanding Possibilities for Individual Self-Definition

Again, I offer three suggestions, some of which will create tensions with the previous three: devise governmental policies permitting individual self-identification for temporary or specific purposes; try achieving governmental purposes, other than remedying group harms, without deploying group categories; and strengthen and enlarge public support for the arts. Self-invention necessarily works with givens, the found circumstances of culture, history, and memory; through self-invention, we each express a self that was shaped in part before we knew we had one. Yet fostering materials for self-expression and chosen or reaffirmed affiliations most directly acknowledges the dignity of each person. If individuals in turn reinvigorate existing groups, or form new ones, these can be cherished sources of meaning.[402]

*A. Devise governmental policies that permit individuals to affiliate or identify themselves with groups temporarily and for specific purposes rather than have governmental assignment to fixed groups.*

If one of the problems behind identity politics is the assignment of individuals by government or powerful actors to groups beyond their own control or choice, renewed assignments to groups even for remedial purposes can reinstall the injury and the incoherence, constraint and mythology of forced group identity. One alternative worth exploring is for governmental structures that permit people to identify themselves in temporary groups, for specific purposes.

Consider rules for electing representatives to Congress or another legislative body.[403] Two kinds of voting rules are at stake: the rules about what constitutes a voting district for purposes of aggregating votes, and the rules about how to count votes for purposes of declaring winners and losers. The conventional rules determine which votes to aggregate, and divide the electorate into geographic districts; and the selected geographic lines may split a given group of voters into ineffective minorities between more than one district. Yet, equally troubling are districting plans that concentrate a group within one or a few districts, removing their views from any influence in other districts, and ensuring thereby that their elected representatives become a minority among the entire group of representatives. The conventional rule determining how to count votes is majority rules, which means 51 percent of the votes determine 100 percent of the outcome.

The Voting Rights Act specifically permits challenges to voting districting that dilutes the voting power of racially identified groups.[404] Civil rights advocates have supported the enforcement of these provisions with the particular hope of increasing the number of minority representatives elected to office. Critics of race consciousness attack the Act and its implementation for designing districts artificially to yield more minority representatives. The Supreme Court has ruled that legislative districts drawn where race is the "predominant factor" are suspect, even when drawn under the Voting Rights Act directive to produce districts in which minorities can be majorities.[405]

Professor Lani Guinier's scholarship has led a different kind of challenge to pre-existing districts as neither natural nor neutral, and questions the majority-take-all method for counting votes. She proposes instead the creation of multi-representative districts, or at-large elections, in which all the voters in the district vote to elect more than one representative, and proportional voting, which mathematically determines the minimum number of votes necessary to produce a winner and devises a randomized method for distributing the "losing votes" to other candidates so that some of them may also win enough to meet the minimum number of votes to be elected.[406]

When Guinier was nominated to serve as the head of the Civil Rights Division of the Justice Department by President Bill Clinton, a right-wing campaign successfully defeated her by portraying her as a "Quota Queen."[407] Critics maintained that Guinier wanted the electoral rules to produce fixed numbers of black, Hispanic, Asian, and white representatives. In fact, Guinier's scholarship challenges precisely those conceptions, but she was never given a chance to explain her position before President Clinton withdrew the nomination. Her proposals seek to make each vote have equal value, and therefore to prevent majority groups from freezing out minority group members from exercising an effective vote.[408]

Guinier specifically endorses cumulative voting, the method commonly used within corporate governance, which gives each voting member the same number of votes as there are open seats, and allows the voter to assign more than one vote to a given candidate to reflect her own intensity of preference.[409] Guinier notes that this method would permit minority group voters to obtain their preferred candidate if they work together—but the method immediately also permits any kind of group to coordinate that way. "*[A]ll* voters have the potential to form voluntary constituencies based on their own assessment of their interests. As a consequence, semiproportional systems such as cumulative voting give more voters, not just racial minorities, the opportunity to vote for a winning candidate."[410] Further, "[r]acial-group interests become self-identified, voluntary constituencies that choose to combine because of like minds, not like bodies."[411] The goal is to produce a voting method that allows individuals the freedom to move beyond artificial groups based solely on residence, race, or any other feature beyond the individual's choice to affiliate with other like-minded voters.[412]

Thus, individuals may identify themselves, through their vote, with others who share a race, a gender, a concern for the environment, or any other factor. The grouping occurs on the act of voting.[413] This conception of voting thus exhibits the possibility of structures to permit self-identification by individuals as temporary, contingent members of self-formed groups.[414] This conception is especially helpful in supporting the conception of American pluralism that acknowledges people's membership in and affiliation with multiple groups.[415]

Would this conception have application elsewhere? One hotly contested context is the U. S. Census; in 1997, a mini-survey in preparation for the census of the year 2000 will test a new category, "multiracial," in response to demands of those who want to identify themselves that way.[416] The standard classifications of white, Asian American, African American, Hispanic-nonwhite, and Native American/ Pacific Islander are themselves arbitrary and certainly confining for those who identify with more than one, or none of these categories.[417]

Powerful articulations of difficulties faced by persons of mixed-race attest to the cruelties as well as the incoherence of standard distinctions.[418] Yet, the practical uses of the census, for example, to enforce school desegregation, fair housing, and employment laws, make the choice of categories and method of assignment significant and politically charged.[419] This simply exposes the multiple uses of the census; it can be used to remedy discrimination—but it can also be used to inflict it. The census can afford people a chance to help define themselves, but it also can employ definitions imposed on people by subgroups and by the larger society. It is difficult to know who would be helped or hurt if people could identify as "multiracial" (or bi-gendered, for that matter), but I find compelling this poetic comment by Michael Gorra: "the box on the census form of the self does need to be checked, if only to make sure there's someone at home. And it would be better if you could always do it yourself, but too often other people's pencils get there first."[420] The move to self-identification, rather than labeling by a Census official, is a crucial reform.

A more basic alternative would eliminate inquiry into race; Canada, for example, gathers no census information on "race," but does inquire into the ethnic or cultural identities of the individual's ancestors.[421] Canada did not, however, have slavery or Jim Crow laws excluding African Americans from suffrage, so its experience with race is different from that of the United States. Given the particular history of the United States, and the multiple purposes of Census information, Ruth Colker proposes modifying the Census forms to ask three different types of questions:

1. What is your self-identity?
2. If your self-identity is different than your community identity, what is your community identity?
3. What are the countries of origin of your parents, to the extent that you are aware of them?[422]

Then information will be available about the numbers of people in a given area who are treated as if they are "black" while individuals would retain the ability to contribute to their own identifications.

Professor Colker acknowledges that this proposal implies a degree of trust in the government and its use of information that may not be warranted.[423] A more basic problem is that the questions are not likely to be clearly understood.[424] Many people have never thought about the notions of self-identification and community identification, much less the contrasts between them, and thus have no way to answer the questions. Others would have answers—in terms of religion, sexuality, occupation, or avocations—that are not what this portion of the Census seeks.

I propose instead that people be directed to check as many boxes regarding race and ethnicity as seem relevant.[425] The total, or regional, responses can be divided by the actual numbers of people counted by the Census. The resulting fractions will help remind anyone using Census information of its source in self-identification and of the roughness of its truths.

*B. For prospective governmental action outside of efforts to remedy group harms, work to achieve governmental purposes without deploying group-based categories while remaining committed to overturning the effects of categorical exclusions in social and political realms.*

This is not a call for color-blindness, gender neutrality, or other pretenses that we already have achieved a world free from the legacies of group-based exclusions.[426] Instead it is an invitation to invent ways to achieve governmental purposes that do not deploy the group-based identities yet again. Here are three examples:

> 1) peremptory challenges: after a lengthy struggle by civil rights and defense attorneys, the Supreme Court adopted the view that uses of peremptory challenges by prosecutors that resulted in excluding persons of a particular race could violate the Equal Protection Clause.[427] The Court quickly extended this decision to behavior of defense attorneys and then to both sides in civil cases and to exclusions; then the Court extended its analysis to exclusions based on gender as well.[428] Why should the Equal Protection scrutiny stop at race and gender—rather than extend to ethnicity, linguistic minority, religion, sexual orientation, disability, and age, not to mention intersectional categories such as immigrant woman?[429] Alternatively, why not adopt quotas to assure racial, gender, and other categorical representation on juries?[430]

Before we go down that path, however, it is worth considering whether we can achieve the goals behind equal protection and behind the jury system another way. At stake in the composition of juries is a conception of the decision-making body as a representative cross-section of society who are also peers of the parties.[431] Longstanding legal and social practices excluded certain groups from jury service altogether.[432] Discriminatory practices may occur in the gathering of names for the general jury pool, the selection of particular individuals from the pool to serve on juries, and the exclusion of particular individuals from a jury through the process of voir dire.[433]

Such exclusions interfere with the parties' rights to have a representative jury and the citizen's right and duty to serve on the jury.[434] Besides providing the appearance of fairness through representation, the cross-sectional jury also can generate insights based on a range of experiences and perspectives.[435] The historic right of the parties to strike a specified number of jurors without stating a reason risks undermining these purposes.[436] On this basis, the Court developed Equal Protection scrutiny of use of the peremptory challenge. Yet, an alternative and better solution would be to eliminate the peremptory challenge altogether.[437]

Several benefits could emerge from this elimination of the peremptory challenge. The messy administration of the Equal Protection challenges and the strategic gamesmanship surrounding jury selection would end, or at least be forced into the "for cause" exclusions, which require reasons and judicial approval. Eliminating peremptories would end the unresolved debate about which groups deserve this kind of equal protection.[438] Eliminating peremptory challenges would reduce the parties' (and lawyers') abilities to shape the jury and seek to influence their results, which could both help but also significantly hurt members of disadvantaged groups. The very practice of trying to shape the jury through peremptory challenges has been deeply characterized by stereotypic predictions about how members of particular groups would respond to the topics on trial. Ending the peremptory challenge would, at least symbolically, rule all such thinking out of bounds, at least in this setting.

Indeed, parties, and lawyers, commonly seek to remove jurors based on their group characteristics because they load many presumptions—and prejudices—onto those identities.[439] The prosecution tries to exclude people who look like the defendant on the assumption of undue sympathy; the defense tries to exclude those whose racial and ethnic membership differs from that of the defendant. Why permit peremptory challenges that presume that people *cannot* empathize across lines of difference? Not only is such a rule untrue to human possibilities, it might also be a self-fulfilling prophecy.[440]

Eliminating peremptory challenges would not halt attention to group-based categories, for aggressive antidiscrimination enforcement would still be needed at the systemic levels defining the pool of available jurors and calling specific people to serve.[441] Eliminating peremptory challenges would afford one way to restrict the use of governmentally imposed group-based categories while still achieving the underlying governmental purpose. It would send a signal that a practice must end if it plays into or reinforces group stereotyping.

> 2) reasonable person:[442] Scholars, lawyers, and judges have justly attacked this pervasive legal concept for installing the views and beliefs of only some people—typically, middle-class, white, Protestant, able-bodied men—rather than helping to create new common-law categories for setting standards of care or reasonableness. But should the "reasonable person" standard be replaced now with the "reasonable woman" when a woman is the defendant or plaintiff, or "the reasonable Caribbean American gay male," or further efforts to articulate sub-group identities? These may well be improvements over a pretended universal but partial notion better called the reasonable white-middle-class-Protestant-able-bodied man. Yet the practical problems posed by proliferating subgroup standards are immense, and so are the symbolic and psychological risks of confining individuals to governmentally prescribed group categories.

Is it possible to devise an alternative that also avoids sliding back into the faulty neutrality of the "reasonable person" standard? One route would retain "reasonable person" but link it to "the circumstances," where circumstances include encountering the meanings of group identity in a given community during a specific time period.[443] This route would permit testimony and even expert evidence about such meanings while resisting the easy but faulty route of assigning individuals to group categories that then acquire the force of a legal norm.[444]

Another route would press to articulate more fully the standards of care the law means to demand, or shift burdens of care to those best able to anticipate them. An early case ruled against a complainant who sued a city after a broken bridge collapsed, killing his horse and damaging his goods.[445] The city had posted a sign in English indicating that the bridge was broken; the complainant spoke German and could not read English. The court ruled that any reasonable person would have been able to read English and thus the city violated no duty of care. But the city was in the best position simply to place a barrier before the bridge that would require no particular language literacy. Similar assessments of ways to allocate burdens of care could avoid debates over what kinds of persons should be viewed as reasonable under the law.

3) hate speech codes: colleges and universities for several years have debated, and some have adopted, codes of conduct that proscribe "hate speech."[446] Students of color and women had argued that they often feel silenced in classrooms and injured elsewhere on campus by epithets and other speech stereotyping and degrading members of their groups. Some white male students countered that they feel silenced by the implicit demand for "politically correct" speech. The intense campus and public debates surrounding proposed speech codes tend to polarize communities.[447] Arguments against regulation tend to assert the First Amendment as the end of the discussion, while arguments for the codes tend to identify opponents as insensitive, prejudiced, or hostile. Richard Abel has characterized the debates this way: "If the dominant trivialize the harm they inflict, the subordinate abuse their moral leverage by playing identity politics, claiming exclusive rights to speak for or about their group."[448]

Of course, restrictions on speech are extensive throughout college campuses—in professors' rules about who speaks and when in class, in rules confining public assemblies and posters, and in the usual rules of libel and defamation that govern the entire society. Informal norms present in the general culture or cultivated in the local one also powerfully regulate what people think they should say, and what people do say. No one is truly in favor of completely unfettered speech in college settings. In addition, even defenders of codes carve out exceptions to assure freedom of speech, and sometimes invite test cases at the boundaries of the restrictions.[449] So the debate, although usually not characterized this way, could be viewed as one over which kinds of restrictions are justified, not over whether to have any.[450]

In the analogous area of hate crimes, the Supreme Court has rejected on First Amendment grounds laws that focus exclusively on groups that have historically suffered from discrimination.[451] According to one commentator, the Court seemed to construe the First Amendment as forbidding governments from telling the world that "violence driven by racial hatred is more destructive than violence driven by class hatred, political animosity, labor strife or just plain greed."[452]

Rather than join the debate about degrees of victimization,[453] and about which kinds of categories should or should not receive protection through speech codes or hate-crime statutes, I would like to consider the ways in which the debates over these issues distract attention from the conditions that permit hateful expression.[454] The greater diversity of students on college campuses over the past decade means that many students encounter, for the first time, people who are very different from themselves. They do so in the intense and often intimate settings of classrooms and dorms. Yet colleges have not taken many steps to acknowledge these encounters. Most have not diversified faculties as much as student bodies nor altered curricular offerings. Nor have most developed ways to teach students about the displacement of economic insecurity—in the current global economy—onto issues of group difference.

The focus on disciplinary codes and First Amendment defenses does not address the sources and forms of hate nor the institutional contexts that could alter hateful expressions. Colleges should articulate and enforce codes of conduct that prohibit acts that injure others; students, faculty, and administrators should protest and condemn statements of hatred. But more basic reforms to the structures of important centers of learning should proceed to address the causes for hateful expressions in what should be places of civility and respect.

*C. Enlarge public support for art and artistic opportunities to address topics of past and present identities and affiliations, oppressions, and resistances.*
Alexis de Tocqueville may have been the first, but surely not the last, to

observe the American tendency to convert social issues into legal debates.[455] Law provides crucial settings and vocabulary for working out issues and dilemmas in a society that shares little besides a Constitution and the civic culture that surrounds it.[456] Yet perhaps the dominance of law grows also from inadequate opportunities for expression in other settings and vocabularies. One vibrant alternative is art. Theatre, visual arts, dance, music, fiction, public memorials, documentary films, and other forms of creative expression can provide avenues for provocation, catharsis, remembrance, and invention, all of which would enhance richer and more complex renditions of identity and all it does and could mean for people.[457]

Maya Lin's Vietnam Memorial and the debates it triggered provide a vivid example. Her vision of a wall placed as a gash in the land, a wall polished and engraved with the names of those Americans who died in the Vietnam War, offended many who sought greater majesty and appreciation for those who served in that most contentious war.[458] In response, veterans groups organized to fund and commission a more representational sculpture of men in combat; another group of women veterans organized to fund and commission a similarly representational sculpture.[459] Meanwhile, the crowds visiting the wall found that it permitted stunning occasions for personal and collective grief. Many have commented on the power of seeing themselves reflected in the polished marble. One ritual of producing paper rubbings of the names and another of leaving distinctive personal objects as tributes to those named have themselves stimulated new kinds of art and expression.[460]

Sadly, these possibilities for the public dimensions of art are seldom offered in defense against cost cutting and attacks on art as frivolous, offensive, or dangerous.[461] Cultivating greater appreciation for the possibilities of the arts—and greater opportunities for public participation in the creation as well as the appreciation of art—may be one of the most significant ways to enhance people's abilities to be for others as well as for themselves. It is through imaginative identification with others unlike oneself that art can transport; it is through the suspension of disbelief required to engage with the fiction of theater that people can discover their own deep sensibilities through temporary connections with others unlike themselves.

Greater attention to the history of the arts in America would also enhance understanding of the complex interconnections among people of different groups in forging artistic expression. From jazz to American fiction, the mutual influences of blacks and whites, men and women, immigrants and natives is a wondrous story of interconnection and strife.[462] The tales of the unmelted ethnic, the compound identity, may be distinctively American.[463] Artistic forms allow creators and viewers to explore group identities in complex and subtle ways that challenge simple labels; art also invites people to cross over gender, racial, and generational lines, lines between self and other, and to stretch imaginations.

## III. ADJUDICATION

I will not now adjudicate among these six strategies; I think we need them all, or at least debates about them all. The injuries that animate identity politics call for a variety of responses.

Ignoring historical and ongoing patterns of group-based oppression would be a supreme and cruel act of denial. Mindlessly repeating those very group lines will not overcome the psychological and social consequences of that oppression, nor expand the chances for individual freedom that oppression squelches. Yet, telling people to "get beyond it" neglects the hunger for memory and acknowledgment that people know—or believe—can afford a sense of place and meaning. Simply invoking unity to bypass group identities does not heed this hunger for recognition. Remembering, forgetting, reproaching, and forgiving do the work of making human meaning no less than eating, sleeping, growing, and reproducing do the work of making human existence. We need more, not fewer, settings for naming and articulating felt harms on the basis of group status.

Yet, when the government acts to install group-based categories for any purpose other than remedying group-based harms, we have a further problem. Governmental force gives words an apparent reality, backed by police and by bureaucratic practice. When governmental words refer to group identities, that force implies that identities are fixed, singular, and coherent. Remedial use can be defended, but would be improved if the process of constructing group categories became the focus for inquiry and response. When the purpose is not remedy, we should wrack our brains to find alternatives.

It is quite a different matter when an individual wants to claim a group identity, and to affiliate with others on that basis. This is the stuff of culture, and comfort—if we accept the poet William Stafford's definition: "Comfort: we think it is calm here, or our storm is the right size."[464] Group identities can, and should, be claimed and celebrated by individuals. Should we be able to claim, and assign, group identities to the next generation? To draw the state into this activity? To resist exposing children to other identities, and other options for their own development? These are among the most difficult and contested issues involving identity, and for good reason: children are the future. This is the next chapter's topic.

# CHAPTER 5
## *Generations*

<>

It is no accident that issues surrounding identity so often surface in decisions about children and schooling. In those decisions, parents often express their most vigorous attachments to a group identity and their deepest hopes for the future course of that group itself. Maintaining a culture, a religion, a language, or a nation depends on the cultivation of attachment and knowledge within the next generation. Identities are not given, but produced as individuals negotiate their ways through the webs of familial, social, and governmental attitudes and practices. Parents, and other adults, join the effort to influence each child's development of religious, racial, ethnic, and gender identities; they, and the child him- or herself, encounter some play in the joints and opportunities for resistance to identities that others seek to impose.

Given the larger society's attitudes toward some identities, however, some parents may try to resist the assignment of particular group identities to their children, especially when those labels spell stigma or disadvantage. They may seek assimilation into a dominant culture for, and through, their children. The polity—usually represented by public officials or representatives—also has a crucial stake in the identities of children and the educational experiences that help to shape them. Philosopher Michael Walzer notes, "All nation-states act to reproduce men and women of a certain sort: Norweigian, French, Dutch, or whatever."[465] In a nation whose motto is *E Pluribus Unum*, the public stake in children's development is complex. Ideals of unity and commonality compete with ideals of pluralism and particularity. The dream of common institutions that would create a "melting pot" or even a "mosaic" for a society composed of diverse communities clashes with the vision of a free country in which individuals can practice their religions, pursue their own visions of the good life, and raise children to advance those visions.[466]

How much should children's upbringing be an extension of their parents' freedom and how much instead an opportunity for collective, national policy? Governmental policies may have a more obvious and justified scope where children's physical well-being is jeopardized by parental choices and behavior, as when some parents consult their religious beliefs and refuse to authorize medical treatment and others plan painful, disabling, or disfiguring rituals for their children.[467] Social choices, made by adults, inevitably shape landscape within which each generation negotiates these alternatives. As philosopher K. Anthony Appiah puts it, "We have to help children make themselves, and we have to do so according to our values because children do not begin with values of their own."[468]

How much, then, should the United States, now, aspire to match with prospective parents the races or religions of children available for adoption?[469] When parents disagree between themselves about a child's affiliations, should the state intervene, and if so, how?[470] If the state does interpose a choice for the child, it then inevitably enters the activity of defining children's identities. Public neglect of these topics also produces potentially momentous consequences, including potential disintegration of particular cultural, religious, or racial groups. Neglect allowed numerous adoptions of Indian children by white families; neglect jeopardized some children's proficiency in the language other than English spoken at home. Yet, debates persist over legislation according Indian tribes rights in the adoption of Indian children and public school bilingual and bicultural programs.

Nowhere are the choices between parental and governmental control more significant for the cultivation and imposition of group identities than in schooling. As philosopher Elizabeth Minnich observes, "It is in and through education that a culture, and polity, not only tries to perpetuate but enacts the kinds of thinking it welcomes, and discards and/or discredits the kinds it fears."[471] As the ticket to adulthood, schooling also provides a crucial arena for efforts to remedy past and ongoing inequities in the society. These public efforts clash at times with the goals or choices of individual parents.

Already, I have urged efforts to enhance private choices about the shape and meaning of group affiliations, while restricting to remedial purposes any governmental assignment of individuals to group identities. What should happen when some individuals—parents—want to make private choices about the shape and meaning of the identities of other individuals—notably, children? Are decisions about one's children exemplary of the kinds of private choices people should enjoy[472] or are they exemplary of the kinds of public concerns that justify governmental regulation?[473] These questions are especially difficult given the likely effects of education on what children grow up later to choose.[474]

The answers are complex. This helps to explain the persistence of legal rules requiring a balance of parental and governmental interests. Those rules respect the liberty of adults and the pluralist traditions of the nation while reinforcing governmental authority to set and maintain the structure for ordered liberty and permitted pluralism. Or, to put the emphasis differently, the current legal rules in the United States set limits on the freedom enjoyed by adults to shape or determine the identities of their children, but those limitations arise within a general framework according parents considerable privacy and latitude in their plans and practices for their children. The prevailing rules do not prevent more direct policies to promote the capacities of children to be both for themselves and for others. I explore such possible policies after sketching the current state of legal rules governing parents, children, and schools. The results of current arrangements do not always advance either governmental or parental purposes, and raise serious questions about the place of children in American society.

## I. Pluralist Schooling and Choice
Three sets of overlapping questions frame parental control over their children's schooling. First, how much choice should parents have over where their children enroll in school? Must the school be public, run by the government, or may it be private, including religious and other specialized schools? May parents educate their children at

home or must they send them to a place recognized by the government as a school?

Second, how much control should parents exercise over what their children learn, or at least over the topics and methods of instruction? Should parents be allowed to veto or shape curricula used in public schools? Should the state be able to prescribe any of the content and methods for instruction in private schools or home schooling by parents?

Third, how much control should parents enjoy over selecting the peers with whom their children learn? To some extent, the issue of peers will necessarily reflect latitude of choice over public and private options. It will also, though, involve alternate designs within the public system: is there a plan for racial desegregation or integration in the school system? Does such a plan involve public assignment of children by race to particular schools, or parental choice subject to racial balance guidelines? Should the public system allow all-girl or all-boy schools? If the government regulates private schools, should it permit single-sex private schools? Forbid racial discrimination by religious schools? Or otherwise govern the student composition of private schools? Should parents be allowed to opt for home schooling even if this means their children will never be exposed to other kinds of children?

## A. Current U.S. Law

Contemporary American constitutional law can generally be described as a balancing act; competing values, such as respect for individual liberty and commitment to equality and collective safety, appear as worthy weights in judicial assessments.[475] Individual liberty is valued for itself and also as a means to sustain a vital society of plural traditions. Yet, protection of individual liberty and restraints on pluralism to assure social vitality and individual freedom require delicate governmental actions. Thus, the answer to almost any constitutional law question is, it depends. Case by case determinations of contested issues has yielded a long series of balances of private liberties and public interests in the context of schooling.

The state's traditional power to act as *parens patriae*, or as guardian for minors, and the democratic public's interest in producing an educated, well-socialized citizenry, add to the concerns that weigh against private, parental liberty. In essence, parents retain liberty to choose from among schooling options that satisfy minimum regulations set by the states. If the dream of a "common school," attended by all students, ever took hold in the imagination of Americans, it has been replaced by a rhetoric of choice. Parental choices are themselves constrained by public and private finances. Parental control over the child's peer group is similarly constrained by public commitments to equality—and by residential patterns, and borders dividing urban, suburban, and rural districts.

### Choosing Schools

Parents can within certain bounds select schooling for their children. In *Pierce v. Society of Sisters*, the 1925 touchstone precedent, the Supreme Court rejected a state compulsory education law that compelled attendance at public schools run by the government. A Roman Catholic school and orphanage, and a private military academy for boys challenged the statute. Holding such a law to be a violation of parental liberty to direct the education of their children, the Court's opinion included these sentences, which often have been repeated in later cases: "The child is not the mere creature of the State; those who nurture him and direct his destiny have the right, coupled with the high duty, to recognize and prepare him for additional obligations."[476]

If parents can pay or qualify for a limited number of scholarships, they can select a private school that satisfies the state's own regulations concerning the certification of teachers and instruction in required subjects such as preparation for citizenship. The courts still accept challenges, though, to state regulations on the ground that they unacceptably burden parental liberty. Parents prevailed, for example, against a Kentucky law specifying the same instruments of education, certified teachers, and state-approved textbooks in private schools.[477] Yet courts have upheld, even against religious liberty claims of parents, other state compulsory schooling laws that require private school instruction to be "substantially the same" as public-school instruction.[478] Again, the law has produced a balancing test, comparing the sincere religious beliefs of parents with the state's legitimate and compelling interests in educating people. Regulations that appear reasonable to courts and that do not seem to judges to be *unwarranted* intrusions on parental religious freedoms (note the implicit balancing judgments) will survive, unlike regulations that are too specific and cannot be supported by the state's general interests.

A remarkable Supreme Court decision in 1972, *Wisconsin v. Yoder*[479] is the leading modern American legal hymn to pluralism. Like any hymn sung by real people, however, it does not resolve all dissonant voices. Wisconsin, like all other states, adopted a law requiring children to attend school until they reach the age of sixteen. Parents of children who did not attend school would be subject to a fine.[480] Members of the Amish community in Wisconsin, who opposed schooling for their children past the eighth grade,[481] challenged the law as an intrusion on their right to exercise their religion freely, a right guaranteed by the First Amendment to the U. S. Constitution. The Amish parents argued that their religion called for a way of life tied to the local farming activities and shielded from the heterogeneous world of industrial and material distractions.[482] The courts considering the case did not doubt that these beliefs were religiously motivated and deserving of constitutional protection.[483]

Nonetheless, the state government had the opportunity to demonstrate that its concerns could override even the important constitutional commitment to free religious exercise. Wisconsin maintained that it represented the interests of the broader community, and of the Amish children themselves, in seeking to assure that all children in the state received the same minimal amount of educational instruction.[484] The Supreme Court concluded that the burdens placed on the constitutionally protected religious freedoms of the Amish could not be justified by the state's espoused interests, especially because, in the Court's view, the Amish already fulfilled many of the state's purposes by raising their children to become productive and law-abiding individuals.[485]

The majority opinion for the Court, written by Chief Justice Warren Burger, finessed many of the tensions in the case. The opinion suggested that the rest of the community faces no sacrifices in respecting the Amish parents' request for an exemption because this subgroup so resembles the majority in its ability to teach its children just what the majority hopes its public schools will teach: to be productive, self-sufficient, and law abiding, like the archetypal yeoman farmer and family.[486] In essence, the opinion maintained that the state must respect religious and cultural differences because the Amish really are fundamentally the same as the larger society. Moreover, the majority avoided facing up to the question of parental, or subcommunity, power to curtail the freedom of individual children. The majority was content to point to the success of individuals raised within the Amish way of life.

A separate, partial dissent by Justice Douglas chided the majority for failing to require consideration of the children's own views. For Douglas, concern for the Amish children's interests should include efforts to present and preserve options for individuals who might decide to leave the Amish community—and who then might need the extra years of school instruction required by the state.[487]

Parental decisions might not match choices the children themselves would make. Deferring to parents, rather than to individual children, does stand as the one nearly universal exception from the Constitution's commitment to individual self-determination.[488] The majority assumed that the Amish parents spoke for their children, but Justice Douglas urged direct questioning of the children to learn their views.[489] He acknowledged the potential conflict between world views, and the difficulties in selecting who would resolve it.[490] Of course, the Amish had submitted their case to the U.S. courts for resolution, but the Supreme Court itself acknowledged that if Amish litigants had lost, they said they would have left the United States in search of a more tolerant place.[491]

A critic of the decision in *Wisconsin v. Yoder* could object to its failure to protect the rights of individual Amish children to develop abilities and acquire experiences that would enable their own choices about how to live.[492] A defender could celebrate the Court's willingness to sacrifice a liberal value of individual choice in order to respect a religious subcommunity's preferences about how to raise its children.[493] Even this high-water mark for religious and ethnic pluralism under American constitutional law attests to the balance of private and public purposes. Tolerance and private freedom win as long as they comport with goals approved by the majority.

Home schooling stretches the limits of public regulation. Between 1980 and 1995, private groups successfully persuaded over half of the state legislatures to permit home schooling. This is instruction in the home, typically by a parent. It does not assure interaction with other students, or access to libraries, laboratories, and other facilities.[494] Home schooling, which by some estimates involves some 300,000 children each year, has been sought by some because of religious beliefs, by others because of disappointment with other school options, and by still others due to opposition to established institutions.[495] Yet, even the home-schooling option remains subject to state regulation. States may require certification or demonstrated competence of teachers, and states are authorized to monitor the quality of home schooling by mandating testing of students. The states' interests in assuring that students learn must be balanced in these regulations by the parental interests in guiding the development of their children and protecting their free exercise of religion.[496]

### Choosing Curriculum

Being able to choose home schooling, or private schooling, considerably enhances parental control over the content and methods of instruction. These options are meaningful chiefly to those families that can afford the money or time involved, although scholarships and recruitment efforts may help diversify the families involved. Those who use the public schools either adhere to the vision of the common school, integrating a pluralist society, or else cannot afford or find a preferable alternative. Parents may still try to influence the curriculum by pressing the local school board or state legislature to restrict the use of certain textbooks or library books, offer instruction in a subject, or forbid instruction in a subject.[497] School board and legislative actions in these arenas have especially focused on books alleged to insult or hinder particular religious traditions, materials that are viewed as obscene, immoral, or vulgar, and courses on evolution and sex education.

Courts, in turn, have reviewed school board and legislative decisions by trying to balance not only private parental liberties and public purposes but also teachers' and students' freedoms of speech and academic inquiry.[498] A state may not forbid instruction about evolution nor require balanced exposure to "creation science" alongside evolution science.[499] A school board may require sex education courses, although some districts make them optional or permit a student to be excused on parental request.[500] A school board can discontinue instruction about Aristophanes' *Lysistrata* and Chaucer's *The Miller's Tale*; the board's concerns about excessive vulgarity in the books are reasonably related to legitimate pedagogical concerns.[501] Yet, removal of books from a school library in order to limit the available spectrum of knowledge or points of view may violate freedoms of expression and inquiry.[502] Again, courts engage in contextual inquiries, weighing competing values of individual freedoms, socialization goals, and deference to teachers and school boards.[503]

All states currently require instruction about the U. S. Constitution; most require education about American history.[504] Beyond these elements, public school curricular plans vary widely and states vary a great deal in the requirements they impose.[505] State requirements range from teaching the accomplishments of Leif Erickson,[506] and the political and economic contributions of women[507] to instruction in cooperative marketing and consumers' cooperatives.[508] Moral education and character education programs attract many local supporters.[509] Yet efforts to promote—not require, promote—education to instill values such as honesty, kindness, and responsibility have failed to succeed in Congress.[510] Conservatives fear a liberal agenda and liberals worry about right-wing or religious values seeping into public education.[511]

### Choosing Peers

Officially, parents do not retain control over the exposure of their children to other children who differ from them, whether in terms of race, ethnicity, gender, or disability. Public schools or schools receiving public financial support cannot segregate by race, and those that do so remain subject to court-ordered plans to desegregate.[512] Yet parents with financial resources can, in effect, select the racial composition of their children's public schools by moving to districts with the racial composition they prefer. Similarly, parents may press for their children's entrance into programs for gifted children or into private schools where the racial composition departs from that of the regular urban public school classroom.[513]

The law governing sex-segregated schooling is in flux.[514] Sex discrimination is clearly forbidden in any school receiving financial assistance from the federal government, but equal access to comparable programs does not violate this rule.[515] The Supreme Court recently rejected the Virginia Military Institute's defense of its exclusion of women as a violation of equal protection.[516] The Court found the school failed to articulate "important government objectives" for the exclusion of qualified women or to show that this exclusion was "substantially related to the achievement of those objectives."[517]

A public school that could proffer strong reasons might justify single-sex schooling, although all-male schools have mainly failed to convince courts that they have good reasons.[518] All-female schools might be justifiable based on grounds of remedying past mistreatment or based on evidence that girls get less attention from teachers in coeducational settings;[519] all-male schools have been advocated as ways to reduce sexual tensions that interfere with students' learning and as settings for providing positive male role models.[520] Some schools experiment with single sex classrooms within a coeducational school as a measure to eliminate distractions.[521] Still, any reasons that look like sex-based stereotyping will fail to justify single-sex schools.[522] Private schools that do not receive any public financial support may avoid these concerns altogether.[523]

State and federal laws assuring equal educational opportunities for children with disabilities authorize appropriate programs, which may be separate from mainstream classrooms.[524] These laws at the same time require placement in the "least restrictive" settings. Therefore, these laws press toward inclusion in regular classrooms. Some parents of children with special needs prefer inclusion of this sort while others worry that their children will not receive tailored teaching and services as a result. Congress adopted the central statute in the area after noting that more than half of the eight million children with disabilities in the country were not receiving appropriate education and that approximately one million were excluded entirely by the public schools.[525] Some courts have ordered school districts to reimburse parents for the tuition of private schools selected by parents when the placement or placement process provided by the state can be proven inadequate under governing law.[526] The design of special education programs must always guard against misuse of testing to treat as disabled nonwhites or those whose primary language is not English.[527]

In addition, local public education officials must assist private schools in meeting the needs of local children with disabilities; thus, parents of children with disabilities can choose—subject to their financial abilities—private schools, and still receive some public benefit.[528] Parents of children who are not disabled may be unhappy with the inclusion of children with disabilities in their children's public school classrooms; they may fear disruption or loss of attention to their own children. The law gives them no particular claim in the matter, although they can make their concerns known to the relevant teachers and administrators.

Children whose primary language is not English may be grouped in bilingual education classes. Some parents seek such separate instruction; others oppose it. The relevant policy is set by local school authorities under the influence of federal regulations.[529] Local rules and practices must struggle to accommodate competing values. Segregating students whose primary language is not English or whose race is not white[530] conflicts directly with constitutional commitments to guard against racial and ethnic segregation in the schools.[531]

Finally, public school systems may provide for some degree of choice over kinds of schools, content, and peer students.[532] One method establishes "magnet" schools with specialized programs. Another method awards charters to groups of parents and teachers who propose new kinds of schools with particular missions in the hope of breaking out of perceived mediocrity or banality of common public schools. Still subject to general requirements governing racial equality and opportunities for children with disabilities, these specialized programs may nonetheless produce substantial racial segregation or other sorting of students because of transportation issues and the use of admission criteria.[533]

Thus, parents who have enough resources may select private schools or home schooling or suburban schools, and in those ways influence the content of schooling and the peers encountered by their children. Parents in public urban systems may secure a modicum of choice through magnet programs and charter schools. Some twenty-two states have adopted charter school legislation since 1990, which permits groups of parents, teachers, and other community members to create new schools and receive a public charter and financial support.[534] Dissatisfaction with homogenized schools and hopes that competition will improve school quality also motivate voucher programs, through which parents receive a voucher representing all or a portion of the tuition associated with public and private schools, and then select the school that will receive their child's voucher. Most proposals and experiments in this vein exclude private parochial schools in order to avoid potential violations of the First Amendment's prohibition against state establishment of religion. Yet, Cleveland, Ohio, recently, has included private religious schools in a voucher plan; Milwaukee, Wisconsin, dropped private parochial schools from its voucher plan, but private donors raised the money to cover 5,000 students whose parents had selected religious schools.[535]

A hard case illuminates restrictions on parental choice framed both by the Establishment Clause and by federal and state commitments to extend educational opportunities to children with disabilities. The case is difficult in part because of the collision between norms involving religion and disability; it is also difficult because prior interpretations of the Establishment Clause confine the room for reconciling these norms. Yet, while the case exhibits the historical and political process of balancing public and private interests, and subgroup and majority interests, it also demonstrates the profound challenges to any vision of integration that is presented by residential segregation.

### B. A Hard Case

Are legal efforts to promote exposure in schools to a range of ideas and to diverse fellow students counterproductive? Do such offers tip the balance too much toward state control and away from parental control—or do they fail adequately to assure opportunities for individual children to encounter ideas and people? Does the process of balancing public and private interests go any distance in promoting a next generation whose members can be for themselves, and also for others?

The recent, difficult case, *Board of Education of Kiryas Joel Village School District v. Grumet*[536] highlights these questions. I think it also affords an occasion for identifying if not right answers, at least some wrong ones.

When the story began is itself a likely subject for dispute, depending on which side is consulted. Did it start when residents of the Village of Kiryas Joel successfully pressed the New York State Legislature to adopt a statute to create a school district for the village, composed entirely of followers of Satmar Hasidim? Or did it start when a group of Satmar Hasidim, a group of ultra-Orthodox Jews, moved to upstate New York and faced charges of zoning violations in the city of Monroe? The Satmar used housing in ways that reflected their close-knit group practices and their prior experiences of dense urban living. They ultimately avoided the zoning issue by seeking, gaining, and defending incorporation as a separate local government under New York law.[537]

Members of the Satmar community would probably say that the story began with the history of the Jews, or at least with the history of the Teitelbaum family leadership of a sect of Hasidic Jews in Hungary in the nineteenth century.[538] Emerging in hostile, non-Jewish settings, this Orthodox sect in Europe, and then in the United States, subscribed to the idea that the Law of the land is the Law—but only as a choice of law rule within Jewish law.[539] The Satmar are the largest traditional Hasidic community. They established themselves in the United States to honor the memory of those murdered in the Holocaust by trying to re-create separate communities resembling the Eastern European villages that the survivors fled after World War II.[540]

The community resisted the assimilation of modern secular Europe, and promoted as well the economic and civic opportunities afforded in the United States.[541] Members of the Satmar view the United States as a government of grace that is just and kindly disposed to them, but which is also a threat because of the larger society's lures and lawlessness.[542] The Satmar believe that "[t]he Torah forbids the new."[543] They transported their way of life from Hungary to Brooklyn, and then some moved to what became Kiryas Joel. They speak Yiddish; they dress in clothes more typical of eighteenth-century than late-twentieth-century America; they segregate the sexes outside the home; they eschew television, radio, and English-language publications.[544] They vehemently oppose the establishment of the state of Israel.

The Satmar community educates its children in private, single-sex religious schools.[545] The disabled children in the community, however, are entitled under federal and state law to special educational services using public funds.[546] Briefly, during the mid-1980's, those services were provided by the state in the religious schools, but Supreme Court decisions announced at the time forbade the provision of such direct public services on the site of religious schools.[547] Some of the parents of disabled Hasidic children then sent their children to the public schools in the next town,[548] but found it unacceptable because of the "panic, fear and trauma" experienced by children sent away from their community to be with people so different.[549] Some of the parents had challenged the provision of services in the public schools as inadequate and insensitive to the needs of their children.[550]

At the request and urging of residents of Kiryas Joel, the New York State legislature authorized the Village of Kiryas Joel to establish public schools. The village exercised this authority solely for disabled students because the Satmar Hasidim in the village had no interest in any other public schools. Citizen taxpayers and the New York School Board Association sued, claiming that the statute creating this special school district was not neutral, and violated the First Amendment's requirement to separate church and state.[551] Viewed in this way, the case presents a problem squarely within all three questions left unanswered by the history of Jews in Western constitutional societies: the education of children, the governance of families and care of dependents, and the acceptable degree of accommodation of religion in public settings.

It may well be that the Hasidic community had complex motives.[552] Many outside observers think that the Satmar are a contentious and difficult group, with authoritarian rabbis, internal schisms, and a willingness to use devious tactics of appeasement, bribery, and manipulation.[553] They have had recent occasions of internal violence and allegations of voting fraud.[554] In an earlier, prolonged controversy, residents in Kiryas Joel sought publicly funded transportation for children attending private religious schools but protested the assignment of women bus drivers for buses carrying boys.[555] Some outside observers argue that the Satmar never really wanted the public school at issue ultimately in the Supreme Court. Instead, they wanted the state to pay for a private school, entirely segregated from the rest of the world.[556]

There is evidence outside the court record of preferences for self-segregation by the community. One Satmar residing in New York City was quoted as saying: "If we have our kids learning with [others], they'll be corrupted. We don't hate these people, but we don't like them. We want to be separate. It's intentional."[557] Jerome Mintz quotes another Satmar from Williamsburg, New York, who said:

> If you raise a child for eighteen years, sacrifice and sweat blood, and someone comes along and tries to influence them in a different way from yours, what would you do? . . . Our community is built on religion. You can't understand it with your mind. It's more important than any other thing.[558]

Significantly, this defense of separatism was offered to defend the Satmar against another Hasidic group, the Lubavitch. Indeed, this particular statement was offered in defense of Satmars in Williamsburg who assaulted a Lubavitch rabbi for offering lessons to an eighteen-year-old Satmar. This certainly portrays a vivid sensibility of the outside world as a threat, the inside world as very particular to the Satmar Hasidic community, and the plausibility of any means, including violence, to further true belief.[559]

Yet "separatism" is not an accurate way to describe the Satmar, who engage in commercial activities, such as the diamond industry, both in New York and in the rest of the world.[560]

The community did request authorization for a public school. The school they set up was administered by people from outside the community and offered entirely secular instruction by teachers from outside the community.[561] The superintendent, who had direct control over the school, is a person with twenty years of experience in the field of bilingual/bicultural education in the New York City public schools—and a person who is, himself, not Hasidic.[562] No religious instruction occurred at the school. The school was co-ed, despite the community's religiously mandated sex segregation in the religious schools.[563]

In its lawsuit, the New York School Board Association claimed that it was not the school per se, but its creation by the state, which violated the Establishment Clause. As it turns out, the majority of the organized Jewish community, and most Jews I know, agreed with this position and disagree with the creation of the special district for Kiryas Joel. In amici briefs filed with the Supreme Court, some representatives of the Orthodox Jewish community supported Kiryas Joel, but all other Jewish groups—and 500 citizens of Kiryas Joel itself—opposed the special school district on constitutional grounds.[564]

A deeply religious Jewish professor suggested to me that the Satmar should not ask for special education from the state, but should instead take care of their own, and secure their independence. Other Jews might worry that accommodating members of the Kiryas Joel community could unleash Christian animosity toward all Jews. Even if accommodation helps in the short run, in the long run it breeds jealousy and resentment. Some may even fear that non-Jews will think that all Jews are like the Satmar: bearded, intense, antisecular, and rigid. Others may fear that letting pro-Jewish legislation go forward will prompt a backlash against religious Jews or Jews in general.

In the long run, permitting the special school district could have further negative results for Jews, including the Satmars. Accommodation of this Hasidic community could lead to accommodation for other fundamentalist groups—and the others are very likely not to be Jews. This prospect threatens the liberal, secular state with takeover by enclaves of illiberal, fervently religious groups. In an era of growing Christian fundamentalist political movements, these are not imaginary worries. For many Jews, the commitment to separate church and state is so basic a precondition for freedom from state-sponsored oppression that the analysis stops there. Anything that smacks of state-sponsored religion—no matter what the religion—must be stopped.[565]

The point might be put as a response to Hillel's teaching that inspires this book: We must be for neutrality in order to be for ourselves. Some Jews also support this conception of separation apart from its instrumental value to Jewish communities, simply seeing it as a principled opposition to state-sponsored or even state-favored religion.

This conception of a strict separation between church and state underlies the decision of the state trial court in *Grumet v. New York State Education Department* rejecting the school district in Kiryas Joel.[566] The U. S. Supreme Court affirmed, though the Justices could not agree on a single opinion.[567] There was also a vigorous dissent. A majority joined Justice Souter in concluding that the special school district gave too much authority over a secular function of society to a religious group, and thereby unconstitutionally delegated a secular function to a religious body. Justice Kennedy's opinion, in contrast, analogized the problem to recent disputes about apportioning voting districts along racial lines.[568] This opinion reasoned that the special school district simply looked too artificial, too carved out, to be neutral toward religion.[569]

Justice Scalia wrote an impassioned dissent, joined by Chief Justice Rehnquist and Justice Thomas.[570] Anyone who knows me knows this is not my crowd. But I think the dissenters rightly argued that the rest of the Court in this case was overly suspicious of, or even opposed to, religion. The dissent reasoned that the state of New York came up with a reasonable accommodation for a special case. Nothing in the record or in experience suggests that the State would refrain from accommodating another religious group that asked for it. A fair concern is unequal abilities of different groups to mobilize sufficient legislative support for a special statute. Nonetheless, even this worry gives no grounds to conclude that the legislature acted with unacceptable favoritism toward the Satmar and would disfavor another religious group's request for a similar accommodation.

The immediate response of the New York State legislature was to adopt new legislation encompassing something like the Kiryas Joel special district into a statute that looks more general and more neutral.[571] New York thus took up the suggestions in some of the Justices' opinions to avoid an appearance of favoritism by changing the form, but not the substance, of the law authorizing the Kiryas Joel school district.[572]

The problem of the Kiryas Joel School District can be discussed as an example of the narrow, or nonexistent, distance between the constitutional command to avoid establishing or favoring religion and the constitutional command to protect religious liberty. As many observers note, government efforts to accommodate religious individuals run the risk of looking like favoritism or preference for religion.[573] The case could also be examined in terms of the relative power of different groups in legislative politics. The judicial response might be defended as an effort to restrict unfair advantages secured by a group when similar advantages have not—or have not yet—been secured by others.[574] These are familiar moves and countermoves in the development of constitutional doctrine in the context of religion.

A different frame of analysis, though, highlights the tension beteen parental and community prerogatives regarding schooling. The government assures special education entitlements to every child who needs them. To get them, how much must the Satmar parents forgo their preferred way to raise their children?[575] The Supreme Court's decision suggests that parents in Kiryas Joel must choose.[576] On the one hand lies separatism—and refraining from exercising the statutory right to public support for the education of children with disabilities. On the other lies assimilation into the mainstream society, and access to public education benefits.[577] The state in this view has no choice: it must either respect private decisions about private schooling, or control public schooling and thereby refuse to endorse any particular religion in that undertaking.

Yet, the public school created in Kiryas Joel triggers issues beyond the delicate balance between private religious exercise and public neutrality toward religion. At issue here are competing views of how best to achieve equal educational alternatives for children with disabilities. One view advocates inclusion,[578] and would seek instruction for the Satmar children with disabilities in the least restrictive setting, the one most like a mainstream classroom with exposure to other kinds of children.[579] These provisions reflect the struggle to overcome two kinds of discrimination experienced by people with disabilities— the total exclusion from opportunities afforded to others, and the failure to adjust and to alter existing opportunities so that those with disabilities can take advantage of them. Both imply particular visions of equality. Separate, specialized instruction can respond to particular needs while also creating a space in which the children with disabilities are not "different" and marginal.[580] Even the strong vision of inclusion does not and should not place the burden of overcoming prejudice on the backs of the most vulnerable in the society. Disabled children of a minority religion and culture seem easy candidates for a position of extreme vulnerability. The school in *Kiryas Joel* thus posed a choice between visions of equality for children with disabilities as well as the difficulties in assuring free exercise of religion without producing governmental preference for any one religion.[581]

For me, the most powerful and most troubling perceptions in the Supreme Court opinions are two points made by Justice Stevens. He stressed, and I support, the public school's duty to prevent trauma from inclusion. He reasoned that the adults in the situation had to be able to produce more choices than exposing the disabled Hasidic children to ridicule, "panic, fear and trauma" in the neighboring public school system or creating a special, segregated school district for them.[582] Instead, "the State could have taken steps to alleviate the children's fear by teaching their schoolmates to be tolerant and respectful or Satmar customs."[583A] Such steps would not risk violating the Establishment Clause. At the same time, they would advance the larger vision of inclusion represented by the public schools.

Yet Justice Stevens also concluded, contrary to my own view, that the parents should not be able to shield their children from competing religious influences. He said that the separate school system wrongly shields the disabled children from association with their neighbors and disabled children from association with their neighbors and thereby gives "official support to cement the attachment of young adherents to a particular faith.[583B] Justice Scalia understandably, though sarcastically, responded in the dissent, "[s]o much for family values. If the constitution forbids any state action that incidentally helps parents to raise their children in their own religious faith," this is a "manifesto of secularism" and "hostility to religion."

How could Justice Stevens simultaneously call for measures to alleviate the Satmer children's fears through teaching tolerance *and* deny their parents any protection against competing religious influences? The two positions are compatible because they arise from a notion of cosmopolitanism, or what historian David Hollinger calls a "postethnic" conception of individual freedom: Individuals should be free to affiliate and disaffiliate from groups within a democratic society.[584]

While there is much to commend this view, especially as against the assignment of individuals to groups with no exit, I worry about the assumption that cosmopolitanism is always better—for individual children, and for society as a whole. Cosmopolitanism affords no space for conceptions of group membership insoluable in the sea of chosen individuality.[585] It implies a melting pot or rootlessness that would eliminate distinctive, particular cultures and the smaller groupings that nurture norms.[586] Especially given the homogenizing forces of a global economy, the vitality of subgroups faces substantial jeopardy.[587]

Marge Piercy addressed this issue in her novel, *Woman on the Edge of Time*.[588] The book intertwines two stories. The first tells of a poor woman of color who, through a series of misfortunes, finds herself in a mental hospital where she is repeatedly subjected to shock treatments. The second story concerns either this woman's delusions or— it being science fantasy—the utopia where she periodically finds escape, only to return to the mental hospital. In the utopia, the main character finds many surprising practices. Children are born only through test tubes; parents sign up for the opportunity. Parents and children thus are commonly of different races and hues. Upon reaching adolescence, each individual moves to a new household and stays with a new guardian who shepherds her through that transition to adulthood. In addition, gender makes no difference in childbearing or childrearing.

In this utopian society, however, people worried about losing distinctive cultures and about resisting historical stigmas and status differentials associated with less powerful groups. The society decided to preserve traditional groups, and to promote the development of new groups, but made membership in any group entirely voluntary. An adult could choose to join a group devoted to preserving the traditions of the Iroquian Indians, or another group interested in developing Reformation Protestantism. A child would participate in a group, or multiple groups, chosen by his parent. Upon reaching adolescence, he or she could try any group. In this way, the society maximized options for entrance, while preserving options for exit. At the same time, the society avoided converting all cultural traditions into either museum artifacts or shopping-mall displays of fashions and foods.

Unless and until childbirth and childrearing separate from the identity of parents, this vision remains remote. Yet, to forgo any protection for or encouragement of traditional groups could undermine them or fuel a reactionary fundamentalism opposed to a liberal state. Decisions about schooling again become the meeting ground for parents and community; what visions of group identity and individual self-creation should inform the selection of schools and the design of their programs?

In the case of *Kiryas Joel*, receipt of public benefits might draw the children from Kiryas Joel into a world more diverse than their own secluded community. Indeed, as operated in the system rejected by the Supreme Court, this was the case. The faculty of the public school was itself ethnically and religiously heterogenous.[589] Young, impressionable students had role models, helpers, and mentors from backgrounds quite different from their own. Yet they lacked peers who were different.

Rather than focus on the uniqueness of the public school district created in Kiryas Joel, the Court could, and should, have addressed its seclusion, its segregation from other kinds of children. The public school officials responsible for the entire state plan for special education could expand the diversity of students in the Kiryas Joel school district. Greater diversity in peers would enlarge the social worlds and room for imagination for the disabled Satmar children. Secular programs at the school could include nondisabled Satmar children, welcomed to join in common projects with the disabled children on the site of the public school. English language instruction and exercises using English might provide a good topic. Or the school could draw non-Satmar children with disabilities, where appropriate. It could be a "magnet" school attracting students from neighboring communities. Devising incentives to promote integration across varied divides would not eradicate difference, but instead nurture self-conscious acknowledgment of identities, and the grounds for tolerance itself. For tolerance has no occasion to be tested, or strengthened, in the absence of differences that trigger genuine disagreement.[590]

Schools where children do not encounter children unlike themselves could only arise due to artificial segregation, for ours is a world of difference. Segregation of children with disabilities remains a troubling aspect of the solution sought by the community of Kiryas Joel. Yet more profoundly, residential segregation produced homogeneity in that school, as it does in schools around the country. Residential segregation is a humanly made practice. In some instances, the government plays a direct or indirect role. The issues at Kiryas Joel would not have arisen had the state of New York denied a religious community to become a legally recognized municipality.[591] Here segregation stems not from the law but from private choices;[592] in other circumstances, public policies and private choices converge to produce racial, ethnic, and religious segregation.[593] How much can public authorities acknowledge the public dimensions of residential segregation, and override parents' residential choices to produce integrated schools, or at least settings in which children can get to know others unlike themselves?

The Supreme Court has refused to authorize remedies for racial segregation in the schools if those remedies require crossing municipal borders absent a showing of intentional segregation by the authorities in the relevant communities.[594] While this ruling itself may prompt white flight from central cities, rewarding self-segregating white com-munities with immunity from desegregation efforts, a contrary ruling directing cross-district integration could also stimulate white flight from public to private schools. Some communities voluntarily participate in efforts to overcome residential segregation through cross-district busing and other programs.[595] The most basic step toward tolerance and mutual respect is the sheer creation of integrated settings. Psychologists have argued that when people change behavior so that it is incongruent with their attitudes, those attitudes will change to harmonize with the behavior.[596] On this theory, integrated schools will be more likely than segregated schools to elicit mutual tolerance even among groups that distrust one another.[597]

But other steps are important to promote mutual respect even in integrated school settings. One review of the literature on the efficacy of racial desegregation programs concludes that reduction of racial prejudice is most affected by significant contact with members of other groups "under conditions of equal status that emphasize common goals and deemphasize individual and intergroup competition."[598] Important kinds of contact include group academic projects and shared membership on athletic teams.[599] Contact with nondisabled children is especially important for children with disabilities if they are ever to learn how to interact with others and find out what behaviors are viewed as normal by other students.[600]

Making the matter more difficult, prejudices are more readily decreased where there are few points of difference between groups. Pre-judice about racial difference, for example, may be more easily altered where there are not also social class differences among the groups.[601] Support from the community,[602] especially from neighbors and family members, is important in influencing the attitudes of students toward the experience of integration.[603] It is probably not unfair to infer that the Satmar parents gave little effort to make the integration effort work for their children who tried the neighboring public school. Other communities resisting desegregation across district lines are no more, but also no less, commendable.

## III. SCHOOLING FOR PLURALISM

Parents, communities, schools, legislatures, and courts will continue to struggle with the balance of private choice and public plans affecting where children are schooled, with what content, and with which fellow students. In the meantime, because even private schools and home-schooling options require some degree of public regulation, let us focus on that basic issue: what minimal regulation should address issues of identity formation, stigma, and inequality?

Nothing in the requisite balance between parental and governmental interests gets in the way of this basic goal: schools in the United States, of whatever sort, should try to promote intergroup understanding and the capacities of young people to be both for themselves and for others. This comports with respect for both parental choices to instill pride about heritage and identity and with public commitments to promote equality and exposure to different kinds of people. Parents and children may choose private and public educational programs that reflect and strengthen religious, racial, or gender identities but still face requirements for courses and activities with demonstrated success in promoting intergroup tolerance.

One promising approach calls for joint projects, whether academic, recreational, or cultural, that involve diverse groups of children in engaging activities and emphasize common goals.[604] In school systems with considerable segregation, such projects may be devised to bring together students from different schools either during or after school hours.[605] No particular student need participate, but schools of all sorts could participate, and could make it easy and attractive for students to join.[606]

Some programs may be conducted with partners outside the schools. Recently, a group of New York judges organized "Blacks and

Jews in Conversation," a series of forums, discussions, and an essay contest.[607] Started by Justice Jerome Hornblass, an Orthodox Jew, and Justice William C. Thompson, who is black, the program grew from the judges' perceptions that group conflicts in the city needed a creative response. The judges also found inspiration in the earlier partnership between blacks and Jews in the civil rights movement. The program has expanded to include some 200 judges and lawyers, and includes Asian, Hispanic, and homosexual participants. Sessions have addressed racism and violence, slavery, and art. Many of the events afford students their first chance to speak to someone of another race.[608]

A participating student who won an essay contest award, and the strongest applause at the award ceremony, said: "I am scared of expressing myself, but I'm trying to change. I am Hispanic and I was taught not to like white people, black people, and Asians, but I can't accept that. Everybody is not the same. Everybody is different. I know this program will be successful. It won't stop racism, but it will lower it to a good level so everyone can live in peace."[609]

Community service projects that bring together students from urban, suburban, and rural areas also can forge friendships amid common challenges and purposes. Proposals to mandate such service for all young people after high school have not succeeded, but voluntary programs can be designed to assure real diversity.[610]

Besides promoting programs that bring diverse students together in and outside of schools, states can impose basic requirements for instruction that at least address information and ideas to enhance respect and tolerance across groups. Just as states have lawfully required private as well as public schools to provide basic instruction in American history, health, and other specified subjects, states could require learning about diverse cultures, American pluralism, intergroup relations, or struggles to overcome group bias and oppression.[611]

Courses and texts ostensibly advancing these ends have sparked volatile controversies, to be sure. Especially if "multiculturalism" seems to require a particular political viewpoint or appears to elevate some traditions at the expense of others,[612] curricular requirements to promote tolerance or values of equality will ignite controversies and jeopardize public support.

Nonetheless, states and local school officials could permit a range of courses or materials to satisfy the requirement while still establishing a universal commitment to cultivating appreciation for human equality and the struggles to achieve it. The project of devising a range of courses and materials to satisfy the legal requirement would itself be educational for teachers, students, and policy makers. Leaving room for a particular school or community to select its way to fulfill the requirement would not undermine the symbolic and practical benefits of having one.

A state could, for example, specify that all schools, public and private,[613] assure instruction in any ONE of the following: 1) contribution of diverse cultures to the development of the United States; or 2) U. S. judicial decisions enforcing religious freedoms and racial and gender equality; or 3) study of social movements to overcome group hatred in the United States; or 4) examination of the sources and confusions behind stereotyping and prejudice; or 5) studies of slavery, the Holocaust, genocide, racial apartheid, or caste systems—and the efforts by people to resist or overcome them.[614]

One curriculum I admire has elicited insistent critics. "Facing History and Ourselves," according to its Executive Director, Margot Strom, uses "the history of the Holocaust to educate students and teachers about the meaning of human dignity, morality, law, citizenship and human behavior and to help them make connections between history and their own lives. The lessons provided by this piece of twentieth-century history about bigotry, dehumanization, the roots of violence, individual and collective responsibility, are examined to illuminate the role individual citizens have in a democracy to preserve justice."[615]

Phyllis Schlafly and other leaders of New Right organizations criticize programs such as "Facing History" as psychologically invasive and likely to promote moral relativism.[616] The critics express the belief that children should not be exposed to controversial and conflictual subjects that could produce inner struggles, and that education should teach clear recognition of right and wrong, based on traditional and unquestioned faith in God and Western civilization.[617] I disagree with these views but leave the disagreement for another day. Instead, I challenge Schlafly and others to propose affirmative alternatives to meet a public requirement of instruction in what are after all fundamental principles of American law and civic values: due process, equal protection, religious freedom, and access to court to protest injustice. If there are those who maintain that no educational experiences would be appropriate to teach children about these principles, or the five alternative topics listed above, then the ensuing public debate should be a stirring civics lesson, and a controversy I would be proud to join.

## A. Current U.S. Practice

States and school boards will contest the desirability of a range of curricula and programs intended to promote tolerance and multicultural respect for some time to come, just as courts will continue to muddle through the process of balancing parental and public interests over school choice, curriculum, and the composition of student bodies. In the meantime, a reality check about the actual conditions of American schooling is in order, and will help put the "culture wars" in perspective.

Considerable racial segregation—whatever the cause—continues in American schools. More than forty years after *Brown v. Board of Education* declared intentional official racial segregation violated the guarantee of equal protection, patterns of resegregation appear in most urban areas. Although integration grew substantially during the 1970s and 1980s, studies have documented growing resegregation in many areas.[618] Moreover, courts increasingly require desegregation only at the level of the school building, permitting considerable race segregation at the classroom level.[619] Private parental choices, including choices about where to reside, contribute to racial and class segregation. Lawyers and judges have proved unable, or unwilling, to respond.[620] Other forms of segregation exist on limited bases.[621] Segregation not only can harm individuals, by depriving them of social contact and acceptance, but also can also undermine political cohesion.[622]

At the same time, current practice also reveals powerful pressures for increasing parental choice in education—whether through magnet programs or voucher plans letting parents use public dollars to select private schools. Middle-class and poor parents join in coalitions for such programs. The explosion of legislation authorizing charter schools in twenty-two states indicates frustration with existing schools and faith in choice as a mechanism for change.

These demands for choice reflect pervasive disappointment with American schools. A series of commissions meeting periodically over the past twenty-five years all conclude that America's children could reach much higher standards, as evidenced by children in other countries.[623]

The problem is not simply one of averages, but nearly universal underachievement.[624] For example, high achieving American student math scores approximate low math scores for children growing up in China or Japan.[625] Differences in student accomplishment within the United States reflect parental expectations and involvement more than any other factors.[626] Perhaps most distressing of all, aspirations and achievement for immigrant children and their families reflect—inversely—the amount of time spent in the United States. Asian American, Caribbean American, and Hispanic American children are more likely to hold higher goals and register higher school achievement the less time they and their families have spent in the United States. After two generations, the children of these immigrants blend into their nonimmigrant peers in terms of lowered aspirations and achievement.[627] Something happens in the process of becoming American, or is it from learning historically negative views and low expectations for members of minority races and ethnicities in America? The message that intelligence is innate and success is fore-ordained seems to be received effectively.[628]

## B. Whose Children?

Schooling in this, the wealthiest country in the world, falls far behind other countries. Our rates of innoculation and literacy also notably trail those of other industrialized countries, while we lead in rates of reported child abuse, teen pregnancy, and teen violence, and we near the top in teen suicide.[629] Efforts to mobilize political movements for children are stymied by charges of adult self-interest. Standing for children is viewed either as a front for old liberal governmental programs[630] or as an excuse for cutting them.[631]

These circumstances reflect two fundamental aspects of American society: intergroup divisions and a commitment to treat children as primarily the responsibility of their own parents. Middle-class and wealthy parents opt out of urban public schools and the tax base that supports them. "Other people's children" are other people's problems. Constitutional, and cultural, commitments to respect the privacy of each family and the prerogatives of parents similarly insulate the circumstances of children from public scrutiny or responsibility.

Yet, no estimate of the future makes any sense without central attention to children—all children. They are future workers, consumers, criminals, taxpayers, dissidents. The current Social Security system is based on the assumption that for every three beneficiaries of old-age insurance, there will be ten workers in the paid labor force, contributing to the insurance fund. Demographic shifts indicate that by the year 2020, the actual ratio will be five beneficiaries for every ten workers. The entire system will collapse unless all ten of those individuals actually hold good jobs and are able to contribute to the Social Security fund.[632] In major urban areas in this country, however, half of all poor and nonwhite students drop out of school, and those students leave school with few skills or job prospects.[633] The picture for those who do graduate from high school is not much better; thirty-five percent of all eighteen year olds in 1994 could be described as functionally illiterate.[634] The Business Roundtable, representing Fortune 500 companies, has concluded that American self-interest and world interests turn on the future quality of American public schools.[635] What does it take to convince others? If the financial estimates do not move people, would estimates of failed democracy, crime rates,[636] or human despair help?

We can't be for ourselves unless we are for others; and if we are not for all children, what are we?

# CHAPTER 6
## *Ties*

<>

Some say that ours is a time of unusually high conflict among groups. Tensions between generations[637] help explain why local community after local community cuts funding for schools and children's services while maintaining support for senior citizens.[638] Other disconnections seem at work here. Cutting public resources for children tends to manifest failures of concern across ethnic, racial, and income groups. Distrust across such social groups foments conflict. New regionalisms arise even as global communication surges.

Is national unity at risk? How do assertions of group identities affect politics across the nation? What does, or could, bind Americans together—or is that the wrong question? As an initial comment, I note that the contrast between group identities and an American identity is itself a contrast of identity politics. The assertion of an American identity as a necessary unifying trait for citizens of this nation invokes a subgroup identity, in relation to humanity, and threatens divisive chauvinism and nationalism compared with a unity of all humanity. The relative priority or trump of alternate identities—national or subnational, ethnic or gender, or a range of others—bears little relation to forging a common future. More crucial to that enterprise is devising settings for social interchange that nurture criss-crossing ties and experiences across groups that differ, and come together, on many different bases.

## I. DISUNITY?

In his best-selling book, *The Disuniting of America*, Arthur Schlesinger Jr. warns that "the division of society into fixed ethnicities nourishes a culture of victimization and a contagion of inflammable sensitivities."[639] Moreover, "when a vocal and visible minority pledges primary allegiance to their groups, whether ethnic, sex-ual, religious, or, in rare cases (communist, fascist), political, it presents a threat to the brittle bonds of national identity that hold this diverse and fractious society together."[640]

These charges, which center for Schlesinger largely on fights over what version of U.S. history should be taught in schools, actually entangle several different strands. The first is a defense of the values of Western civilization against critics who condemn it as racist, sexist, imperialist, and otherwise oppressive.[641] Those critics, writes Schlesinger, want history to nurture group pride and self-esteem for children of minority groups; this search for "feel-good history" misunderstands how children develop self-esteem and how history must tell the negative as well as the positive about each group.[642]

Historians and social critics have made debates over the teaching of American history a growth industry, and it will terminate, or continue, in venues other than this book.[643] Many observers—including Schlesinger—converge in the aspiration for rich, complex understandings of U. S. history and present. This would include the mutual influences of diverse cultures, the shortfall or violation of ideals in practice, and the continuity of concern over the relative balance of unity and plurality in the nation devoted to *E pluribus unum*.[644]

Historian Eric Foner, for example, explains his admiration for new histories giving increased attention to the experiences of previously neglected groups, such as women and members of racial minorities.[645] "But when history moves from recognition of the irrefutable fact that different peoples have had different historical experiences, to an effort to locate supposedly primordial characteristics shared with other members of one's group and no one else, it negates the study of change that is the essence of the discipline itself," just as it ignores the influences of different cultures on one another to shape America.[646] Foner reports that he shares some of the worries that modern scholarship wrongly emphasizes what divides Americans, rather than what unites Americans, and contributes to fragmentation that undermines national cohesiveness.[647]

However, then Foner parts company with Schlesinger and others who decry group divisiveness in American history debates. Foner notes the divisiveness comes at least in part from its supposed critics. He argues that the effort to turn history into psychological uplift, and to emphasize innate and immutable group differences, better characterizes the political right than the political left.[648] "[W]itness, for example, *The Bell Curve*, or *Alien Nation*, Peter Brimelow's recent screed against nonwhite immigration as destroying America's 'ethno-cultural community,' grounded, according to him, in a shared European ancestry." The strongest advocate of "feel-good" history designed to promote self-esteem, according to Foner, is "Lynne Cheney, former head of the [National Endowment for the Humanities], who condemns the new history standards for neglecting the greatness of the Western tradition and offering a 'depressing' portrait of our nation's past."[649]

The intensity of this fight reflects how much the official stories about the nation and the past matter to the present and the future.[650] Debates over what young people should learn reflect identity politics on many sides, not a fight between identity politics and neutrality or truth. A political landscape that hides this fact traps people in fruitless finger-pointing. In addition, it is a faulty American history that neglects the longstanding American experiment with pluralism, including successive waves of fears and defenses of it.[651]

The standards raising Cheney's ire tried to redress the traditional neglect in American history texts and courses of the experiences of America's minority groups. Surely, truth demands some changes in that direction, although a new sort of "victors' history," just with different victors in charge, is not the answer. Promoting understandings of complexity would help. So would expanding the arenas for discussing and debating the shape of past and present group experiences.[652] Then decisions over school curricula would not have to bear all the weight of pent-up fury, resentments, and fear.[653]

It is not only debates over American history teaching that make Schlesinger worry about "the disuniting of America." His argument combines three other claims. He warns against tribalisms and ethnic or linguistic apartheids that are stirred by demagogic hucksters and projected by mass media.[654] He invokes an American national identity as either a reality or an aspiration, uniting diverse residents of the continent over time.[655] Finally, he tries to summon a vision of civic culture uniting diverse Americans in commitments to self-government, freedom of expression, and individualism.[656]

Tangled in these themes are anxieties about what could tie together a nation of diverse, and often mutually suspicious, people. Because of the fear of social division, Schlesinger embraces successful assimilation to an existing, though gradually evolving, American identity. Suppose for a moment that the problem of social division is as severe as Schlesinger suggests, though analogies to wartorn Bosnia seem considerable exaggerations.[657] Remote as they may be, unscrupulous and ambitious demagogues have too often fed insecurities and grievances, producing political splinters and schisms that benefit only the demagogues, if anyone. So, for discussion, take concerns about social division, founded in or exacerbated by public discourse, as genuine and worth attention. Schlesinger's solution merges the issue of civic values with the issue of personal identity. He implies that only some people have to change in the melting pot of America, those whose language, customs, or preferences seem "different" from the "norm," which itself, to be frank, is the result of the last political battle over whose ways should prevail.[658]

There are other promising and palpable alternatives for holding Americans together besides trying to articulate and elevate a singular American identity. One alternative disentangles "American identity" and American civic culture.[659] Another looks to new developments in consumer culture; a third emphasizes the power of cross-cutting affiliations.

*Civic culture.* In this view, to be an American a person needs no particular national, linguistic, religious, or ethnic background, but need only commit "to the political ideology centered on the abstract ideals of liberty, equality, and republicanism."[660] The ideals binding the civic to a culture call for political participation representation offered to all, *and* freedom for religious pluralism and other private pursuits.[661] Amish parents seeking to exempt their children from compulsory schooling and Satmar Hasidic Jews seeking to accord their children public special education benefits could subscribe to these ideals sufficiently to work through the political and judicial systems to achieve their goals. Some people may subscribe to the civic culture only for short-term, or even long-term, reasons of self-interest, but that is enough, if their behavior comports with the principles at stake.

It would be difficult to maintain that civic culture as national glue accurately and fully describes the past and present. Even defenders of Americanism as civic culture acknowledge lapses, or hypocrisies, in the exclusions of blacks, Indians, Chinese, and then Japanese immigrants.[662] Yet, its failure as a full summation of practices to date does not disprove its abilities, periodically in the past and potentially in the future, to hold together the diverse residents of this nation. When compared with other potentially plural nations, the United States at least includes pluralism as one of its traits. "The United States *is* a nation of immigrants; France is a nation that attracts and incorporates immigrants."[663] The gap between practice and the ideal of an inclusive American pluralism founded in individual freedom and basic equality persists, but constitutionalism affords resources to redress that gap.

Reverence for, at least preoccupation with, law has often seemed an attribute of Americans.[664] This attachment to law need not signal great unanimity or high levels of accord, and indeed, may indicate instead considerable amounts of conflict that seems to require adjudication. Similarly, even elevation of the U. S. Constitution through almost religious devotion would not necessarily carry with it easy agreement about its meanings. Indeed, Sanford Levinson, a leading theorist who has treated the U. S. Constitution as the key feature of American civil religion, proceeds to argue that constitutional interpretation has been as great a source of disunity and disagreement as has biblical interpretation.[665] Yet, conflict over the potential meanings of the Constitution and high-volume uses of and imaginative references to litigation indicate remarkable levels of unity or convergence in the place accorded to the Constitution and to legal resolutions of disputes. We can fight hard within the ideological and institutional framework that we take for granted and reaffirm daily by use.

The emphasis on rights, enforced by a kind of winner-take-all litigation, may seem to worsen group conflicts in America. Mary Ann Glendon has advanced an eloquent critique of this and other consequences of the emphasis on rights in American culture. Yet, Glendon has also noted that "The very heterogeneity that drives us to seek an excessively abstract common language may indeed be one of our most promising resources for enriching it."[666] If the civil constitutional culture tilts more toward individualism and liberty than toward community and responsibility, it nonetheless affords a common starting point for discussion and debate by diverse and divergent individuals and groups.

Empirical studies of rights consciousness suggest that the civil constitutional culture is not reserved to a limited band of elites.[667] Trends in this area are not easy to establish, but awareness of constitutional rights and popular discussions about them burgeoned during the Bicentennials for the Constitution and the Bill of Rights. Curricular programs for high school and even elementary school students increasingly model judicial action and focus on contemporary legal issues.[668] If only as a point of departure, the language of law and constitutionalism can provide a common set of reference points for people in this country who otherwise feel little in common.

*Consumer culture of difference.* Whether one celebrates or bemoans them, consumer marketing strategies of leading advertisers and merchants appeal to and reinforce images of tolerance and respect for diversity that contribute to American civic culture. Sociologist Todd Gitlin observes, "Today it remains true that immigrants want to assimilate, but the America into which they hope to do so is not the America of white bread. It is an America where the supermarket shelves groan beneath the varieties of bagels, sourdough, rye, seven grain, and other mass-produced loaves. One belongs by being slightly different, though in a predictable way."[669] The United Colors of Beneton advertising campaign appealed to both the federation dimensions of a multiracial United States and the features of international law by showcasing multiethnic individuals wearing Beneton clothing.

Malls across the country replace restaurants with "food courts" that array mass produced, fast-serve food with distinctive ethnic presentations. Consumers buy the food they choose and then sit down in a common eating area; one table may be eating Mexican food while another consumes Japanese fish; at another table, individual family members each relish different ethnic foods. When General Mills decided to replace its picture of Betty Crocker, used on its syrup and cereal packages, it substituted for the white housewife a computer-generated composite of seventy-five American women of various racial and ethnic backgrounds; someone in marketing discovered that this reflects America.[670] Does this also suggest some greater sense of inclusion emerging within a civic culture devoted to individual freedom, equality, and consumer purchasing?

Putting aside questions about the durability of popularized constitutional culture and consumer marketing of civic images, more persistent criticisms can assault the desirability of these forms of civic culture. Legalisms can be abstract and divisive; consumerism can emphasize material values over all others, divide by class, and fuel insatiable desires for commodities that deplete other resources for building meaning and a sense of community.

Beyond these worries, civic culture, whether inflected by constitutionalism or consumerism, may seem ultimately too thin and intellectual to provide social glue. To define "American" in terms of civic culture is to assert that "[t]here is no American people, merely an American Idea."[671] This, say critics, misses the crucial sense of belonging that people need. Cultural glue needs more than ideas. Especially in the face of heated disagreements, solidarity and respect may require more than experiences and aspirations, something more textured than abstract commitments.[672] Empirical tests would be necessary to resolve this dispute, but the critique is sobering.

*Criss-crossing commonalities* Perhaps, alternatively to civic culture, or compatible with it, Americans are bound together by criss-crossing commonalities: not any one unity, but overlapping communities, the way a family may extend across marriages, divorces, and other intimate relations.[673] A community of communities can evoke sufficient allegiance to the ground-rules that let the subcommunities thrive.[674] Certainly one way to become American has long been to affirm a particular religious or ethnic identity.[675] Americans also ironically claim commonality as a nation of strangers. Claiming outsider status is a familiar American practice.[676] The "one" of American is yoked to "the many." Rather than either/or, we should acknowledge "both/and."[677] Especially American may be the unsettling of even these identities through the tradition of undermining tradition.[678]

On this view, unity is less important than solidarity. Unity implies coherence, which may actually be illusive or elusive. Solidarity is possible only where there are differences. It does not require unity, identity, or similarity. Solidarity puts differences aside in the name of affection, self-interest, or short-term or long-term purposes.[679] It may grow from interactions, rather than commonalities.[680] Criss-crossing commonalities grow when people work together on a school bake sale; recognize shared passions for basketball or hip-hop dancing that cut across differences in race, gender, or age; meet the extended family of a friend and discover how families often bridge religions, ethnicities, and races. Rather than a community of common identity or interests, repeated interactions and exposure among heterogeneous peoples can provide social glue.[681]

The virtues of this theory include its consonance with powerful observations by anthropologists, sociologists, and historians. Complementarity, interacting differences, integration through internal trades and swaps across groups with different strengths and resources—these converging phrases appear in works by observers of pluralistic cultures that seem to function well.[682] Moreover, students of culture increasingly question a presentation of any culture as homogeneous.[683] In a famous examination of solidarity, Clifford Geertz studied villages marked by a communal sharing of food within neighboring households, despite diverse belief systems; those ties were disrupted when people moved to larger towns, and similarity based identities seemed to matter more.[684] This kind of work implies not only a futility in a search for the common culture of a diverse society, but even danger in the creation of myths about national identity.[685] Myths of unity in national identity work to justify channeling people into singular identities, or else eliminating any person who does not conform.[686]

Important examinations of American history expose the notion of the "melting pot" as mythical and highlight long-standing features of unstable pluralism.[687] English officials had tried unsuccessfully to impose uniformity on the untidy, diverse, and unstable variety in colonial life, laws, and polities.[688] Myths of the melting pot emerged with the new nation, but perhaps applied only to American Negroes, who did indeed overcome regional, linguistic, and tribal differences during and after slavery.[689] Traditions of governance and cultural renewal that emphasized the local and resisted central authority made uniform laws, customs, and even coinage often unavailable prior to the revolution. The preservation of state sovereignty alongside federal supremacy marked an ingenious compromise in the founding of the nation. Protected by the rule of law as well as a complex constitutional structure, the nation preserved and promoted a plural society, despite fears of its risks of instability. "Americans continue to celebrate pluralism in the past, but are reluctant to honor it in the present."[690] Ambivalence about our pluralism is itself an American tradition.[691]

Exposures of the plurality, even within seemingly homogeneous cultures, also dislodge the mistaken assumption that unity is necessary for stability. Associations, subgroups, can be defended as democratic bulwarks against centralized power.[692] Ties of cooperation and respect, and the work of self-governance through democratic politics can be enhanced by overlapping but disconnected ties among different groups of people. Perhaps the very multiplication of people's felt alliances affords enlarging grounds for solidarities.

Constitutional scholar Kenneth Karst suggests that the proliferation of each individual's connections to groups defined by race, religion, family, occupation, and hobby affords chances for new kinds of commonality. The multiplication of every individual's group connections

> holds to unify a national society that might otherwise torn apart by cultural divisions. If the Catholics and Protestants who did bloody battle in mid-nineteenth century Philadelphia had continued to live in two adjoining but separated (and homogeneous) communities, the long-term results might have been bloodier still. But market individualism went about its usual work of multiplying selves with the result that both homogeneity and separateness were destroyed. Each of the groups became stratified by class and otherwise differentiated within itself, making new integrations possible for succeeding generations. Opportunity called individuals and families, both Catholic and Protestant, to join the move West; in their new surroundings they formed communities in which the old divisions just didn't matter so much. Their grandchildren intermarried and produced children of their own. As daily life in Hawaii

makes beautifully clear, nothing else integrates quite so effectively as a baby.[693]

The solidarities afforded by criss-crossing connections may never seem as strong or coherent as a unity directly tied to an overarching value, like nationalism (though that one, too, is an affiliation to a sub-group, among the family of nations). Yet, these solidarities may well be strong enough to withstand hate and to permit mutual aid against fractionalizing violence. Perhaps, cross-cutting connections offer something both more fragile and more reliable than unity. Connections based on intermarriage, overlapping group memberships, or a recognition that this particular stranger is actually in the soccer team that plays against your cousin's team are founded in experiences of exchange and concrete encounters rather than idealized histories or imagined shared heroes. The tentative quality of such ties would never lull people into believing there is no work to do, to build respect and communality, while the fact of some connection provides the yeast for more to grow.

Illusions of unity cannot sustain tolerance and respect when differences between people and groups inevitably surface. Aviam Soifer, an insightful scholar of groups in American history, concludes:

> Tolerance, ironically, must be bound to group struggle. It requires recognition of the guilt and fear we all encounter, rooted in uncertainties about our own identities. We strive for independence, yet any meaningful freedom is deeply dependent upon our social networks. To be real, tolerance requires recognition that we all use groups to define ourselves and others, inescapably and differently.[694]

For tolerance, respect, and democratic politics, unity is neither the necessary precondition nor the crucial means. Instead, engagement in the process of debating the future affords the ties of shared struggle.

## II. POLITICS

The distinguished and iconoclast theorist Hannah Arendt emphasized that politics cannot wait for unity, or love.[695] Practical problems of governance arise every day. Unity is evanescent, or mythical; love is even more fragile and more difficult to spread beyond a limited few. Nonetheless, democratic, participatory politics is not only possible, in Arendt's view, but also the most promising setting for heroic action, self-invention, and creation of a good larger than the vision of any one person or group.

Neither identity politics nor its critics who seek national unity would find comfort in the conception of politics offered by Hannah Arendt. She celebrated politics as an area of action in which "people create, through words and deeds, the power they need to initiate new projects or response to shared predicaments."[696] To Arendt, politics at its best affords a field on which diverse individuals, in their very plurality, express ideals of freedom and equality.[697] To express an opinion requires imagination and communication with others. Politics requires connection, not always happy and harmonious; politics requires the presence and acknowledgment of others who are located differently in the world.[698]

Arendt's conception of politics both invites and challenges notions of identity, whether of an individual or a group. For Arendt conceived of the political sphere as the setting in which individuals "show who they are, reveal actively their unique personal identities and thus make their appearance in the human world."[699] Arendt would oppose reducing individuals engaged in political action to pre-existing social categories of race, gender, and so forth. Those categories imply that people act because of what they already are and "express a prior, stable identity." In contrast, the political actor imagined by Arendt is "an unstable, multiple self that seeks its, at best, episodic self-realization in action and in the identity that is its reward."[700] Power, energy, and creativity stem from each individual's complexity and multiple dimensions.

Political claims and statements founded on prior, allegedly stable, identities founded on race, or gender, or religion, or another category, threaten to close political spaces and cut off discussion and differences.[701] A Jewish reader, shocked by Arendt's analysis of the Nuremberg trials, *Eichmann in Jerusalem*, appealed to Arendt as "a daughter of our [Jewish] people"; Arendt responded that her Jewish identity was an indisputable fact about her life, but did not wholly define herself.[702] This exchange addressed the subtle but powerful connection between group identities and homogenized views, and between group loyalty and suppression of independent judgment.[703]

At the same time, Arendt's vision should discomfit those who would invoke a national identity and press group identities to the margins. A national identity, no less than a religious or racial one, implies a pre-existing, stable frame that suppresses differences and prevents political freedom. Preoccupation with what it means to be an American is no less constraining than preoccupation with being Chicano, or a woman. Both preoccupations try to summon a solidarity prior to political action; both try to skip the hard work of inventing, crafting, and often straining for understanding and connection in the very process of deliberating and judging. Solidarity does not arise from understandings prior to politics, but instead politics permits its construction, in particular moments.[704]

Political action must occur in real time, with real, other people. A just politics should try to do justice to the differences among people.[705] Any identity, even one that seems given and not chosen, is not irrefutable nor able to control all the beliefs and desires of an individual person. Each hand can be played out differently.

Arendt herself used terms remarkably evocative of Rabbi Hillel's questions, "If I am not for myself, who will be for me? And if I am not for others, what am I?"[706] In *The Human Condition*, she wrote: "the moment we want to say *who* somebody is, our very vocabulary leads us astray into saying *what* he is; we get entangled in a description of qualities he necessarily shares with others like him . . . with the result that his specific uniqueness escapes us."[707] For Arendt, the "what" reduces the individual to membership in a category; the "who" invites self-definition through performance in public action.[708]

By resisting the use of the political realm to simply display "what" we are, in terms of identities framed elsewhere, we avoid crude impositions of ill-fitting limitations. We avoid merely re-presenting what we already are. We gain the chance to generate ourselves anew in connection with others, similarly engaged in politics.[709] One student of Arendt pushes the point still further. "When allegiances cease to be taken for granted as either rationally or intuitively necessary, the task of political organizing changes. Rather than defining *what* we believe in or declaring *who* we are, we now need to assess *how* we are implicated in a worldly event."[710]

Thus, Arendt suggests that telling people to put aside their group affiliations in the name of national identity is no better—or worse—on this view than urging people to pay fealty to other group identities. Attachment to the abstraction of "nation" or "race" will not sustain people and should not suppress disagreements. Sentiments of affection are too fickle and incomplete to forge an arena of commitment and respect.[711] There is no already existing glue to hold us all together, only the demanding project of inventing our contiguous lives and forging neighboring futures.[712]

What, then, can offer sufficient hope that a diverse society can share enough to be self-governing? Again, Arendt's work offers insight. Lisa Disch explains:

> For Arendt, the courage and respect that make politics possible do not spring from our feelings for each other so much as from a kind of care for the world. It is the world that we share, that relates and separates us, the human artifice that is built up on earth and populated by us humans: the houses, the office buildings, the vacant lots, the parks; the hospitals, factories, restaurants; the schools, the shelters, the streets. We share this world together, and we cannot evade that togetherness if we want to preserve a world with space for the exercise of distinctively human capacities, and the perhaps distant possibilities of a just politics.[713]

The links of a common fate or future do join those who occupy this nation. Historian David Hollinger emphasizes: "The national community's fate can be common without its will being uniform, and the nation can constitute a common project without effacing all of the various projects that its citizens pursue through their voluntary affiliations."[714] This insight could and should be amended to acknowledge pursuits through affiliations that are not always or fully voluntary. And, at least sometimes, should we not acknowledge the common fate of those who share the globe, not only the nation? Group identities are not sacred glue; nor are they corrosive to it. Instead they are some of the material affording people a sense of self and purpose in and out of the process of shaping a collective future.

## III. For Selves and Others

Facing and forging the future can be terrifying. Contemporary identity politics seems to offer people life rafts in the turbulent search for meaning, home, acknowledgment, and redress. Joining with some others to seek recognition may be easier than going it alone. Recognition, of course, is not the only stake.[715] Physical safety, when you are gay, or brown-skinned, or female, in the contemporary United States, is definitely at stake.[716] When the injuries inflicted by others predictably fall more often on some, it makes sense to resist along those very lines. And when some people have specifically targeted others *because* of their race, or gender, or sexual orientation, or religion, or disability, demanding redress and acceptance *on those very grounds* is the only way not to concede those grounds are natural or legitimate targets for injury.[717]

Hence, out of this arises identity politics. Efforts to resist mistreatment on the basis of a trait shared by the group become efforts to celebrate the trait, and to seek recognition and redress on its basis. Lively and intense, identity politics combines very public concerns with resources and justice with private concerns for meaning, healing, and self-respect. Yet identities can be flimsy, and at times stunting, grounds for organizing people and framing political debates.

The problem is less the risk of divisiveness than the risk of false and constraining roles or scripts.[718] We do not need arcane theories to recognize the way that stereotypes persist even when embraced by those they describe. Reducing a person to one trait shared by a group of others misses much of what matters, and invites demands for conformity. One trait can never convey the crucial interactions among an individual's memberships in multiple groups, or the special experiences of being not only Chinese American but also female; not only African American but also Baptist; not only male but also gay and Catholic. Mobilizing around identities forces people to pick sides when the lines are themselves so often arbitrary, shifting, mythical, or nonexistent. The San Francisco public schools now have a rule permitting a parent to change the racial identification of a child only twice—a rule that tries to cabin the unavoidable movements across lines that do not work. More and more children have, and claim, multiple racial ancestors; more and more people marry a person of a different race.[719]

Is there a way to acknowledge the complexity of identities without pretending that race, gender, disability, religion, and sexual orientation do not matter in this society? For they have mattered, and they still do.[720] Within the memories of people today are the legal rules excluding African-Americans from voting—and the violent responses of whites to those who fought for change.[721] In 1990, young blacks and young whites with equivalent resumes and trained to behave identically tested the job market; whites did substantially better.[722] Whites on average earn sixty percent more than blacks.[723] Hispanics have continually risked loss of jobs, land, and language.[724] Japanese Americans—many of whom were citizens—lost property, homes, dignity, and health when corralled into internment camps during World War II.[725] Indians lost land and children, self-government, and language through explicit and implicit policies since before the nation began.[726] Women of all backgrounds were denied participation in juries in some parts of the country until 1975, and refused admission to private schools and clubs onto the present; women still face risks of domestic violence, bias in the courts, and sexual harassment in the workplace.[727] Gays and lesbians encounter explicit job and housing discrimination with little protection.[728] Persons with disabilities have been denied education, employment, and housing, and also have been confined in often brutal and disgusting institutions.[729]

The injuries that result are more than the facts of exclusion, economic hardship, and humiliation. In addition, "a web of narratives develop[s] along with these specific exclusions, narratives that attempted to legitimize those exclusions by constructing an identity of the excluded group to explain why members of that group could not enter those fields."[730] Yet, the sources of those narratives in social practices often remain unknown. Both those they describe and those they do not are then easily able to conclude that there are inherent defects in people with those particular identities.

Vast societal ignorance about or indifference to the past and present severe mistreatment of people along these group lines are matched in scale only by constant categorization into groups.[731] Law, bureaucracies, and mass culture contribute to this concept. The constant use of group categories feeds stereotypes and offers homes for floating fears and anxieties.[732] Although group identities often afford a basis for pride, they too often become portals for societal degradation, portals even into the minds and hearts of children.

An unscientific sample, but nonetheless true story, gives a sobering example centered on race. Law professor Charles Lawrence wrote about it after the *Washington Post* published a story about it.[733] A white sixth grade teacher in a suburb of Washington, D.C. taught a class of 29 students; all but two were black or Hispanic, and all but three were from poor families. The teacher showed a film, based on a story by Langston Hughes, about a young black boy who tries unsuccessfully to steal from an elderly black woman. The woman takes the boy into her home and heals him with time and love. The teacher wrote about the class discussion following the film:

> I turned on the lights and asked if anyone wanted to share their reactions to the film. An '"A" student, who is black, raised his hand and said, "You knew something bad was going to happen when it started. As soon as you see a black boy you know he's gonna do something bad."
>
> Me: "Just because he's black, he's bad?"
>
> Student: "Everybody knows that black people are bad. That's the way we are."[734]

The teacher checked out whether the student meant "bad" as "evil" or instead as "cool," but evil it was, and the cause was inherent in black identity. The teacher found a near consensus on the following statements of racial attributes:

- Blacks are poor and stay poor because they're dumber than whites (and Asians).
- Black people don't like to work hard.
- Black people have to be bad so they can fight and defend themselves from other blacks.
- As students, they see their blackness as natural. They don't mean any disrespect to me personally: It's "just how we are."

- They don't need to work hard because it won't matter in the end.
- Black men make women pregnant and leave.
- Black boys expect to die young and unnaturally.
- White people are smart and have money.
- Asians are smart and make money.
- Asians don't like blacks or Hispanics.
- Hispanics are more like blacks than whites. They can't be white so they try to be black.
- Hispanics are poor and don't try hard because, like blacks, they know it doesn't matter. They will be like blacks because when you're poor you have to be bad to survive.
- Black kids who do their school work and behave want to be white. White kids who do poorly or dress cool, want to be blacks.[735]

As Charles Lawrence concludes, this report gives evidence of "the transmission and internalization of racist cultural symbols that inflict dehumanizing psychic injury." A Lou Harris poll indicates that this classroom of nonwhite children seems even more convinced of racial stereotypes than the nonblack community; forty-six percent of non-blacks reported that they believe that "African-Americans are more likely to commit crimes and violence," but forty-four percent deny this view.[736] Internalizing negative views often works more perniciously and powerfully than projecting them onto others.[737]

Charles Lawrence concludes that color-blindness has moved from an ideal to a condition of societal denial, notably in judicial decisions against affirmative action and the political climate producing those cases.[738] Denial and ignorance are close cousins. They also prove gracious hosts for repetition. Thus, unacknowledged group oppression does not cast out but instead accommodates constant group categorization. These are linked mistakes.[739] They call for linked, but contrasting, responses. Such responses will not cure or fix the underlying tensions but instead acknowledge and work with the tensions. Framing linked responses, and even debating in these terms, can at minimum prevent the repetition of disappointment with partial and contradictory strategies; at best, working on linked responses can move the society more in the direction of hanging in for the long-term struggle with the contradictions of group experiences and aspirations for individual liberty.

What would linked, but contrasting responses look like? I have suggested these examples:[740]

- Use group-based categories (race, gender, disability, ethnicity, sexual orientation) to announce and enforce vigorously forbidden grounds of discrimination in employment, education, public accommodations. *But also* promote opportunities for self-expression and definition by designing voting districts and methods not in terms of group categories but instead based on opportunities for individuals to affiliate, in the act of voting, with the groups of their choice;

- Expand opportunities for groups to claim, and debate, reparations for group-based injuries. *But also*—direct individuals to check all categories they believe apply in census collections of group-based identities;

- Proliferate settings for debates and exchanges of stories about the histories and experiences of individuals as members of groups.[741] *But also* eliminate the use of group categories in lawyers' challenges to jury membership, in legal standards of reasonableness, and in hate-speech regulations.

- Strengthen public support of the arts to permit expression of group-based experiences, *but also* to stretch, reinvent, render more complicated and multiple any particular understanding and recognition of individuals in terms of groups.

- Permit parents to select schools, and thus student peers, for their children. *But also* subject those choices to constraints and incentives to promote exposure to diverse others, not selected by the parents or by the happenstance of their residence.[742]

Immerse in the use of group categories, and resist them. Using group categories seems antithetical to aspirations for individual self-definition; yet, individual self-definition is impossible in a world that makes group categories basic to how others see us, and often to how we see ourselves. There is no *solution* to such a circumstance, but perhaps there are next steps to take. Any next steps will create, or expose, more difficulties. "To light a candle is to cast a shadow," writes Ursula K. Le Guin, a master of futurist fiction.[743] But new difficulties, emerging from expanded participation in struggles over group affiliation and democracy, open the horizon. At least new difficulties will take a new form and invite new engagement.

IV. TRIBALISM OR SEGREGATION? AFFIRMATIVE ACTION OR REACTION? If this turbulent century is a period of renewed tribalism, patterns of segregation seem better subjects for such pronouncements than the "culture wars" over university curricula, hate-speech regulations, or even public school history texts. The biggest threat to America comes not from the unraveling of a mythical American identity, but from the efforts by those with privilege to wall themselves off from others. They huddle in suburbs and private residential developments, with private security, garbage collection, and after school entertainment for children.[744] Few encounters bring these suburbanites in contact with those in urban and rural areas. Highways carry cars, windows up, doors locked.[745]

Solidarity in a diverse society could come from criss-crossing ties, or from enough repeated encounters that people come to realize they share circumstances and futures. These chances dim as patterns of racial, economic, and other segregations persist.[746] Criss-crossing connections cannot grow when people do not encounter one another. The courts have clearly set limits on the use of children to desegregate this society, and the options of private and suburban schools are thriving. Judicially-ordered housing desegregation has prompted ingenious efforts at avoidance, and some, small successes.[747]

This new pattern of self-segregation, largely by economically advantaged whites, compounds longstanding patterns of racial and class-based residential segregation in this country. These patterns, I believe, should be the starting point for discussions about the barriers to an inclusive, integrated society; these patterns, therefore, must be part of any responsible analysis of affirmative action. Hotly debated, and currently under vigorous challenge in courts, legislatures, and referenda around the country,[748] affirmative action seems to have become an "essentially contested concept,"[749] plausibly conveying different meanings by different users.

Let us remember its origins: affirmative action offered a vague name for the specific insight that simply removing explicit racial and gender barriers would not produce an integrated, inclusive society embracing members of historically excluded groups. First announced by President John F. Kennedy,[750] and then advanced and enlarged by subsequent presidents, affirmative action expresses the simple acknowledgement that full opportunities—in employment and education, in commerce and industry—do not arise by merely removing explicit barriers in a society that has entrenched racial, ethnic, and gender exclusions. This acknowledgment reflected not only general, abstract commitments to equality, but also concrete experiences with the rage, frustration, and wasted human talents resulting from continuing practices of exclusion. Ironically, perhaps, affirmative action has become the lightning rod for economic frustrations of members of the baby boomer generation, regardless of race.[751]

Although these economic frustrations neither stem from affirmative action nor would be cured by its elimination, the use of racial, ethnic, and gender categories to allocate jobs, government contracts, or admissions to universities seems to many observers to violate the very vision of a barrier-free world of equal opportunity. I agree with those who wonder why anyone finds it hard to distinguish color-conscious, sex-conscious criteria that aim to overcome exclusion from those that enforced exclusion.[752] To take the most obvious case, in a society that has made race matter so pervasively, color-blindness simply leaves in place racialized thinking that benefits whites, and seems rational because it is so familiar.[753] Ignorance or denial of longstanding racial discrimination contributes to the easy embrace of faulty neutralities.[754]

So do people's desires to hold onto privileges they have enjoyed under discriminatory regimes.[755] When places like Harvard Law School never, in their entire histories, find it possible to identify at least one woman of color qualified to serve as a professor, the criteria and selection processes in place become at best suspect and warrant investigation. Conceptions of race, disability, sex, religion, ethnicity, and sexual orientation that animate patterns of exclusion or mistreatment deserve attention not because they capture an ineluctable reality, but because our social practices have made them seem real, and determinative.

Yet time's passage, and mounting political and litigative campaigns against set-asides, preferences, or quotas, require an honest assessment that these versions of affirmative action are increasingly vulnerable to challenge.[756] Set-asides, preferences, or quotas will fail under equal protection analysis, according to reviewing courts, in the absence of specific, demonstrated exclusionary behavior and a demonstration that only those measures will cure the past, although preferential programs will remain lawful when done with care, absent further word from the Supreme Court.[757] In the time ahead, many, many resources will be spent documenting and contesting patterns of exclusion in the context of preferential selection programs. The costs and benefits of pursuing that strategy for inclusion will have to be weighed by its defenders even if the courts and the political process refrain from outlawing it altogether.

Moreover, difficulties categorizing individuals in terms of a particular group identity raise worries even for those who share the vision of an inclusive society. Who should be in or out under the category of African American? Should Hispanic include immigrants from Cuba? Argentina? Spain? Sephardic Jews? Should efforts to reach out to persons with disabilities be satisfied by finding individuals with back pain, rather than visual impairment, or mental retardation? And if remedying disadvantage is the underlying motive, how is it advanced by offering a position to an African American male whose family includes four generations of college graduates and who already enjoys an upper-middle class status? The use of quotas, set-asides, and preferential selection processes highlights the difficulties of assigning an individual to a group that lacks clear boundaries, shows internal incoherence, or ignores an individual's membership in multiple groups.

The attacks on affirmative action have not been limited to quotas, set-asides, and preferential selection process, however. As Assistant Attorney General for Civil Rights Deval Patrick noted upon discussing his plans to leave the Clinton Administration, "I think the debate that is unspoken, but is really at issue, is whether ultimately in this country integration is still a national objective."[758] This debate should become explicit; it would expose to view the danger of fragmentation that comes not from identity politics but from continued and innovative exclusionary practices.

Integration—to overcome exclusions based on race, ethnicity, gender, and also economic disadvantages—simply does not occur without reforms of longstanding selection methods. Conducting outreach to expand the range of applicants, affording special preparatory sessions to enhance the chances that previously excluded groups will succeed in existing selection procedures, can make real strides towards integrating schools, workplaces, and economic transactions. So can redesigning selection procedures to value diversity for its own sake or as relevant to the task at hand.[759] Revamping selection methods so that they do not produce patterns of exclusion along the lines of race, ethnicity, and gender—and for that matter, disability—can advance the goal of integration while also updating and improving the match between selection criteria and the tasks of the schools, employers, or commercial exchanges at issue.[760]

When integration seeks not only to overcome past exclusion or remedy past disadvantage, but also to promote greater contact across varied groups, refining the categories becomes less important than when it is justified as a remedy for past discrimination.[761] Similarly, diversity along lines of income or economic status is as valuable as diversity by race, gender, and disability, when the goal is to promote contact and mutual exposure across groups—and to thereby undercut tendencies to stereotype or demonize the "other." The name of affirmative action has included precisely such efforts.

Perhaps "affirmative action" has become both meaningless and a magnet for negative fears, and another name is needed for deliberate efforts to create an inclusive, integrative future. The term is unimportant; the vision is key. What would it take to make the ideal of a land of opportunity a reality rather than a remote possibility or a cruel joke?[762] If selection criteria for schooling and jobs, or for government contracts and licenses, leave out identifiable groups of people without extremely good reasons, the long-term interests of the society as a whole are jeopardized.[763] Affirmative action should be reclaimed, or renamed, to signify not preoccupation with the past but instead a collective effort to create the future we want to inhabit, with as inclusive a we as possible.[764] If we are for others in this way, we invent what we will become, and what kinds of selves we will have to be for ourselves.

Interfaith, sports, music, and other groups can bring together students from different elementary and high schools; reasonable efforts can be made to include children with disabilities in the classrooms and activities of other children; and curricular requirements can be made to address the roots of prejudice and the experiences of group oppression and resistance.[765] Yet, remaking a segregated society cannot, and should not, depend solely, or even largely, on children, especially as long as parental prerogatives also deserve some respect.

Why does contemporary American politics make it seem so difficult to face up to the complex, ongoing patterns of group harm and also to debate and discuss the meanings of group differences in the lives of people in different and multiple groups? Why is it hard to encourage and welcome individual self-invention? Why do children figure so oddly in public discourse—either absent, or instead the place holders for inconsistent adult purposes? No doubt the sources of our current fix are multiple. The rise of the sound-bite and decline of attention spans[766] render sustained public conversation a dim memory. The cost of media time limits the range of views at least in national, and often state-wide politics. Deeper problems, though, persist. Economic insecurity creates a breeding ground for distrust. Distrust leads low-skilled white men to blame nonwhite Americans and immigrants for economic dislocation more likely due to decisions made in board rooms to use cheaper labor—in other countries. Political contests soak up anger, frustration, and short-term crises, leaving little space for big issues, or lofty ideals.

One more factor contributes, but it is not a new feature of the American scene. A longstanding method for becoming American has involved putting down more recent newcomers—and also African Americans, or others who seem vulnerable to put downs. Reporter Ron Grossman tells the story: "A few years back, my father and my uncle were strolling through a shopping mall that reverberated with a dozen and one different languages. At the time, boatloads of Southeast Asian refugees were pouring into this country. Turning to my uncle, my father said, '*Gantsn tog, men hert nit ein vort* English,' which roughly translates from Yiddish as, 'In a whole day, you wouldn't hear one word of English.'"[767]

Grossman continues, "When the episode was recounted, the family doubled over in laughter: It seemed deliciously funny to condemn others for not using the country's dominant language—and to do so in a foreign tongue. Yet father could not see the humor. To his way of thinking, he hadn't been using a foreign language. Yiddish and English were equivalent in his mind. It was the 'others'—those Thai, Hmong, and Vietnamese shoppers—who needed to recognize that in America everyone ought to speak English. That view reflects a peculiar ground rule of American society. To be accepted into the mainstream, each successive immigrant group has had to demonstrate it is prepared to look down on more recent newcomers."[768] This tradition is a costly one in terms of group tensions and individual shame, and does not produce the unity it might seem to seek.

Yet I do not think we should underestimate the impact of sheer ignorance and inexperience about people who seem different. It can be difficult to be for others, unlike yourself, when you do not know them. People you do not know, who seem different, become screens for the projection of anxieties; they can become abstract rather than real individuals. Imagining the range of people who share the future requires some actual knowledge of people, and ideally, actual conversations with them.[769]

Identity politics ties us in knots. Yet even without unity in the sense of a single, shared American identity, the peoples of this nation can recognize and deepen ties, sufficient to enhance self-governance. Those ties are enlivened by the paradoxes of our shared experiences as unique individuals with varieties of affiliations. We all have made differences matter; we all must sense freedoms for self-invention would help. Promoting daily contact across lines of differences in schools, jobs, and communities would strengthen the kind of ties that permit a solidarity sufficient for sustaining debates over the future. The important question is not just what to do, but when.

# Notes

<>

1. Mervyn Rothstein, "Producer Cancels *Miss Saigon*; 140 Members Challenge Equity," *New York Times*, 9 August 1990, sec. C15. The union has authority over all performers appearing on Broadway. Actors from foreign countries need union approval before appearing unless they are considered British "stars." Michael Kuchwara, "*Miss Saigon* Canceled Over Casting of White Actor," *Boston Globe*, 9 August 1990, 79. The union said it had not reached the question of whether the British actor was a "star" for these purposes. Id.

2. See Kuchwara, *Boston Globe*.

3. Mervyn Rothstein, "Equity Council Approves Accord on 'Miss Saigon,'" *New York Times*, 18 September 1990, sec. C14.

4. Mervyn Rothstein, "Dinkins Offers to Help in 'Miss Saigon' Dispute," *New York Times*, 10 August 1990, sec. C3. See Robert Armin, "Miss Saigon: Not the Final Word," *Theater Week*, 10-16 September 1990, 37–38. ("If *Miss Saigon* did not have such a tremendous advance sale . . . very few people outside of the theatrical profession would have batted an eye over Equity's decision.")

5. Mervyn Rothstein, "Equity Will Reconsider 'Miss Saigon' Decision," *New York Times*, 10 August 1990, sec. C3.

6. See Frank Rich, "Jonathan Pryce, *Miss Saigon* and Equity's Decision," *New York Times*, 10 August 1990, sec. C1 (analogizing Actors Equity's decision in "Miss Saigon" to denial of funds by the National Endowment for the Arts for art depicting homoerotic and sexually explicit images).

7. See generally Louis Menand, "Illiberalisms," *New Yorker*, 20 May 1991, 10 (reviewing Dinesh D'Souza's *Illiberal Education: The Politics of Race and Sex on Campus* (New York: Free

Press, 1991); see also Virginia Durr, *Outside the Magic Circle,* ed. Hollinger F. Bernard, (Tuscaloosa: Univ. of Alabama Press, 1985) (discussing racism in the United States).

8. See, e.g., *City of Richmond v. J.A. Croson Co.,* 488 U.S. 469 (1989). But see *Metro Broadcasting, Inc. v. FCC,* 110 S.Ct. 2997 (1990).

9. Making a similar connection to underscore his own viewpoint, Robert Brustein, the director of the American Repertory Theater in Cambridge, Massachusetts, commented:

> Everyone's in the casting business. You have to cast a black woman in a law school as a law professor.... You have to cast Asians, homosexuals, everyone, in order to get sufficiently diverse multicultural representation. That is what Yeats called the "mad intellect of democracy," thinking that democracy means there has to be equal representation for everything that happens. Richard Bernstein, "The Arts Catch up with a Society in Disarray," *New York Times,* 2 September 1990, sec. 2, p. 12 (quoting Robert Brustein).

10. See Debbie Howlett, "Harvard Hit with Bias Suit," *USA Today,* 21 November 1990, sec. 3A. The plaintiffs, an unincorporated student organization, claimed that Harvard Law School's faculty hiring practices discriminated against minority groups and thus violated a state antidiscrimination statute and a state statute guaranteeing equal rights in the context of contracts. The trial court granted the defendant's motion to dismiss the case. Memorandum of Decision and Orders on Defendant's Motion to Dismiss and Other Pending Motions, *Harvard Law Sch. Coalition for Civil Rights v. The President and Fellows of Harvard College,* No. 90-7904-B (Super. Ct. Feb. 22, 1991). Curiously, in light of the themes explored here, the decision largely rested on conclusions that the students could not represent the interests of minority lawyers who might be victims of employment discrimination by the law school. Thus, the court ruled that the plaintiff group lacked legal capacity to sue; that it lacked standing to assert the claims of any person wrongfully denied employment by the school; and that it could not assert a breach of contract regarding existing contracts between the school and its faculty, nor a breach regarding nonexistent contracts with minority candidates. Id.

11. Two law professors have commented from contrasting perspectives on the analogy between the *Miss Saigon* controversy and minority preference policy in comparative licensing proceedings undertaken by the Federal Communications Commission. Compare Charles Fried, *Metro Broadcasting, Inc. v. FCC: Two Concepts of Equality,* 104 Harv L Rev 107, 121–122 n.82 (1990) with Patricia Williams, *Metro Broadcasting, Inc. v. FCC: Regrouping in Singular Times,* 104 Harv L Rev 525 (1990).

A more general analogy between law and theatre is vividly explored by Milner Ball, *The Promise of American Law* (Athens, GA: Univ. of Georgia Press, 1981).

For a provocative treatment of the law school hiring issue, see Duncan Kennedy, *A Cultural Pluralist Case for Affirmative Action in Legal Academia*, Duke L J 705 (1990).

12. *United States v. Virginia Military Institute*, 116 S. Ct. 2264 (1996).

13. Jacques Steinberg, "Plans for a Girls-Only School Raises Questions About Bias," *New York Times*, 16 July 1996), Sec. A1 col. 1; see also David Firestone, "See Girl School May Violate Little-Known City Law," *New York Times*, 17 July 1996, sec. B7, col. 1 (city ordinance may forbid single-sex school).

14. See Nanette Asimov, "San Francisco Schools Sued Over Enrollment Restrictions," *San Francisco Chronicle*, 12 July 1994, sec. A13 (Chinese American parents claimed that federal court consent decree, ending NAACP challenge to school selection methods, discriminates by requiring higher entrance test scores for Chinese American students than other students seeking admission to competitive Lowell High School). The city sought unsuccessfully to dismiss the suit; then the Superintendent of Schools proposed an alternative admissions plan by which eighty percent of the class would be admitted according to one universal standard, while twenty percent of the class would be admitted based on a variety of other factors, including race. See Associated Press, "New Admissions Policy Offered," *New York Times*, 11 January 1996, sec. B10, col.

5. Actually the Chinese American community is divided over Lowell High School; one group seeks to eliminate "standards by race," but another group called Chinese Americans for Affirmative Action disagrees.

15. Pam Belluck, "College's Head of Jewish Studies Resigns, Blaming 'Bigotry' of Jews," *New York Times*, 16 July 1996, sec. B1 col. 1. Some of his opponents emphasized the nominee's lack of knowledge of Hebrew, rather than his religion, as the important failing. Jonathan Helfand, "Letter to the Editor," *New York Times* 20 July 1996, p. 18, col. 1.

16. See *Texas v. Hopwood*, 78 F.3d 934 (5th Ci)., cert. denied, 1996 US LEXIS 4267 (July 1, 1996). For comprehensive discussions of affirmative action debates, see Christopher Edley, Jr., *Not All Black and White: Affirmative Action, Race, and American Values* (New York: Hill and Wang, 1996); George E. Curry, *The Affirmative Action Debate* (Reading, MA: Addison-Wesley, 1996).

17. Judy Rakowsky, "Learning Disabled Sue, Saying BU Hostile To Their Needs," *Boston Globe*, 16 July 1996, p. B5, col. 1.

18. See Theresa Glannon, *Race, Education, and the Construction of a Disabled Class*, 1995 Wis L Rev 1237.

19. See chapter 4.

20. Arthur Schlesinger, Jr., *The Disuniting of America* (New York:

Norton, 1992).

21. See Fried, *Metro Broadcasting.*

22. Rothstein, "Producer Cancels," C15.

23. Frank Rich, "Jonathan Pryce," C1, C3. He continued: "This is a policy that if applied with an even hand would bar Laurence Olivier's Othello, Pearl Bailey's Dolly Levi, and the appearances of Morgan Freeman in 'The Taming of the Shrew' and Denzel Washington in 'Richard III . . .'" Id. at C3. Others in response call for asymmetrical cross-casting, so that members of historically excluded groups can play the majority of existing roles without giving members of historically privileged groups opportunities to play the relatively more scarce minority roles. See Ellen Holly, "Why the Furor Over *Miss Saigon* Won't Fade," *New York Times* 26 August 1990, sec. 2, p. 7.

Rich, and others, also argued that opposing the casting of one lead part in *Miss Saigon* was counterproductive because the production of the play would itself open thirty-four Asian, black, and Hispanic roles in the musical, and not all, he claimed, would be minor roles. Rich, "Equity's Decision," C.3. It was not clear why Rich or anyone else thinks that the other roles depicting racial minorities are any more likely to be cast with nonwhite actors, or any more appropriately so, and if so, why.

24. See, e.g., Randall Kennedy, *Racial Critiques of Legal Academia,* 102 Harv L Rev 1745 (1989); Abigail M.

Thernstrom, "On the Scarcity of Black Professors," *Commentary,* July 1990, 22, 25. Cf. Kathleen Sullivan, Speech to the Harvard Law School Visiting Committee, 15 March 1991 (discussing reporter Lisa Olsen's charge of sexual harassment in the men's locker room of the Patriot football team and acknowledging that some people don't think a woman reporter belonged in the men's locker room. Sullivan then noted that based on that theory, perhaps women would not belong at Harvard Law School either.)

25. To round out the analogy, one could simultaneously have argued that just as African Americans teach contracts and tax, whites should be allowed to teach about race relations. Yet this argument has the awkward implication that teaching contracts and tax are "white" roles and teaching about race relations is a "minority" role.

26. Holly, "Furor Over *Miss Saigon,*" sec. 2 at p. 7, 27. Bernard Marsh, an actor, criticized the virtually all-white casts of contemporary Broadway productions and noted, "We're trained to believe an actor is an actor. We've found that it only applied when the actor is white." Id. (quoting Bernard Marsh).

27. August Wilson, "I Want a Black Director," *New York Times,* 26 September 1990, sec. A25; August Wilson, "I Don't Want to Hire Nobody Just 'Cause They're Black," *Spin,* October 1990, 70, 71. Wilson elaborated this view recently in a highly publicized

debate with Robert Brustein, artistic director of the American Reperatory Theatre. See Jack Kroll, "And in This Corner . . . ," *Newsweek*, 10 February 1997, p. 65.

28. Student posters, bulletin boards, Harvard Law School, 1990.

29. Anita Allen explores the persistence of merit even within role model claims. See Anita Allen, *On Being a Role Model*, 6 Berkeley Women's L J 22 (1990/1991). See also Adeno Addis, *Role Models and the Politics of Recognition*, 144 U Penn L Rev 1377 (1996).

30 See Oliver Sacks, *Seeing Voices*, (Berkeley, CA: Univ. of California Press, 1990), 127-63.

31. This may be more like the notions of political representation in legislatures, and the implicit idea here is that the representatives will redirect resources. See Duncan Kennedy, *A Cultural Pluralist Case for Affirmative Action in Legal Academia*, 1990 Duke LJ 705, 728-730.

32. Kevin Kelly, "M. Butterfly, Miss Saigon and Mr. Hwang," *Boston Globe*, 9 September 1990, p. B89. Journalist Kelly in turn commented that Hwang "might be considered Confucian. 'The superior man,' Confucius says, ' . . . does not set his mind for anything or against anything; what is right he will follow.'" Id.

33. Shirley Sun, "For Asians Denied Asian Roles, 'Artistic Freedom' Is No Comfort, *New York Times*, 26 August 1990, sec. 2, p. 7.

Should arguments about the chance to "depict ourselves" be any different if the question involves an actor with disabilities? Perhaps there is a possibility of believable portrayal that the actor with a disability uniquely has to offer. It is tempting to argue that so few have the chance to play any theatrical role or to be taken seriously for any role of a character without a disability. When the few roles calling for a person with disabilities are given out to someone without those disabilities, the rare opportunity to perform is eclipsed, and prejudice or ignorance about persons with disabilities may be the reason for the decision not to cast or even audition an actor who has a disability. See Andrea Wolper, "Beyond Tradition: Ethnic and Disabled Actors Assess the Present, Plan for the Future, *Back Stage*, 23 February 1990, sec. A1, 29 (producers tell an actress who uses a wheelchair not to audition for the role of a person in a wheelchair because they feared she would not be strong or well enough). But this relative rarity of good roles resembles the situation for Asian, African American, Hispanic actors, and female actors over the age of forty.

34. See Hanna Feinchel Pitkin, *The Concept of Representation* (Berkeley, CA: Univ. of California Press, 1967) 26.

The relative scarcity of such opportunities to create illusions through acting may be especially underscored when a member of one minority group is cast as a member of another minority group. Allan Wallach, "Casting Color Aside; Must Nonwhites be Limited to Roles Written Specifically for

Them?", *Newsday*, 1 July 1990, Part II, p. 4–5.

35. Curiously, few people considered the possibility of casting a Eurasian actor for the role; both white and Asian commentators suggested that the Eurasian character would have to be played either as Asian or European. Thus, the white actor cast in the role, Jonathan Pryce, declared that "If the character is half Asian and half European, you've got to drop down on one side of the fence or the other, and I'm choosing to drop down on the European side." Rothstein, "Producer Cancels," C15.

36. The Non-Traditional Casting Project defines four types of non-traditional casting: (1) societal, in which nonwhite and/or female actors are cast in roles of characters with their ethnicity or sex; (2) cross-cultural, which transposes an entire play to a different culture; (3) conceptual, which casts an ethnic, female, or disabled actor in a role to give it greater resonance; and (4) casting of the best actor for a role, even if this departs from the script. See generally Andrea Wolper, "NonTraditional Casting: Definitions & Guidelines," *Back Stage* 23 February 1990, p. 29.

Zelda Fichandler, the producing director at the Arena Stage Theater in Washington, D.C., has maintained that theater's task, "while not stretching credulity to the breaking point, is to stretch it as far as we can." Zelda Fichandler, "A Theater Should Live on the Cutting Edge," *Washington Post*, 13 December 1990, sec. A22. Under her leadership, that theater has pursued non-traditional casting: actors are cast to play roles not written for someone of their race or ethnicity. See generally Zelda Fichandler, "Casting for a Different Truth," *American Theater*, May 1988, 8.

A multiracial cast in a performance of Thornton Wilder's *Our Town*, directed by Douglas Wager at the Arena Stage, led one reviewer to comment: "standing in a mass on the stage, the cast's racial mix has seemed utterly unexceptional, but as the actors begin to step into character, it's suddenly startling. Emily and George, the two young lovers who will court, marry, and experience tragedy together, have both been cast with white performers, but each has been given a black sibling. George's father is Hispanic and speaks with a pronounced accent. Nothing whatever is made of this. This mix is casual, but also crucial, because it serves to point up the play's universality with the same understatement and lack of fuss that eliminating sets and artifice did in that original 1938 production [of *Our Town*]. By suggesting that the New England village be represented on stage by a non-specific void, Wilder made his play universal. By transforming New England into an idealized global village in microcosm, Wager is doing the same thing." Bob Mondello, "Rival Revivals," *City Paper*, 30 November 1990, 30.

37. See Josephine R. Abandy, A Message From the Artistic Director, in the Cleveland Play House, The Glass

Menagerie (*Playbill*, April 4–May 7, 1989) (announcing first professional all-black production of *The Glass Menagerie*). Reviewer Tony Mastroianni acknowledged that this all-black production reflected Abandy's effort to remedy past neglect of the black community by the Play House, but maintained that a better approach would be to produce "good new plays by black playwrights." Tony Mastroianni, "The Casting Cracks This Glass Menagerie," *Akron Beacon Journal*, 15 April 1989, sec. B5, Cols. 1–3.

38. Some steps in this direction are taken by the Voting Rights Act, 42 U.S.C. §§ 1971–1974e (1988). The Act adopts the notion of vote dilution—that groups can be wrongly deprived of political clout by the electoral methods used. Some criticize this approach, see, e.g., *Holder v. Hall*, 114 S. Ct. 2581, 2618 (1994) (Justice Clarence Thomas, concurring in the judgment); others advocate electoral processes to assure effective election of constitutive groups, see, e.g., Iris M. Young, "Polity and Group Difference: A Critique of the Ideal of Universal Citizenship," 99 *Ethics* 250 (1989).

39. Anne Phillips, The Politics of Presence (Oxford: Clarendon Press 1995).

40. Ibid. at 6.

41. See Pitkin, *Concept of Representation*, 62, 88 (1967). Pitkin herself identified the tension between the idea of the representative as a mirror, and contrasting notions of the representative as actor, trustee, agent, deputy, or symbolic substitute for the represented. Id. at 125–43.

42. Phillips, *Politics*, 7. See also id. at 57–83 (describing quotas and targets used by Nordic countries, as well as by the African National Congress and the British Labour Party).

43. Ibid. at 8.

44. Michael Sandel, *Democracy's Discontent* (Cambridge, MA: Harvard Univ. Press, 1996), 340–50.

45. I have written in this vein. Martha Minow, *Making All the Difference: Inclusion, Exclusion, and American Law* (Ithaca, NY: Cornell Univ. Press, 1990).

46. *Geduldig v. Aiello*, 417 U.S. 484 (1974). Congress responded to this view with the Pregnancy Discrimination Act, but the Act only deals with statutory requirements and leaves in place *Geduldig*'s holding about what the Constitution requires.

47. Susan Estrich, *Real Rape* (Cambridge, MA: Harvard Univ. Press, 1987), 29-56

48. *Patterson v. McLean Credit*, 491 U.S. 164 (1989). Congress responded with the Civil Rights Restoration Act of 1987, Pub. Law N. 100-259, codified at 29 U.S.C.A. 706 (8) (1) (West Publishing, Supp. 1990).

49. Robert L. Burgdorf, Jr., *The Americans with Disabilities Act: Analysis of a Second Generation Civil Rights Statute*, 22 Harv CR-CL L Rev 413, 418–19, 460–63, 470–81 (1991).

50. Americans with Disabilities Act, 42 U.S.C. §§ 12101–12213; and Civil Rights Restoration Act of 1987, Pub. L.

No. 100–259, codified at 29 U.S.C.A. 706 (8) (1) (West Publishing, Supp. 1990). The Supreme Court opinion giving most attention to the failure of neutrality may be *Loving v. Virginia*, 388 U.S. 1 (1967) (rejecting as unconstitutional a ban on interracial marriage although it banned members of both races from intermarriage).

51. Before contemporary identity politics, Edmund Burke wanted representatives who formed independent views of the interests of constituents. The representatives, he thought, should be drawn from an aristocracy presumed to produce superior men, not typical ones. Pitkin, *Concept*, 168–9. Those representatives, in turn, should seek to serve the entire nation, not the particular district or group of constituents, and thereby act as a trustee caring for the interests of others. This conception presumes that interests can indeed be discovered in an objective and impersonal way, though direct consultation with constituents would contribute in only a limited way toward this end. Edmund E. Burke, *Works and Correspondence*, Vol. III (London: Rivington, 1852), 354.

52. See Fried, *Metro*. See also Jane S. Schacter, *Review Essay: Skepticism, Culture and the Gay Civil Rights Debate in a Post-Civil Rights Era, Review of Andrew Sullivan, Virtually Normal: An Argument About Homosexuality* (1995) and Urvashi Vaid, *Virtual Equality: The Mainstreaming of Gay and Lesbian Liberation* (1995), 110 Harv L Rev 684 (1997) (distinguishing liberal and critical critiques of identity politics).

53. This is the position increasingly adopted by a fractured Supreme Court. See *Shaw v. Hunt*, 116 S. Ct. 1894 (1996) (North Carolina redistricting plan violates equal protection in subordinating racial neutrality to race consciousness); *Bush v. Al Vera*, 116 S. Ct. 1941 (1996) (rejecting Texas plan according to varied theories); *Miller v. Johnson*, 115 S. Ct. 2475 (1995) (Georgia redistricting plan violates equal protection in subordinating racial neutrality to race consciousness).

54. Alfie Kohn, *The Brighter Side of Human Nature: Altruism and Empathy in Everyday Life* (New York: Basic Books, 1990), 188–124; Jane J. Mansbridge, ed. *The Rise and Fall of Self-Interest in the Explanation of Political Life, in Beyond Self-Interest* (Chicago, IL: Univ. of Chicago Press, 1990), 3, 20-21.

55. See Elizabeth Spelman, *Inessential Woman: Problems of Exclusion in Feminist Thought* (Boston, MA: Beacon Press, 1988) for an elegant exploration of these issues and a call for politics based on mutual consultation and struggle.

56. See chapters 2 and 3. See also Steven Epstein, "Gay Politics, Ethnic Identity: The Limits of Social Constructivism," 17 *Socialist Review* (May–August 1987): 10 (identifying conflict between academic arguments that gay identity is fluid and socially constructed and political arguments that gay identity is natural and determined).

57. For an exploration of people

who do not fit bipolar categories, see Ruth Colker, *Hybrid: Bisexuals, Multiracials, and Other Misfits Under American Law* (New York: New York Univ. Press, 1996). See also Michael Marriot, "Multiracial Americans Ready to Claim Their Own Identity," *New York Times*, 20 July 1996, p. 1, col. 5; Eunice Mosoco, "Mixed-Race Americans Want New Census Category," *Atlanta Journal and Constitution*, 10 July 1996, A12.

58. See *New York Times* News Services, "House Panel Will Examine Rash of Fires at Black Churchs in South," *Chicago Tribune*, 21 May 1996, 14. At the same time, many black leaders noted that white leadership was more ready to respond to the church burnings than to the chronic economic disadvantage of large numbers of African-Americans, or to the bigotry and hatred that made the climate ready for the church burnings. See Bob Herbert, "Burning Their Bridges," *New York Times* 21 June 1996, sec. A 27, col. 1 (op ed).

59. Jane Jacobs, *The Question of Separatism: Quebec and the Struggle over Sovereignty* (New York, NYX: Random House, 1980), 115.

60. See generally *Conflicts Within Feminism*, Marianne Hirsch and Evelyn Fox Keller (New York, NY: Routledge, 1990). A different kind of division exists among women over abortion, because it is so deeply influenced by other religious and class divisions, and over whether feminism is good or bad for women.

61. Compare Henry Louis Gates, Jr., *Critical Race Theory and the First Amendment, in Speaking of Race, Speaking of Sex: Hate Speech, Civil rights, and Civil Liberties* (New York, NY: Univ. Press, 1994) (against restrictions) with Mari J. Matsuda; Charles R. Lawrence, III; Richard Delgado; and Kimberle Williams Crenshaw, *Words that Wound* (Boulder, CO: Westview Press, 1993) (supporting restrictions).

62. Compare Paula Ettelbrick, "Since When Is Marriage a Path to Liberation," *Out/Look*, fall 1989, 9, reprinted in ed. William B. Rubenstine, *Lesbians, Gay Men, and the Law* (New York, NY: New Press, 1993) with Thomas Stoddard, "Why Gay People Should Seek the Right to Marry," *Out/Look* fall 1989, 9, reprinted in Rubenstein. See also William B. Rubenstein, 106 Yale Law Journal (1997).

63. Frank Pommershiem, *Braid of Feathers* (Berkeley, CA: Univ. of California Press, 1995); Allison M. Dussais, *Geographically-Based and Membership-Based Views of Indian Tribal Sovereignty*, 55 U Pitts L Rev 1 (1993). Mary Sanchez, "Indians Fear Cultures Will Fade as Tribes Grow," *Kansas City Star*, 22 September 1996, A1 (discussing tribal debates over whether to define membership solely in terms of blood, and over how to calculate blood membership). The Cherokee Nation does not require any proof of Cherokee blood but instead descendency from a list of people identified as Cherokee in the early 1900s, some of whom had no American Indian lineage. Id.

64 See Gary Jeffrey Jacobsohn, *Apple of Gold: Constitutionaism in Israel and in the United States* (Princeton, NJ: Princeton Univ. Press, 1993) (discussing Israeli Supreme Court interpretation "who is a Jew" under the Law of Return, permitting emigration of Jews).

65. Compare Schlesinger, Jr., *Disuniting America*, with Colker, *Hybrid*.

66. Joan Wallach Scott offers a nuanced treatment of the notion of paradox in *Only Paradoxes to Offer: French Feminists and the Rights of Man* (Cambridge, MA: Harvard Univ. Press, 1996). Scott observes: "Technically, logicians define [paradox] as an unresolvable proposition that is true and false at the same time . . . In rhetorical and aesthetic theory, paradox is a sign of the capacity to balance complexly contrary thoughts and feelings and, by extension, poetic creativity. Ordinary usage carries traces of these formal and aesthetic meanings, but it most often employs 'paradox' to mean an opinon that challenges prevailing orthodoxy (literally, it goes against the *doxa*), that is contrary to received tradition. Paradox marks a position at odds with the dominant one by stressing its difference from it. Those who put into circulation a set of truths that challenge but don't displace orthodox beliefs create a situation that loosely matches the technical definition of paradox." Id. at 4–5. Scott's book specifically addresses a variety of paradoxes expressed by French feminists who faced a democratic politics that equated individuality with masculinity.

67. Practice with paradox may also help to cultivate an aesthetic appreciation for, or comfort with, complexity. Cf. Thomas C. Grey, *The Wallace Stevens Case: Law and the Practice of Poetry* (Cambridge, MA: Harvard Univ. Press, 1991) (examining the poetry of Wallace Stevens as invitations to cultivate pragmatic and metaphoric sensibilities).

68. David Mura, *Where the Body Meets Memory: An Odyssey of Race, Sexuality and Identity* (New York, NY: Anchor Books, 1996).

69. Jonathan Rauch, "Where the Body Meets Memory: Books," *International Hearld Tribune*, 9 August 1996.

70. In a classic moment of internal struggle over whether to claim women's difference or similarities to men, Stanton said, "Man cannot speak for us—because he has been educated to believe that we differ from him so materially, that he cannot judge of our thoughts, feelings and opinions by his own." Nancy Cott, *The Bonds of Womanhood: "Woman's Sphere" in New England, 1780–1835* (New Haven, CT: Yale Univ. Press, 1977) p. 95 (quoting Stanton's speech to the Waterloo Convention on August 2, 1848). Men and women thus differed in their understanding of women because men were taught to think that men and women differ, while women could consult their own experiences to know their commonality with men.

71. *Hearing of the Woman Suffrage Association, Hearings Before the House*

*Comm. on the Judiciary,* 47th Cong., 1st Sess. 3–4 (1892) (address of Elizabeth Cady Stanton, President, National Woman Suffrage Association). See also Scott, *Feminists,* 147 (discussing Madeleine Pelletier's commitment to imagining an original, solitary self still dependent on others and to gaining recognition of women's individuality by defending suffrage for women as a group).

72. Gary Larson, *Far Side: A 10th Anniversary* (Kansas City, MO: Andrew & McMeel, 1989), Exhibit 132.

73. For a discussion of this and related issues, see Martha Minow, *Putting Up and Putting Down: Tolerance Reconsidered,* 28 Osgoode Hall Law J 409 (1990). For a pungent critique of tolerance as a stance in a history of domination, see Herbert Marcuse, Barrington Moore Jr. and Robert Paul Wolff, *A Critique of Pure Tolerance* (Boston, MA: Beacon Press, 1965).

74. See Michael Kamman, *People of Paradox: An Inquiry Concerning the Origins of American Civilization* (Ithaca, NY: Cornell Univ. Press, 1972) ("a dialectic of pluralism and conformity [lies] at the core of American life").

75. Pirke Avot 1:14; see generally Yitzchak Buxbaum, *The Life and Teachings of Hillel* (Northvale, NY: Jason Aronson, Inc., 1994).

76. See Ruth Wisse, *If I Am Not For Myself... The Liberal Betrayal of the Jews* (New York, NY: The Free Press, 1992) 18–19.

77. Ibid.

78. See Seyla Benhabib, "The Gen-

eralized and the Concrete Other: The Kohlberg-Gilligan Controversy and Feminist Theory," in *Feminism as Critique*. Eds. Seyla Benhabib and Drucilla Cornell (Minneapolis, MN: Univ. of Minnesota Press, 1987).

79. See ibid. (describing relational approach).

80. See Joan Tronto, *Moral Boundaries* (Routledge, NY: 1993). See also Elizabeth V. Spelman, *Fruits of Sorrow* (Boston, MA: Beacon Press 1977) (criticizing ethics of care theories for failing to attend to which others deserve or receive care).

81. As one commentator suggests, coming to know that I should be the kind of self who cares for others (question two) modifies the kind of self I am, and should defend (question one). See Buxbaum, *Teachings of Hillel,* 269–270. This is one of many readings that emphasizes the dialetical quality of Hillel's questions.

82. We would be fools not only by missing the benefits of cooperation, but also by missing the centrality of human interdependence to thinking, talking, and creating human cultures. See Hannah Arendt, The Human Condition (University of Chicago Press: Chicago 1958).

83. Martin Niemoller, quoted in *Bartlett's Familiar Quotations,* ed. Justin Kaplan (Boston: MA: Little, Brown, 16th ed. 1992) 684.

84. Some children give evidence of empathy before they are two; many are moved by the happiness or sadness of others by the time they are three years

old. See M. L. Hoffman, "Empathy, Its Development and Prosocial Implications," in C. B. Keasey, ed., *Nebraska Symposium on Motivation*, vol. 25 (Lincoln: Univ. of Nebraska Press, 1977) 169–218; C. Zahn-Waxler, M. Radke-Yarrow, E. Wagner and M. Chapman, "Development of Concern for Others," 28 *Developmental Psychology*: (1992), 126–36. See also Michael Schulman and Eva Mekler, *Bringing Up a Moral Child*, rev. ed. (New York, NY: Doubleday, 1994), 52–88.

85. Debates over the names of each group reflect the struggles over group self-definition. Contemporary identity groups also organize around disabilities, religions, nationalities, regions, and experiences of surviving traumas such as rape and involuntary civil commitment.

86. See Sigmund Freud, *Moses and Monotheism*, trans. Katherine Jones (New York, NY: Vintage Books, 1967); Sophocles, *The Oedipus Cycle: An English Version* (New York: Harcourt, Brace and World 1949). Shakespearian comedies play with identity through cross-gender disguises and contrasts between "legitimate" and "illegitimate" forms of families. *Twelfth Night, or, What You Will* (New York, NY: Clarendon Press, 1994).

87. See generally William Barrett, *Irrational Man* (Garden City, NY: Doubleday, 1958) (discussing modernity and existentialism); Craig Calhoun, ed., *Social Theory and the Politics of Identity* (Oxford, England: Blackwell, 1994); Charles Taylor, *Sources of the Self* (Cambridge, MA: Harvard Univ. Press, 1989).

88. See James Clifford, *The Predicament of Cultures* (Cambridge, MA: Harvard Univ. Press, 1988); Isaacs *Idols of the Tribe. Group Identity and Political Change* (Cambridge, MA: Harvard Univ. Press, 1989), p. 35 ("insecure men who are torn loose from all moorings cling hard to wherever they can find an 'unquestionable place' where they belong" and increasingly people find that place in group identities); Anthony Cohen, *The Symbolic Construction of Community* (New York, NY: Tavistock Publications, 1985).

89. Stephen Steinberg, *The Ethnic Myth: Race, Ethnicity, and Class in America* (Boston, MA: Beacon Press, 1981). See also Regina Austin, 'The Black Community,' Its Lawbreakers, and a Politics of Identification, 65 So Cal L Rev 1769 (1992).

90. One view of this process suggests that many people "find" their individual identities through emotional investment in group identities. See Isaacs, *supra*.

91. See K. Anthony Appiah, "Identity, Authenticity, Survival: Multicultural Societies and Social Reproduction," in ed. Amy Gutmann, Charles Taylor, *Multiculturalism: Examining the Politics of Recognition* (Princeton, NJ: Princeton Univ. Press, 1994) 161 ("if one is to be Black in a society that is racist then one has to deal constantly with assaults on one's dignity. In this context, insisting on the right to live a

dignified life will not be enough. It will not even be enough to require being treated with equal dignity despite being Black, for that will require a concession that being Black counts naturally or to some degree against one's dignity. And so one will end up asking to be respected *as a Black*.")

92. For some, the American experience affords a reference point to describe group divisions, even when the divisions take quite different, and often more violent, forms. See Kwame Anthony Appiah and Henry Louis Gates, Jr., *"Editors' Introduction: Multiplying Identities,"* in *Identities* (eds. Kwame Anthony Appiah and Henry Louis Gates, Jr. (Chicago, IL: Univ. of Chicago Press, 1995), 1, 3.

93. This is Michael Sandel's claim in *Democracy's Distrust* (Cambridge, MA: Harvard Univ. Press, 1996), 339–51.

94. A notable example appears in the advertising campaigns entitled "The United Colors of Benetton," which use multicultural images to sell expensive clothing. See also Linda Alcoff, "Mestizo Identity," in *American Mixed Race: The Culture of Microdiversity,* (ed. Naomi Zack (London: Rowan & Littlefield, 1995), 257, 270–71.

95. See Charles Taylor, *Multiculturalism: Examining the Politics of Recognition,* ed. Amy Gutmann (Princeton, NJ: Princeton Univ. Press, 1994).

96. Richard Bernstein, *Dictatorship of Virtue: Multiculturalism and the Battle for America's Future* (New York, NY: Knopf, 1994); Arthur Schlesinger, Jr.,

*Disuniting of America* (New York, NY: Norton, 1992).

Western political theories have long acknowledged the human tendency toward factions and the human experiences of individual differences but urged conceptions that would subordinate such divisions under a collective unity. "Whether read from the frontispiece of Hobbes' *Leviathan,* in which the many are made one through the unity of the sovereign, or from the formulations of tolerance codified by John Locke, John Stuart Mill and, more contemporaneously, George Kateb, in which the minimalist state is cast as precisely what enables our politically unfettered individuality, we are invited to seek equal deference— equal blindness from—but not equalizing *recognition* from the state, liberalism's universal moment." Wendy Brown, "Wounded Attachments," in *The Identity in Question*, ed. John Rajchman (New York, NY: Routledge, 1995), 199, 204.

97. Schlesinger, *Disuniting.*

98. Ibid. at 137–8.

99. Jean Bethke Elshtain, *Democracy on Trial* (New York, NY: Basic Books, 1994).

100. Elshtain, *Democracy,* 85.

101. Long-standing debates include calls for unity on the one side and objections that unity actually involves domination and suppression on the other. See David Zarefsky, "The Roots of American Community" (The Carroll C. Arnold Lecture, Speech Communication Association, San

Antonio, Texas, 17 November 17
1995). Continuous contests over the
meaning of "American," for example,
may be its one consistency. Sheldon S.
Wolin, *The Presence of the Past: Essays on
the State and the Constitution* (Baltimore:
Johns Hopkins Univ. Press, 1989) 10.
A promising effort to acknowledge the
contests and nonetheless promote a
conception of "we" without labels is
Jodi Dean's *Solidarity of Strangers: Feminism After Identity Politics* (Berkeley, CA:
Univ. of California Press, 1996).

102. Cornel West, "Black Leader-
ship and the Pitfalls of Racial Reason-
ing," in *Race-Ing Justice, En-Gendering
Power: Essays on Anita Hill, Clarence
Thomas, and the Construction of Social
Reality*, ed. Toni Morrison (New York,
NY: Pantheon, 1992) 390, 391.

103. See, e.g., Todd Gitlin, *The
Twilight of Common Dreams (Metropolitan
Books*: New York, NY: 1995). I worry
about this, too. See Minow, *Not Only for
Myself*, Or L Rev (forthcoming). Yet,
wishing we could get beyond the
national preoccupation with group
identities does not work; there is other
work to do first.

104. Jane S. Schacter, *Review Essay:
Skepticism, Culture and the Gay Civil
Rights Debate in a Post-Civil Rights Era,
Review of Andrew Sullivan, Virtually Nor-
mal: An Argument About Homosexuality*
(1995) and Urvashi Vaid, *Virtual
Equality: The Mainstreaming of Gay and
Lesbian Liberation* (1995), 110 Harv L
Rev 684 (1997). Schacter distinguish-
es liberal observers—who fundamen-
tally believe in neutrality, individual

autonomy, and universal principles—
from critical observers—who emphasize the influence of structures of
power and domination even in systems
espousing neutrality, individual autonomy, and universal principles.

105. See generally Kathryn
Abrams, *Title VII and the Complex Female
Subject*, 1994 Mich L Rev 2479 (1994);
Angela Harris, *Race and Essentialism in
Feminist Legal Theory*, 42 Stan L Rev 581
(1990).

106. See Marc Fajer, *Can Two Real
Mean Eat Quiche Together? Storytelling,
Gender-Role Stereotypes and Legal Protec-
tion for Lesbians and Gay Men*, 46 Miami
L Rev 511 (1992).

107. See Elizabeth V. Spelman,
"The Virtue of Feeling and the Feeling
of Virtue," in *Feminist Ethics* ed. Claudia
Card (Lawrence: 1991, Univ. of Kansas
Press, 1991), 213 (describing pain
some women have inflicted on other
women); Id., *Inessential Woman: Problems of Exclusion in Feminist Thought*
(Boston, MA: Beacon Press, Boston
1988).

108. Judith Butler, "Contingent
Foundations: Feminism and the Question of 'Postmodernism,'" in *Feminists
Theorize the Political* eds. Judith Butler
and Joan W. Scott (Routledge, NY:
1992) 3, 15. The words marked by
ellipses above are:

There are those who claim that
there is an ontological specificity to women as childbearers that
forms the basis of a specific legal
and political interest in representation, and then there are

others who understand maternity to be a social relation that is, under current social circumstances, the specific and cross-cultural situation of women. And there are those who seek recourse to Gilligan and others to establish a feminine specificity that makes itself clear in women's communities or ways of knowing. But every time that specificity is articulated, there is resistance and factionalization within the very constituency that is supposed to be *unified* by the articulation of its common element.

Id. at 15. See also Denise Riley, *Am I That Name? Feminism and the Category of "Women" in History* (London: MacMillan, 1988); Spelman, *Inessential Woman* (Boston: Beacon Press, 1989), 39, 46.

109. Gitlin, *Twilight*, 206.

110. June Jordan, "Report from the Bahamas," in *On Call: Political Essays* (Boston, MA: South End Press, 1985) 39, 46.

111. Philip Roth, "Defender of the Faith," in *How We Live: Contemporary Life in Contemporary Fiction* (1968) 602. The story also appears in Philip Roth, *Goodbye, Columbus* (Boston, MA: Houghton Mifflin, 1959).

112. Roth, "Defender," 625.

113. Roth, "Writing About Jews," *Commentary*, December 1963 (quoted in *How We Live* 626).

114. See also John Sayles' "Lone Star," a movie depicting in part the shifting positions taken by a leading Mexican American business woman in a border Texas town over whether to turn over to authorities Mexicans who cross the border illegally.

115. For an illuminating examination of the crucial roles of memory and history in group identity, see Aviam Soifer, *Law and the Company We Keep* (Cambridge, MA: Harvard Univ. Press, 1995).

116. Kimberle Crenshaw's work is pivotal in this analysis. See Crenshaw, *Mapping the Margins: Intersectionality, Identity Politics, and Violence Against Women of Color*, 43 Stan L Rev 1241 (1991); Crenshaw, *Demarginalizing the Intersection of Race and Sex: A Black Feminist Critique of Antidiscrimination Doctrine, Feminist Theory, and Antiracist Politics*, 1989 U Ch Legal F 139. See also Kathryn Abrams, *Title VII and the Complex Female Subject*, 92 Mich L Rev 2479 (1994).

117. Crenshaw, *Demarginalizing* 157–59.

118. Crenshaw, "Whose Story Is It Anyway?: Feminist and Antiracist Appropriations of Anita Hill," in *Race-ing Justice, Engendering Power* 402.

119. See Johnetta B. Cole, " Commonalities and Differences," in *All American Women: Lines that Divide, Ties that Bind* ed. Johnetta B. Cole (New York, NY: Free Press, 1986) 1–20.

120. See Daina C. Chiu, *The Cultural Defense: Beyond Exclusion, Assimilation, and Guilty Liberalism*, 82 Cal L Rev 1053 (1994).

121. See Patricia Hill Collins:

"White feminists routinely point with confidence to their oppression as women but resist seeing how much their white skin privileges them. African-Americans who possess eloquent analyses of racism often persist in viewing poor white women as symbols of white power.... In essence, each group identifies the oppression with which it feels most comfortable as being fundamental and classifies all others as being of lesser importance." Patricia H. Collins, Black Feminist Thought 229 (Unwin Hyman: Boston 1990).

122. See Gitlin, Twilight, 223: "The Republican tilt of white men is the most potent form of identity politics in our time: a huddling of men who resent (and exaggerate) their relative decline not only in parts of the labor market but at home, in the bedroom and the kitchen, and in the culture."

123. An alternative formulation looks at each person as an ensemble of social relations with a variety of people in a variety of roles. See Stanley Aronowitz, "Reflections on Identity," in The Identity in Question ed. John Rajhman (New York: NY: Routledge, 1995) 114 (discussing and endorsing views of George Herbert Mead).

124. Mary Waters, Ethnic Options (Berkeley: Univ. of California Press, 1990), 22–51, 250–64. She is careful to note that the latitude for choice about ancestral identity is curbed for nonwhites. Id. at 168. See also Aronowitz, "Reflections," 111, 115–16 (describing creation of Puerto Rican

racial identity as a strategy response to American experiences in the 1940s).

125. Quoted in Gitlin, Twilight, 207.

126. See Dean, Solidarity, 177 ("Many of us have diverse and conflicting identifications that escape categorization yet remain in need of articulation").

127. See Dorothy E. Roberts, Punishing Drug Addicts Who Have Babies: Women of Color, Equality, and the Right of Privacy, 104 Harv L Rev 1419 (1991).

128. Dorothy Bryant, "Blood Relations," in The Graywold Annual Eight: The New Family, ed. Scott Walker (Saint Paul, MN: Graywolf Press, 1991), 75–80.

129. Ibid. at 75.

130. Ibid. at 80.

131. Christopher Ford, Administering Identity: The Determination of "Race" in Race-Conscious Law, 82 Cal L Rev 1231 (1994).

132. See, e.g., Shirlee Taylor Haizlip, The Sweeter the Juice (New York, NY: Simon & Schuster, 1994); Gerald Torres & Milun, Translating Yonnondio by Precedent and Evidence: The Mashpee Indian Cases, 1990 Duke L J 62 (1990).

133. Virginia R. Dominguez, White by Definition: Social Classification in Creole Louisiana (New Brunswick, NJ: Rutgers Univ. Press, 1986); F. James Davis, "The Hawaiian Alternative to the One-Drop Rule," in American Mixed Race, 115–31; Neil Gotonda, A Critique of "Our Constitution Is Color-Blind," 44 Stan L Rev 1 (1991). Anthony Appiah makes the important point, though,

that "the very concept of passing implies that, if the relevant fact about the ancestry of these individuals had become known, most people would have taken them to be traveling under the wrong badge." K. Anthony Appiah, "Race, Culture, Identity: Misunderstood Connections," in K. Anthony Appiah and May Gutmann, *Color Conscious: the Political Morality of Race* (Princeton, NJ: Princeton Univ. Press, 1996), 76–77.

134. See Ian Haney-Lopez, *White By Law* (New York: New York Univ. Press, 1996); Noel Ignatiev, *How the Irish Became White* (New York: Routledge, 1995).

135. Shirlee Taylor Haizlip, *The Sweeter the Juice* (New York: Simon & Schuster, 1994); Judy Scales-Trent, *Notes of a White Black Woman* (Univ. Park, PA: Penn State Press, 1995); Adrian Piper, "Passing for White, Passing for Black," 58 *Transition* (1992): 4. See also *Jane Doe v. State of Louisiana*, 479 So.2d 372 (La. 1985) (state declares that a woman is black based on her parents' answer on birth certificate although her skin is white and she thought of herself as white); Gregory Williams, *Life on the Color Line* (New York: Dutton, 1995).

136. See Gloria Anzaldua, Borderlands/La Frontera: The New Mestiza (Spinsters/Aunt Lute: San Francisco, 1987); Vine DeLoria and Clifford M. Lytle, The Nations Within: The Past and Future of American Indian Sovereignty (Pantheon: NY 1984) (American Indians belong both to tribes and to the United States).

137. See Michel Foucault and Herculine Barbain, *Being the Recently Discovered Memoirs of a Nineteenth Century Hermaphrodite*, trans. Richard Mon-Dongall (New York, NY: Colophon, 1980), originally published as Herculine Barbain, dite Alexina B. presente par Michel Foucault (Gallimard: Paris 1978); Patricia Williams, *The Alchemy of Race and Rights* (Cambridge, MA: Harvard Univ.Press, 1991) (discussing transgendered student who was rejected from each of the single-sex bathrooms).

138. Marjorie Garber, *Vice Versa: Bisexuality and the Eroticism of Everyday Life* (New York: Simon & Schuster, 1995), 65–66. Garber suggests: "If bisexuality is in fact, as I suspect it to be, not just another sexual orientation but rather a sexuality that undoes sexual orientation as a category, a sexuality that threatens and challenges the easy binaries of straight and gay, queer and 'het,' and even, through its biological and physiological meanings, the gender categories of male and female, than the search for the meaning of the word 'bisexual' offers a different kind of lesson. Rather than naming an invisible, under-noticed minority now finding its place in the sun, 'bisexual' turns out to be, like bisexuals themselves, everywhere and nowhere. There is, in short, no 'really' about it. The question of whether someone was 'really' straight or 'really' gay misrecognizes the nature of sexuality, which is fluid, not fixed, a narrative that changes over

time rather than a fixed identity, however complex. The erotic discovery of bisexuality is the fact that it reveals sexuality to be a process of growth, transformation, and surprise, not a stable and knowable state of being." Id.

139. See Kwame Anthony Appiah, "Race," in *Critical Terms for Literary Study* eds. Lentricchia and T. Laughlin (Chicago: Chicago Univ. Press, 1990).

140. See Allan Chase, *The Legacy of Malthus: The Social Costs of the New Scientific Racism* (Urbana, IL: Univ. of Illinois Press, 1980); Stephen Jay Gould, *The Mismeasure of Man* (New York: Norton, 1981); David Hollinger, *Postethnic America: Beyond Multiculturalism* (New York: Basic Books, 1995), 8, 27, 35; Nancy Stepan, *The Idea of Race in Science: Great Britain, 1800-1960* (Hamden, CT: Archon Books, 1982); Anthony Appiah, "The Conservation of 'Race,'" 23 *Black Am Lit F* 36 (1989); Barbara Jeanne Fields, "Slavery, Race and Ideology in the United States," 181 *New Left Rev.* 95, 101 (1990); Dorothy E. Roberts, *The Genetic Tie*, 62 U Chi L Rev 209 (1995). The effort to revive racialist ideas by Charles Murray and Richard J. Hernstein in their book, *The Bell Curve: Intelligence and Class Structure in American Life* (New York: Free Press, 1994) received extensive scholarly criticism. See, Peter Passell, "'Bell Curve' Critics Say Early I.Q. Isn't Destiny," *New York Times* (9 November 1994 A25; *The Bell Curve Wars: Race, Intelligence, and the Future of America* ed. Steven Fraser (New York: Basic Books, 1995), 1617;

Charles Lane, "The Tainted Sources of 'The Bell Curve,'" *New York Review of Books*, December 1, 1994, 14; Symposium on Richard J. Hernstein & Charles Murray, *The Bell Curve* (1994) *New Republic*, October 3 1994.

141. David Theo Goldberg, *Racist Culture: Philosophy and the Politics of Meaning* (Cambridge, MA: Blackwell, 1993), 1–10.

142. Richard Ford, *Urban Space and the Color Line: The Consequences of Demarcation and Disorientation in the Postmodern Metropolis*, 9 *Harvard Blackletter Journal* (1992), 117, 130. He continues: "[T]he maintaining technologies of race [are] primarily economic and spatial."

143. Lopez, *White*. For Indians and Hispanics, shifting Census definitions at times relied on skin color, at times language, at times residence, as well as tribal enrollment, surname, and primary language. See chapter 4. See Hyman Alterman, *Counting People: The Census in History* (New York, NY: Harcourt, Brace & World, 1969); Roland Chilton and Gordon F. Sutton, "Classification by Race and Spanish Origin in the 1980 Census and Its Impact on White and Nonwhite Rates," 40 *American Statistician*: (1986) 197.

144. Haney Lopez, at 2, 96-107. Beyond the factors considered over time by the courts, individuals may prefer to conceive of their identity in terms of culture, socio-economic class, or membership in multiple groups.

145. See Ruth Belier, *Science and*

*Gender: A Critique of Biological and Its Theories on Women* (Oxford, England: Pergamon, 1984); Anne Fausto-Sterling, *Myths of Gender: Biological Theories about Men and Women* (New York: Basic Books, 1985); Carl N. Degler, *Darwinians Confront Gender; or, There Is More to It than History*; John Dupre, *Global versus Local Perspectives on Sexual Difference*; and Ruth Hubbard, "The Political Nature of 'Human Nature,'" in *Theoretical Perspectives on Gender Difference* ed. Deborah Rhode New Haven, CT: Yale Univ. Press, 1990), 33–46, 47–62, 63–73.

146. See Fausto-Sterling, *Myths*; Hubbard, *Globe*.

147. Degler, "Darwinians"; Hubbard, *Nature*.

148. Judith Butler, *Gender Trouble: Feminism and the Subversion of Identity* (New York: Routledge, 1990); Judith Butler, *Bodies that Matter: On the Discursive Limits of 'Sex'* (New York: Routledge, 1993). Bonnie Honig traces the idea of a performative identity to the work of Hannah Arendt, and explores this notion in the context of complex and multiple identities related to gender, religion, nationality, and class. B. Honig, "Toward an Agonistic Feminism: Hannah Arendt and the Politics of Identity, in *Feminist Interpretations of Hannah Arendt* ed. Bonnie Honig (Univ. Park, PA: Penn. State Press, 1995), 135–166. Another early proponent of this view was Erving Goffman, *The Presentation of Self in Everyday Life* (Garden City, NY: Doubleday, 1959).

149. See Mary Joe Frug, *Postmodern*

*Legal Feminism* (New York: Routledge, 1992), 129–153.

150. Akeel Bilgrami, "What Is a Muslim? Fundamental Commitment and Cultural Identity," in Kwame Anthony Appiah and Henry Louis Gates, Jr., *Identities*, 198.

151. W. V. O. Quine, "Natural Kinds," in *Ontological Relativity and Other Essays* (New York: Columbia Univ. Press, 1969), 114.

152. A. R. Luria, *Cognitive Development: Its Cultural and Social Foundations* (Cambridge, MA: Harvard Univ. Press, 1976), 48–49.

153. Ibid. at 98. Yet some categories seem at times to freeze, and people seem to lose the ability to shift their scope and meaning; perhaps this reflects institutional practices and the play of power. See Mary Douglas, *How Institutions Think* (Syracuse, NY: Syracuse Univ. Press, 1986).

154. Harold R. Isaacs, *Idols of the Tribe: Group Identity and Political Change* (Cambridge, MA: Harvard Univ. Press, 1975, 1989), 205–207. Isaacs emphasized that groups are not defined solely by reference to physical characteristics, history, nationality, or language but instead by amalgams of these and other features as well as interactions between inherited and acquired experiences. Id. See also Craig Calhoun, "Social Theory and the Politics of Identity," in *Social Theory and the Politics of Identity* ed. Craig Calhoun (Cambridge, MA: Blackwell Publisher, 1994), 9–36.

155. Bharati Mukherjee, "A Wife's

Story," in *The Middleman and Other Stories* (New York, NY: Grove Press, 1989).

156. Ibid. at 25.

157. Ibid. at 26.

158. Ibid. at 27.

159. Ibid. at 27.

160. Ibid.

161. Mukherjee herself received criticism for implying in an editorial two clear identity options for immigrants to the United States: assimilation or retention of the identity from the nation of origin. The critic explained that "America's appeal through centuries has been to tolerate, even encourage, different ways of being American." Sheila Jasanoff, "Letter to the Editor: To Belong in America . . . Let Us Count the Ways," *New York Times*, 26 September 1996, sec. A26, col. 4 (responding to Bharati Mukherjee, "Two Ways to Belong in America," *New York Times*, 22 September 1996).

162. Ibid. at 29.

163. Ibid. at 31.

164. Ibid. at 29.

165. Ibid. at 32.

166. Ibid. at 33.

167. Ibid.

168. Ibid. at 39.

169. Ibid. at 34.

170. The story does not suggest that emotions or moods are any more "authentic" or free from external influence than are any other feature of identity, such as role or sense of group membership. However, tensions between emotions and role provide clues to a shifting sense of identity.

171. Ibid. at 40.

172. Ibid.

173. Although this degree concerns education for people with disabilities, the author could well mean something more specific about the special education the narrator is receiving about herself.

174. The phrase is Anthony Appiah's. See Appiah, *Race*, at 99.

175. Many claim, or find themselves assigned, the academic group label of "post-modern." I am disinclined to use that or other intellectual labels in order to avoid spending more time fighting over definitions and who belongs in which group than over the ideas at issue.

176. See Appiah, "Race," 96 ("neither the picture in which there is just an authentic nugget of selfhood, the core that is distinctively me, waiting to be dug out, nor the notion that I can simply make up any self I choose, should tempt us. We make up selves from a tool kit of options made available by our culture and society"); Angela P. Harris, *Foreword: The Jurisprudence of Reconstruction*, 82 Cal L Rev 741, 774 (1994); Mari J. Matsuda, *When the First Quail Calls: Multiple Consciousness as Jurisprudential Method*, 11 Women's Rts L Rep 7 (1989). See also Benedict Anderson, *Imagined Communities: Reflections on the Origin and Spread of Nationalism* (New York, NY: Verso, 1991); John and Jean Comaroff, *Ethnography and Historical Imagination* (Boulder, CO: Westview Press, 1992), 50–67; Dominguez, *White by Definition*, 11–16.

177. Barbara J. Fields, "Ideology and Race in American History," in *Region, Race, and Reconstruction* ed. J. Morgan Kousser et al. (New York, NY: Oxford Univ. Press, 1982). See also Cheryl I. Harris, *Whiteness as Property*, 106 Harv L Rev 1710 (1993) (arguing that white racial identity became a form of property).

178. David Hollinger, *Post-Ethnic America: Beyond Multiculturalism* (New York: Basic Books, 1995). See also Michael Omi and Howard Winant, *Racial Formation in the United States: From the 1960s to the 1990s* 2d ed. (New York, NY: Routledge, 1994) (it is wrong to see race as an essence and wrong to see it as illusion; social construction doesn't mean lack of reality); Steven Epstein, "Gay Politics, Ethnic Identity: The Limits of Social Construction," *Socialist Review* (May-August 1987) 9–20. American racism reflects not only the justifications for slavery, but also newer racialist thinking developed after Reconstruction, influenced by the pseudo-scientific theories of intelligence of the 1920s, which have resurfaced in the past decade. See Eric Foner, "Who Is an American?" (unpublished lecture, on being named the New York Council for the Humanities Scholar of the Year).

179. Benedict Anderson, Imagined Communities 110, 149-150, 163, 166-181 (Verso: London, rev. ed. 1991). He also acknowledges yearnings for solidarity that fueled movements by peasants and workers under the heading of ethnicity—which elites in control converted for their own purposes. Id. Stephen Steinberg explores how people use ethnicity as a medium to imagine connections with the past and to fulfill a yearning for meaning in the face of present discontents. Steinberg, *Ethnic Myth*, 262. And Mary Waters finds people ascribing to their ethnic group values held by many others. Waters, *Ethnic Options*, 134. Thus, individuals imagine a group as a basis for both community and individuality against a backdrop of historic practices articulating group identities. Id. at 147–64.

180. Thomas J. Scheff, "Emotions and Identity: A Theory of Ethnic Nationalism," in *Social Theory and the Politics of Identity*, 277–303.

181. See, e.g., Patricia G. Devine, "Stereotypes and Prejudice: Their Automatic and Controlled Components," 56 *Journal Personality & Social Psychology* (1989): 5. See generally Charles R. Lawrence, III, *The Id, The Ego, and Equal Protection: Reckoning with Unconscious Racism*, 39 Stan L Rev 317 (1987); Peggy MacIntosh, "White Privilege and Male Privilege: A Personal Account of Coming to See Correspondences Through Work in Women's Studies," in *Race, Class and Gender: An Anthology* eds. Patricia Hill Collins and Margaret L. Anderssen (Belmont, CA: Wadsworth, 1992).

182. See Hollinger, *Post-Ethnic*, 38–39 (group categories in the United States derive not from biology or culture, but "from the dynamics of prejudice and oppression in U.S. history

and from the need for political tools to overcome the legacy of that victimization").

183. Michael R. Marrus & Robert O. Paxton, *Vichy France and the Jews* (New York: Basic Books, 1981), 85, 205; Richard Weisberg, *Poethics: and Other Strategies of Law and Literature* (New York: Columbia Univ. Press, 1992).

184. Walter Benn Michaels, "The No-Drop Rule," in *Identities*, 401. See also William Connolly, *Identity/Difference: Democratic Negotiations of Political Paradox* (Ithaca, NY: Cornell Univ. Press, 1991) (identity requires difference in order to exist and secure its own certainty). Sometimes, a society simply piggybacks on prior oppression to treat a group-based category as currently meaningful. See Barbara Jeanne Fields, "Slavery, Race and Ideology in the United States of America," 181 *New Left Review* (1990) 95, 97; (discussing Supreme Court acceptance in 1987 of nineteenth-century definition of Jews and Arabs as racially distinct from Caucasians).

185. Catharine A. MacKinnon, *Feminism Unmodified: Discourses on Life and Law* (Cambridge, MA: Harvard Univ. Press, 1987).

186. See Judith Butler, *Gender Trouble: Feminism and the Subversion of Identity* (New York: Routledge, 1990).

187. Marilyn Frye, *The Politics of Reality* (Trumansburg, NY: Crossing Press, 1983), 1016; Peggy MacIntosh, "White Privilege and Male Privilege," in *Race, Class, and Gender: An Anthology*

eds. Margaret L. Anderson and Patricia Hill Collins (Belmont, CA: Wadsworth Publishing, 1992), 76–87; Cheryl I. Harris, *Whiteness as Property*, 106 Harv L Rev 1761 (1993) (whiteness includes the power to make rules and the settled expectation that whites will face no undue obstacles while also controlling the legal meanings of group identity).

188. Avery Gordon and Christopher Newfield, "White Philosophy," in *Identities*, 380, 399.

189. Angelo Falcon, "Puerto Ricans and the Politics of Racial Identity," in *Racial and Ethnic Identity: Psychological Development and Creative Expression*, eds. (Herbert W. Harris, Howard C. Blue, and Ezra E. H. Griffith (New York: Routledge, 1995), 193, 201. There is a curious and unfortunate tendency, though, for scholars who advance this view to treat "power" as singular in its form and direction.

190. Gitlin, *Twilight*, 203. Others may dispute these particular assertions, but group-linked priorities and perceptions about many topics do seem to persist.

191. For related reasons, Harlon Dalton argues that even though the black community is not monolithic, it is still possible to talk about what it needs and believes just as people talk about American aspirations. Dalton, *Racial Healing*, at 163.

192. Janet Malcolm tells this version in a discussion of double binds. See Janet Malcolm, *The Purloined Clinic* (New York: Knopf, York 1992), 108.

193. See Nancy Cott, *The Bonds of Womanhood: 'Woman's Sphere' in New England, 1780-1835* (New Haven: Yale Univ. Press, 1977); Benita Eisler, ed., *The Lowell Offering: Writings by New England Mill Women (1840-1845)* (New York: Harper & Row, 1977); James C. Scott, *Domination and the Art of Resistance* (New Haven: Yale Univ. Press, 1990); James C. Scott and Benedict J. Tria Kerkuliet, eds., *Everyday Forms of Peasant Resistance in Southeast Asia* (London: Frank Cass, 1986); E.P. Thompson, *Whigs and Hunters: The Origin of the Black Act* (Middlesex, England: Penguin, 1990). See also Michel Foucault, *Power/Knowledge: Selected Interviews and Other Writings* ed. Colin Gordon (New York: Pantheon Books, 1980).

194. See Appiah, "Identity," Princeton, NJ: Princeton Univ. Press, 1994).

195. Sherley Ann Williams, "In Honor of Free Women, Meditations on History," in *Midnight Birds* ed. Mary Helen Washington (Garden City, New York: Anchor Books, 1980), 195, 196. She also writes, "I try to elucidate those elements in our lives on which constructive political changes, those that do more than blackwash or femalize the same old power structure, can be built." Id. at 198. Williams reworked the story as part of her novel, *Dessa Rose* (New York: W. Morrow, 1986). Williams did graduate studies at Howard University and at Brown University, but decided not to pursue a Ph.D. because "I didn't want to spend the rest of my life poring over other people's work and trying to explain the world thru their eyes." Williams, *Midnight Birds*, 195, 198.

196. One critic suggests that Williams takes her title from William Styron's note at the beginning of *The Confessions of Nat Turner.* "'Perhaps the reader will want to draw a moral from this narrative, but it has been my own intention to re-create a man and his era, and to produce a work that is less an 'historical novel' in conventional terms than a meditation on history.'" Elizabeth Meese, (Ex)Tensions: Re-Figuring Feminist Criticism 136 (University of Illinois Press: Urbana, IL 1990) (quoting William Styron, The Confessions of Nat Turner ix (Random House: NY 1967).) Meese comments: "Surely the moral Williams cares to draw differs from the one Styron, or many of her (white) feminist readers for that matter, must have envisioned, just as her 'meditations on history' — spoken (of) in the plural and from an/other perspective — take a radically different form and meaning from his." Id.

197. Williams, "Meditations" 211. See also Williams, *Dessa Rose.*

198 Williams, "Meditations," 213–14, 215.

199. Ibid. at 225.

200. Ibid. at 226.

201. Ibid. at 231.

202. Ibid. at 234.

203. Mary Helen Washington, "In Pursuit of Our Own History," in *Midnight Birds*, (Garden City, NY: Anchor Books, 1980), xiii, xxii. .

204. Ibid.

205. Sherley Ann Williams dedicates the story to Angela Davis, and prefaces the story with this quotation from Davis:

> The myth [of black matriarchy and the castrating black female] must be consciously repudiated as myth and the black woman in her true historical contours must be resurrected. We, the black women of today, must accept the full weight of a legacy wrought in blood by our mothers in chains. . . . as heirs to a tradition of supreme perseverance and heroic resistance, we must hasten to take our place wherever our people are forging on towards freedom.

"Meditations," 200 (quoting Angela Davis, *Reflections on the Black Woman's Role in the Community of Slaves*) (brackets in the original).

206. Cf. Mark Twain, *Huckleberry Finn* (Introduction by Justin Kaplan) (New York: Random House, 1996) (main characters play into the stereotypes of gender, age, race, and slave status held by others in order to pursue their own goals); David Leavitt, "Danny in Transit," in *Family Dancing* (New York: Knopf,1984), 95 (a child learns he can avoid adult demands by throwing tantrums but then learns he can claim as his own a parent's recommendation that he go to boarding school—and thereby builds his own sense of dignity).

207. See, e.g., Kenneth S. Greenberg, *Honor & Slavery* (Princeton, NJ: Princeton Univ. Press, 1996) (discussing slave rebellions that challenged culture of honor as well as slavery as an institution); Arthur Koestler, *Darkness at Noon*, trans. Daphne Hardy (Toronto: Bantam Books, 1985); Andre Malraux, *Man's Fate* (New York: Random House, 1934).

208. This approach bears some affinity to the view advocated by some under the term "positionality." See, e.g., Katherine Bartlett, *Feminist Legal Methods*, 103 Harv L Rev 829 (1990); Diana Fuss, "Reading Like a Feminist," 78 *Differences* (spring 1989), 1. The idea of negotiated identity, like positionality, emphasizes the negotiated, interactive quality of relationships and focuses on the social and cultural position of a person. Negotiated identity and positionality therefore both depart from a view that identities are innate, intrinsic to the person and free from relationships and position. See Linda Alcoff, "Cultural Feminism v. Post-Structuralism: The Identity Crisis in Feminist Theory," 13 *Signs* (1988): 405, 433:

> The essentialist definition of woman makes her identity independent of her external situation: since her nurturing and peaceful traits are innate they are ontologically autonomous of her person with respect to others or to the external historical and social conditions generally. The positional definition, on the other hand, makes her iden-

tity relative to a constantly shifting context, to a situation that includes a network of elements involving others, the objective economic conditions, cultural and political institutions, and so on. Negotiated identity emphasizes the continuing interactions among people, and the different patterns of relationship.

209. If people's chances to have and to nurture aspirations and alternative conceptions for themselves are snuffed out by others, I would have to quell this hopeful sense of room for resistance. This helps to explain the crucial importance of the provision of educational opportunities for all children. See chapter 5.

210. See Rosemary J. Coombe, *The Properties of Culture and the Politics of Possessing Identity: Native Claims in the Cultural Appropriation Controversy*, 5 Canadian J L and Jurisprudence 249, 284 (1993).

211. Flannery O'Connor, "The Displaced Person," in *Collected Works* (New York: Library of America, 1988), 285. O'Connor, who attended Georgia State College for women and the writing program at the University of Iowa, spent most of her life in Georgia; her fiction is often described as Southern Gothic. When referring to African Americans, the story uses the term, "Negro," as does my commentary here.

212. See Jean Fagen Yelling, ed. *Incidents in the Life of a Slave Girl, Written*

*by Herself* [1861] (Cambridge, MA: Harvard Univ. Press, 1987). This interpretation of the book draws on the close reading given to it in Elizabeth V. Spelman, *Fruits of Sorrow: Uses and Abuses of Suffering* (Boston: Beacon Press 1997) (chapter 3).

213. See Volume I *Compact Edition of the Oxford English Dictionary 1910* (Oxford, England: Oxford Univ. Press, 1971).

214. See generally Wayne Booth, *The Company We Keep: An Ethics of Fiction* (Berkeley: Univ. of California Press, 1989); James Boyd White, *When Words Lose Their Meaning* (Chicago: Univ. of Chicago Press, 1984).

215. See Gerald Lopez, *Rebellious Lawyering* (Boulder, CO: Westview Press, 1992): 42 ("But time and again our own experiences entirely discredit artificial images of how we construct our lives and everything around them. Most of us eventually come to realize that our identities emerge and evolve much more interactively and much less freely than simple choice can possibly express . . . We struggle constantly to assert what we would become. We struggle with ourselves, with those through whom we construct relationships, and with those institutionalized patterns within which we all operate. And as we struggle we inevitably use and experience the uses of power.").

216. Gish Jen, *Mona in the Promised Land* (New York: Alfred A. Knopf, 1996).

217. Discussing her parents' view that people should not protest injus-

tice, the Rabbi tells Mona: "'Well, of course, nobody likes to yell,' he says, 'But your parents want to be Wasps. They are the only ones who do not have to make themselves heard. That is because they do the hearing.'" Id., at 53.

218. Ibid. at 202.

219. The risk of splintering often is coupled with the possibility of a therapeutic sense of connection. For a discussion of both, see Glenn C. Loury, "One Man's March," *The New Republic* November 6 1995, 18–22; Debra Dickerson, "Queen for a Day?," *The New Republic* November 6 1995), 22.

220. Margaret Beale Spender, Michael Cunningham and Dean Phillips Swanton, "Identity as Coping: Adolescent African-American Males' Adaptive Responses to High-Risk Environments," in *Racial and Ethnic Identity: Psychological Development and Creative Expression* eds. Herbert W. Harris, Howard C. Blue and Ezra E.H. Griffith, (New York: Routledge, 1995), 31, 49.

221. Himani Bannerji, *Thinking Through: Essays on Feminism, Marxism, and Anti-Racism* (Toronto: Women's Press, 1995), 183–84. See also Gitlin, "Twilight," 208: "hasn't history already done its detestable and irreversible work, stamping inferiority on dark-skinned peoples, enslaving them in the name of that classification? Without doubt, the group identities that have lasted longest and cut deepest are the ones that persecution has engraved." Some identities, such as

that of a Christian, have had periods of persecution and periods of relative comfort or even dominance.

222. Franz Fanon, *Black Skins, White Masks* trans. Charles Lam Markham (New York: Grove Press, 1967); Paulo Freire, *Pedagogy of the Oppressed* (New York: Seabury Press, 1970); Albert Memmi, *The Colonizer and the Colonized* (Boston: Beacon Press, 1967). George W.F. Hegel, *Phenomenology of the Spirit* 1 trans. A.V. Miller (Oxford, England: Clarendon Press, 1977), 179–96. See also Toni Morrison, *The Bluest Eye* (New York: Washington Square, 1970) (young black child yearns for blond hair and blue eyes, having internalized racist culture).

223. Freire, *Pedagogy*.

224. Jacques Rancier, "Politics, Identification, and Subjectivization," in *The Identity in Question* ed. John Rajchman (New York: Routledge, 1995).

225. Wendy Brown, "Wounded Attachments: Late Modern Oppositional Political Formations," in *The Identity in Question* ed. John Rajchman (New York: Routledge, York 1995), 199.

226. Ibid. at 202, 220. See also Gayatri Chakravorty Spivak, "Acting Bits/Identity Talk," in *Identities*, 147 (describing identity as a wound).

227. Brown, "Wounded," 215–6. The omitted language is a quotation from Nietzsche's *Zarathustra*: "punishment is what revenge calls itself; with a hypocritical lie it creates a good conscience for itself." Id. In a companion

piece, Judith Butler acknowledges how terms of identity that injure also create social recognition, and how embracing the injurious term is necessary as a stage in learning to resist and oppose it. Judith Butler, Subjection, Resistance, Resignification: Between Freud and Foucault," in *Identity*, 229, 245. See also Martha Minow, *Surviving Victim Talk*, 40 UCLA L Rev 1411 (1993); Robert P. Mosteller, *Popular Justice Review of Fletcher: With Justice for Some*, 109 Harv L Rev 487 (1995).

228. Ibid. at 221.

229. Ibid.

230. Judith Lewis Herman, *Trauma and Recovery* (New York: Basic Books, 1992).

231. Ibid.

232. Harlon Dalton, *Racial Healing* (New York: Doubleday, 1995), 148.

233. Ibid. at 154. "For most of us black folk, the problem is not that we are mired in victimhood; it is that we no longer are able to give a satisfactory account of who we are and why we remain on the bottom."

234. Appiah, in *Multiculturalism*, 163.

235. See Scott, "Multiculturalism," 4, 5. Several scholars have drawn from identity politics the ideas that we each are "other" to others and indeed strangers to ourselves. These ideas could promote openness and a sense of community even with apparent strangers by exposing the common experience of feeling foreign or seeing foreigners. But this somewhat elusive set of notions is not the dominant or even widely understood message of identity politics. See Dean, *Solidarity*; Julia Kristeva, *Strangers to Ourselves* trans. Leon S. Roudiez (New York: Columbia Univ. Press, 1991), 169, 194–5; supra (noting Butler's attention to Cornell, Connolly, Irigaray). Instead, the practices of identity politics are too often characterized by personal testimony that uses experience as authority and grounds for exclusion and silencing of others. See Scott, 10.

236. Scott, "Multiculturalism" at 10. See also Minow, *Victim Talk*, 1411.

237. Cornel West, *Race Matters* (Boston: Beacon Press, 1993), 108.

238. Ibid.

239. See ibid.: "As long as black people are viewed as a 'them,' the burden falls on blacks to do all the 'cultural' and 'moral' work necessary for healthy race relations."

240. There has been a shift from discussion of "identity" to discussion of "identities." See Butler, "Collected and Fracture," in *Identities*, 439. Yet, rather than expanded attention and concern, this continues to limit and confirm the preoccupations of inwardness. "If identity becomes the unit that is multiplied, then the principle of identity is repeated—and reconfirmed—without ever yielding to another set of terms." Id. Butler maintains that some identity theorists pursue its potential for an ethical stance of openness, see id., 441 (citing William Connolly, Kendall Thomas, Drucilla Cornell and Luce Irigary). But the actual unfolding of politics around

identity themes has not had that effect, and the abstruseness of theorists' prose on this point does not bode well for changes in this regard in the future.

241. Butler, "Discussion," in *Identity*, at 139. Implicitly distinguishing philosophical and political analyses, Butler herself resists the idea of surpassing identities, however, given reactionary politics, and instead urges efforts to invoke identity provisionally, for strategic purposes, while questioning notions of identity and emphasizing the contingent and fluctuating aspects of identity. Id., at 129-131.

242. Orlando Patterson, "The Paradox of Integration: Why Whites and Blacks Seem so Divided," *The New Republic*, 6 November 1995 24–27 (describing average improvement for African Americans but increase in percentage living in poverty since 1969, Depression-level unemployment, one in three black men between twenty-five and twenty-nine supervised by criminal justice system; racism in police departments); Gordon and Newfield, *White Philosophy*, 382.

243. Jacqueline Jones, *The Dispossessed: America's Underclass from the Civil War to the Present* (New York: Basic Books, 1992), 292.

244. See E. J. Dionne, Jr., *Why Americans Hate Politics* (New York: Simon and Schuster, 1991), 21. Some observers mourn the decline of class as a meaningful identity category and imagine it could better mobilize political action and challenges to inequality;

for complex economic, political, and psychological reasons, it just has not worked that way. See West, *Race*, 15, 18. Yet, maybe class could become a more vital category for mobilizing people, given the growing disparities between the haves and the have nots.

245. Dean, *Solidarity*, 177: "the critique of identity politics has taught us that we can neither solve the problems of social and legal exclusion nor do justice to the complexity of multiple, shifting, and situated identities so long as we continue to struggle on the terrain of identity politics" and yet identities seem to offer security and belonging.

246. Jen, *Mona*, 118. In addition, Mona realizes that her parents are afraid of turning into blacks, or being treated by whites the way blacks are.

247. Recent scholars devoted considerable energy in demonstrating that law itself is constructed as a product of human imagination. Elaine Scarry, "The Made-Up and the Made-Real," in *Field Work: Sites in Literary and Cultural Studies*, eds. Marjorie Garber, Rebecca L. Walkowitz, and Carl B. Franklin (New York: Routledge, 1996), 214. Unlike art, however, law is then made real in the material world. Id. at 217.

248. See Elizabeth Mertz, *A New Social Constructionism for Sociolegal Studies*, 28 L & Society Rev. 1243–1265 (1994).

249. I take this title, and some of the analysis that follows, from Ian F. Haney Lopez, *White by Law: The Legal Construction of Race* (New York: New

York Univ. Press, 1996).

250. Act of March 26, 1790, ch. 3, 1 Stat. 103. Curiously invoking the notion of "nature" precisely when it does not apply, "naturalization" is the process of conferring the rights of a national, or citizen, on a person not born with those rights.

251. Immigration and Nationality Act of 1952, § 311, ch. 2, 66 Stat. 239 (codified as amended at 8 U.S.C. § 1422 [1988]).

252. Lopez, *White by Law*, 2.

253. Ibid. at 26 (quoting *United States v. Thind*, 261 U.S. 204, 211 (1922)). See generally id. at 5–18.

254. *Ozawa v. United States*, 260 U.S. 178 *(1927).

255. Ibid. at .

256. Lopez, *White*, 91.

257. Ibid. Haney Lopez, 124.

258. Ibid. at 124–132.

259. Ibid. at 91.

260. Ibid. (quoting suicide note of Vaisho Das Bagai).

261. See Neil Gotanda, *A Critique of 'Our Constitution is Color-Blind*, 44 Stan L Rev 1 (1991).

262. Since 1977, the Census Bureau has used four racial categories: white, black, American Indian and Alaska native, and Asian and Pacific Islander; the 1990 census added another category, "other," and also asked whether individuals were of "Hispanic" or "Spanish" origin. Linda Matthews, "More than Identity Rides on a New Racial Category," *New York Times*, 6 July 1996, p. 1, col. 1; p. 7. A discussion of the "other" category appears in Gabrielle Sandor, "The `Other' Americans," *American Demographics*, June 1994, 36-42 ("other" Americans on census are likely to be young, Hispanic, and proud of mixed background). For a history of prior racial categories used in the U.S. Census, see Sharon M. Lee, "US Census Racial Classifications: 1890-1990," 61 *Ethnic and Racial Studies* (January 1993):75–94. According to Lee, the final authority on the selection of racial classifications is the House of Representatives Subcommittee on Census and Population. Id. at 87.

263. Mathews, "Racial Category," p. 1, col. 1.

264. Ibid.

265. Ibid.; Mike McNamee, "Should the Census be Less Black and White?," *Business Week*, 4 July 1994, 40 (business worries that a proliferation of census categories would make compliance with affirmative action guidelines a nightmare). An initial 1995 phone survey using the multiracial category found that the only group declining in identification was Native Americans, but some people thought multiracial would include multiple ethnicity, such as Irish American and Italian American. Matthews, "Racial Categories."

266. Matthews, "Racial Cateogires," (quoting sociologist Mary Waters). By some estimates, most African Americans are multiracial; by others, most whites are multiracial. This may underscore the difficulty of ever using "race"

as a category. See chapter 2 (discussing incoherence of race as a concept); Tom Marganthau, "What Color Is Black?" *Newsweek*, 13 February 1995, 63–65; "Counting Race," *Fortune*, 16 October 1995, 246 (reporting federal Office of Management and Budget acknowledgment of confusion about racial identities of people from Middle East, Indian from Mexico).

267. Noel Ignatiev, *How the Irish Became White* (New York: Routledge, 1995).

268. Ibid. at 2, 34–35 (describing Irish Penal Laws and land-tenant relations putting Irish Catholics in a serf position).

269. Ibid. at 42. See also id. at 41 (Irish referred to as "niggers turned inside out," and Negroes called "smoked Irish").

270. Arthur Mann, *The One and the Many: Reflections on the American Identity* (Chicago, IL: Univ. of Chicago Press, 1979) (quoting Edward A. Freeman), 129.

271. Related studies include David Roediger, *The Wages of Whiteness: Race and the Making of the American Working Class* (New York: Verso, 1991); and Alexander Saxton, *The Rise and Fall of the White Republic: Class Politics and Mass Culture in Nineteenth-Century America* (New York: Verso, 1990).

272. Ignatiev, *Irish*, 96.

273. Judith Butler, "Discussion," in *The Identity in Question* ed. John Rajchman (New York: Routledge, 1995), 139.

274. See Benedict Anderson, *Imag-ined Communities: Reflections on the Origin and Spread of Nationalism* (New York: Verso, 1991) (discussing role of census taking in the creation of group identities); Homi Bhabha, *The Location of Culture* (New York: Routledge, York 1994) 66 ("Fixity, as the sign of cultural/historical/ racial difference in the discourse of colonialism, is a paradoxical mode of representation: it connotes rigidity and an unchanging order as well as disorder, degeneracy and daemonic repetition").

275. Americans with Disability Act, Title I, § 12102 (2)(C). The regulations adopted to elaborate the law further indicate that a "cosmetic disfigurement" can count as a physical impairment. 45 CFR § 84.3 (j) (2) (i) (A) (1985).

276. Bonnie Poitras Tucker, *Federal Disability Law in a Nutshell* (St. Paul, MN: West Publishing Co., 1994), 21–22.

277. Janet E. Halley, *Sexual Orientation and the Politics of Biology: A Critique of the Argument from Immutability*, 46 Stan L Rev 503 (1994).

279. Halley also finds common ground between those who think that sexual orientation is biological and innate with those who think it is influenced by individual choice and cultural context. Even members of these two groups can agree that people definitely and deeply differ in their preferred sexual activities. They may differ not so much over the gender of the other desired person, but instead over how much time to spend in sexual activi-

ties, how important emotional commitment is to sexual activities, what kinds of sexual contact are most enjoyable. Calling this view "weak behavioral constructivism," Halley suggests that it can unite people who otherwise disagree about the immutability of sexual orientation. Ibid. at 558–63.

279. Ibid. at 566 (footnote omitted).

280. For a more extended discussion of this dilemma, see Martha Minow, *Making All the Difference: Inclusion, Exclusion, and American Law* (Ithaca, New York: Cornell Univ. Press, 1990).

281. See Robert M. Cover, *The Supreme Court, 1982 Term—Foreword: Nomos and Narrative*, 97 Harv L Rev 4 (1983); Robert Cover, *Violence and the Word*, 95 Yale LJ 1601 (1985).

282. See Linda Alcoff, "Mestizo Identity," in *American Mixed Race: The Culture of Microdiversity*, ed. Naomi Zack (London: Rowman & Littlefield, 1995) (marketing strategies produce and freeze identities while emphasizing the visible and distinguishable).

283. See Mary Douglas, *How Institutions Think* (Syracuse, New York: Syracuse Univ. Press, 1986).

284. Does family status belong in the same discussion as ethnic, racial, gender, or sexual preference groupings? Aviam Soifer provides a full acknowledgment of the difficulty in devising overarching principles to connect these and other associations, along with a sustained exploration of the dilemmas and features such associations share. See Aviam Soifer, *Law and*

the *Company We Keep* (Cambridge, MA: Harvard Univ. Press, 1995).

285. Natalie Zemon Davis, *The Return of Martin Guerre* (Cambridge, MA: Harvard Univ. Press, 1983). Made into a movie, this story also inspired another movie entitled "Sommersby," which transposed the story from medieval France to Reconstruction-era Southern United States.

286. See "Many Identities Emerge for Amnesia Victim," *New York Times*, 14 March 1990, A26, col. 1 (amnesia victim first identified by family members as one person and then as two other people, based on employment records and employee reports, and three different social security numbers).

287. See Joseph William Singer, *The Reliance Interest in Property*, 40 Stan L Rev 611, 663–99 (1988).

288. Whatever commonsense, scientific, or cultural definitions of fatherhood may have worked in the past, the advent of new reproductive technologies exposes the definition of "father" as a matter of social choice from among a range of possible candidates. Artificial insemination, in vitro fertilization, frozen embryo transfer, and other techniques permit new permutations in parent-child relationships. The person who donates the sperm, the husband of the woman who carries the child, the man who seeks adoption, the man who has undertaken an actual parental relationship with the child—or a second "mother" in a committed relationship with the child's mother—each may be candi-

dates for the second-parent role. That role itself can be defined to include day-to-day caretaking, financial responsibility, spiritual custody (decision making over the child's religious upbringing), decisional authority over the child's schooling and medical treatment, or a mix of these elements.

289. The man's own voluntary acceptance of the parental role means more than engaging in the physical act that produced the child. The Supreme Court has held that for purposes of asserting due process rights to participate in an adoption proceeding that would terminate his claims about a child, an unmarried father must also have undertaken a significant custodial, personal, or financial relationship with the child. *Lehr v. Robertson*, 460 U.S. 248 (1983).

290. Joseph Goldstein, Albert Solnit and Anna Freud, *Beyond the Best Interests of the Child* (New York: Free Press, 1973); Peggy Davis, `There Is a Book Out....': An Analysis of Judicial Absorption of Legislative Facts*, 101 Harv L Rev 1531 (1987).

291. Such presumptions are also sometimes called "conclusive."

292. See *Michael H. v. Gerald D.*, 109 S. Ct. 2333, 2340 (1989) (Scalia, J., plurality opinion) ("A conclusive presumption does, of course, foreclose the persona against whom it is invoked from demonstrating, in a particularized proceeding, that applying the presumption to him will in fact not further the lawful governmental policy the presumption is designed to effectuate.")

293. E.g., Cal. Evid. Code Ann. § 621 (West Supp. 1989). The California rule does allow rebuttal within two years after the child's birth, only at the request of the husband or wife, not a third party. Sec. 621 (c), (d).

294. The California statute was enacted in 1872. 109 S. Ct. at 2338. A similar rule was part of the common-law tradition. E.g., 1 Blackstone's Commentaries 456 (Chitty ed. 1826). Although illegitimacy may still be a stigma in some communities, by law it is not a permissible basis for denying a child inheritance and succession rights. *Lalli v. Lalli*, 439 U.S. 259 (1978); *Trimble v. Gordon*, 430 U.S. 762 (1977). The Constitution also has been interpreted to assure some protected parental relationship for unwed fathers. See *Stanley v. Illinois*, 405 U.S. 645 (1972); *Caban v. Mohammed*, 441 U.S. 380 (1979).

295. See *Little v. Streater*, 452 U.S. 1, 6 (1981) (examining changes in blood test accuracy). Moreover, the 1872 statute was amended several times before the events involved in *Michael H. v. Gerald D.* See *Michael H. v. Gerald D.*, 109 S. Ct. 2333, 2339 (1989).

296. There may indeed be a problem of infinite regress here: if the presumption forecloses consideration of alternative evidence in a given case, does it also foreclose consideration of the presumption itself, and then consideration of the consideration of the presumption?

297. 109 S. Ct. 2333 (1989).

298. 109 S. Ct. at 2339.

299. Justice Scalia rejected the procedural due process objection on the ground that the presumption did not deny Michael procedures but instead represents a classification that survives review as to the fit between its terms and its purposes. 109 S. Ct., at 2341. The opinion also rejected Michael's claim that the presumption violated his constitutionally protected liberty interest in a relationship with his daughter on the grounds that only fundamental liberties are protected, and that only traditional family ties fall within that sphere of protection. Id., at 2341-2345.

300. 109 S. Ct. at 2342. In stressing this look at specific traditions, Justice Scalia's analysis bears consequences for the entire project of judicial interpretation, especially of terms such as due process and liberty. Justice Scalia's effort to clarify this test, based on traditions, prompted sharp dissent even from Justices O'Connor and Kennedy, who otherwise joined his opinion, 109 S. Ct. 2346 (O'Connor and Kennedy, JJ., concurring in part), as well as from the dissenting Justices. 109 S. Ct. 2340 (Brennan, J., joined by Marshall, J., and Blackmun, J., dissenting). See also 109 S. Ct. 2360 (White, J., dissenting).

301. This dimension of the plurality prompted especially sharp dissents from Justices who argued that the Constitution's meaning should evolve in relation to changing social practices and attitudes. 109 S. Ct. at 2349,

2349–51 (Brennan, J., dissenting); Id. at 2360, 2360–61 (White, J., dissenting). See also *Loving v. Virginia*, 388 U.S. 1 (1967) (rejecting state law forbidding interracial marriage as unconstitutional burden on fundamental liberty); *Stanley v. Illinois*, 405 U.S. 645 (1972) (rejecting presumption that unwed father is unfit caretaker for his children).

302. See Katherine Bartlett, *Tradition, Change, and the Idea of Progress in Feminist Legal Thought*, 1995 Wis L Rev 303.

303. See, e.g., Steven Mintz, *A Prison of Expectations: The Family in Victorian Culture* (New York: New York Univ. Press, 1983) ("Demographic historians have found that while in the seventeenth and early eighteenth centuries in England and colonial America the nuclear household (i.e., a husband and wife living in a private, independent household) was predominant, most people, at least in their youth, lived for a time in more complex households, as a servant, an apprentice, a trade assistant, or a boarder"). See also Carol Stack, *All Our Kin* (New York: Harper & Row, 1974) (exploring kin relationships among unrelated people within poor black communities); Lawrence Stone, *The Family, Sex and Marriage in England 1500-1800*, abridged ed. (New York: Harper & Row, 1979), 100–08 (exploring transition from extended family to nuclear family forms); Carol Weisbrod, *The Bounds of Utopia* (New York: Pantheon Books, 1980) (examining nineteenth-

century utopian communities and their use of law to create alternative family and community forms). American law has sometimes recognized plural traditions in family identity, e.g., *Moore v. City of East Cleveland*, 431 U.S. 494 (1977) (plurality opinion) (recognizing extended family as traditional form deserving constitutional protection), and sometimes not, e.g., *Reynolds v. United States*, 98 U.S. 145 (1890) (denying free exercise objection to criminal sanction against polygamy).

304. See Statistical Abstract of the United States 51 (1990) (comparing 10.1 percent single-parent households in 1970 with 22.2 percent single-parent households in 1985); David Chambers, "Stepparents, Biologic Parents, and the Law's Perception of 'Family' after Divorce," in *Divorce Reform at the Crossroads* eds. Stephen Sugarman and Herma Hill Kay (New Haven, CT: Yale Univ. Press, 1990) (examining incidence and patterns of step-families).

305. See Martha Minow, *'Forming Underneath Everything that Grows': Toward a History of Family Law*, 1985 Wis L Rev. 819.

306. See Bharati Muhkerjee, "A Wife's Story," in *The Middleman and Other Stories* (1989),23 (discussed in chapter 2).

307. See, e.g., John Boswell, *The Kindness of Strangers: The Abandonment of Children in Western Europe from Late Antiquity to the Renaissance* (New York: Pantheon Books, 1988).

308. See n. 288.

309. See *Children and Families: Key Trends in the 1980's: A State Report of the Select Committee on Children, Youth, and Families*, 100th Cong., 2d Sess. (December 1988).

310. See Goldstein et al., *Best Interest*. But see *In the Matter of Alison D. v. Virginia M.* (N.Y. App. Div. 1990) (rejecting claim by lesbian co-mother for visitation with child born through artificial insemination of her former lover).

311. See, e.g., *Smith v. OFFER*, 431 U.S. 816 (1977) (foster families); *Lehr v. Robertson*, 460 U.S. 248 (1983) (biological relationship plus actual social relationship necessary to obtain legal protection for unwed father).

312. 109 S. Ct. at 2361 (White, J., dissenting).

313. 109 S. Ct., at 2353–54 (Brennan, J., dissenting); Id. at 2362 (White, J., dissenting).

314. This ultimate question could well be answered by reference to the child's best interests rather than any basis for the father's claims. See *Quilloin v. Walcott*, 434 U.S. at 255; *Lehr v. Robertson*, 463 U.S. 248 (1983).

315. Justice Brennan concluded that the plurality's approach allows "the State's interest in terminating the relationship to play a role in defining the 'liberty' that is protected by the Constitution. According to our established framework under the Due Process Clause, however, we first ask whether the person claiming constitutional protection has an interest that the Constitution recognizes; if we find

that she does, we next consider the State's interest in limiting the extent of the procedures that will attend the deprivation of that interest." 109 S. Ct., at 2354. Justice Brennan concluded that the plurality "takes both of these steps at once." Id.

316. Cal. Fam. Code 7611(d) (Derring Special Pamphlet, 1993).

317. *Guardianship of Phillip Becker*, Superior Court of Santa Clara, Cal. No. 10181 (1981), aff, 139 Cal. App.3d 407; 118 Cal. Rptr. 781 (1983). For a discussion of this case, see Minow, *Making All the Difference*, 342-347.

318. Todd Rakoff, *Characterization* (draft, 1996).

319. Filed on August 26, 1976, the case produced three years of litigation. *Mashpee Tribe v. New Seabury, et al.*, 447 F.Supp. 940 (D. Mass. 1978); aff'd 592 F.2d 575 (1st Cir. 1979).

320. Federal law required congressional approval before the sale of Indian lands and sought to assure full compensation. The Passamaquoddy and Penobscot Indians in Maine successfully asserted claims under the Act and received over $80 million, as well as authority to acquire properties through an out-of-court settlement. Paul Brodeur, *Restitution: The Land Claims of the Mashpee, Passamaquoddy, and Penobscot Indians of New England* (Boston: Northeastern Univ. Press, 1985).

321. The very notion of a "tribe" seems itself a myth invented in part by U. S. law, as well as by anthropologists.

See Goldberg-Ambrose, 28 L & Society Rev 1123 (1994).

322. James Clifford, *The Predicament of Culture* (Cambridge, MA: Harvard Univ. Press, 1988), 294–302.

323. See also Francis Hutchins, *Mashpee: The Story of Cape Cod's Indian Town* (West Franklin, NH: Amarta Press, 1979). Hutchins served as the chief expert witness for the defendants at trial.

324. Clifford, *Culture*, 323, 336.

325. Ibid. at 305.

326. Ibid., at 285–293. See also Russell M. Peters, *The Wampanoags of Mashpee* (Somerville, MA: Media Action, 1987) (a member describes the Mashpee).

327. Clifford, *Culture*, 299. This view comported with an attitude held by many whites, embodied in the Dawes Act. See Leonard A. Carlson, *Indians, Bureaucrats, and Land: The Dawes Act and the Decline of Indian Farming* (1981)4 (describing legislation that allocated Indian reservation lands to individual Indians in an effort to encourage "each family to farm its own land and acquire the habits of thrift, industry, and individualism needed for assimilation into white culture.")

328. Clifford, *Culture*, at 308. Under this interpretation, the town members showed how well they knew the paternalistic attitudes of the white politicians toward residents of Mashpee, and played off those attitudes in order to purchase the space and autonomy to pursue their own vision

of governance. This resembles the strategy of the slave woman in Sherley Ann Williams' "In Honor of Free Women, Meditations on History," in *Midnight Birds* ed. Mary Helen Washington (Garden City, NY: Anchor Books, 1980); see discussion in chapter 2.

329. The federal judge asked the jury to answer whether a tribe existed in 1790, 1834, 1842, 1869, 1870, and 1976 because these were critical dates in Mashpee history pertinent to the land claims.

330. The jury found that no tribe existed in 1670, but a tribe existed in Mashpee in 1834 and 1842.

331. The process of reclaiming a name assigned by an oppressor may be followed by transforming that name into a self-invented one, or further resisting the echoes of the preview subjugation. See R. Radhakrishan, "Ethnic Identity and Post-Structuralist Difference," *Cultural Critique* (1987), 199, 208.

332. This is not meant to imply that the legal texts, or even law enforcement, inevitably precludes choices and responses. Despite the U.S. government's effort to force assimilation by Indians through off-reservation boarding schools, for example, many Indians participated in cross-tribal relationships and in forging an "Indian" identity beyond any particular tribe; in addition, on occasion Indian leaders support accommodation to non-Indian governmental forms to secure greater latitude for self-government.

See Goldberg-Ambrose, 28 "Of Native Americans and Tribal Members," *Law & Society* Rev. 1123 (1994).

333. See Allison M. Dussias, *Geographically-Based and Membership-Based Views of Indian Tribal Sovereignty: The Supreme Court's Changing Vision*, 55 U Pitt L Rev 1 (1993).

334. See Joseph William Singer, *Sovereignty and Property*, 86 Northwestern U L Rev 1 (1991). One of the few recent Supreme Court affirmations of tribal sovereignty came at the cost of refusing access to federal court to a female tribe member challenging her tribe's membership rules for including children of a male but not of a female tribe member. See *Santa Clara Pueblo v. Martinez*, 436 U.S. 49 (1978); see Judith Resnick, *Dependent Sovereigns*, 56 U Chi. L Rev 671 (1989).

335. See *Mississippi Band of Choctaw Indians v. Holyfield*, 490 U.S. 30 (1989) (discussing Indian Child Welfare Act, 25 U.S.C. §§ 1901–1963).

336. 25 U.S.C. § 1915(a).

337. Helen Thomas, "Clinton Signs Minimum Wage Hike," 1996 UPI, *BC Cycle*, August 20, 1996 (describving tax credit to promote adopting and ban on race preferences in adoption).

338. See Elizabeth Bartholet, *Family Bonds* (Boston: Houghton Mifflin, 1993).

339. *Mississippi Band of Choctaw Indians v. Holyfield*, 490 U.S. 30 (1989).

340. The Court interpreted the statutory concept of domicile for this purpose.

341. 490 U.S. at 53.

342. Barbara Kingsolver, *Pigs in Heaven* (New York: HarperCollins, 1993).

343. Ibid. 330–31. Rather than revealing a pre-existing truth, the threat to divide the child could be understood as an educative use of force. See Martha Minow, "The Judgment of Solomon," in eds. Robert Cover and Owen Fiss *The Structure of Procedure* (Mineola: NY: Foundation Press, 1979), 447.

344. *Pigs in Heaven*, 338.

345. Where eligibility for a benefit or protection on the basis of group status is at issue, judges are likely to perceive the danger of including someone who does not deserve inclusion or excluding someone who should be included.

346. Theresa Glennon, *Race, Education, and the Construction of a Disabled Class*, 1995 Wis L Rev 1237.

347. At the same time, people who think African Americans and Latinos are inferior to whites do not need the excuse of affirmative action.

348. See Bill Ainsworth, "A Truly Partisan Measure," *The Recorder* 17 January 1996, 1; Clint Swett, "Coalition Praises Utilities," *Sacramento Bee*, 26 April 1996, F1; "Proposed Testimony of Congresswoman Eleanor Holmes Norton before Senate Committee on Labor, Human Resources, Affirmative Action, Preferences, and The Equal Opportunity Act of 1995," *Federal News Services*, 30 April 1996.

349. See Morton J. Horwitz, *The Transformation of American Law:*

*1870-1960* (New York: Oxford Univ. Press, 1993), 193–212 (describing legal realist criticisms of American law).

350. See supra (this chapter) text at notes 275–280.

351. See Kathryn Abrams, *Complex Claimants and Reductive Moral Judgments: New Patterns in the Search of Equality*, 57 U Pitt L Rev 337, 360–61 (1996) (discussing case brought by African-American woman in which she was called "buffalo butt" and another brought by a Chinese American woman called "Chinese pussy"). For a full examination of the second case, see Martha Chamallas, *Jean Jew's Case: Resisting Sexual Harassment in the Academy*, 6 Yale JL & Feminism 71, 74 (1994).

352. Amendment I, United States Constitution.

353. "No religion" is also an option of free exercise.

354. See Martha Minow, The Free Exercise of Families, 1991 Ill. L. Rev. 925; David A.J. Richards, Sexual Preference as a Suspect (Religious) Classification: An Alternative Perspective on the Unconstitutionality of Anti-Lesbian/Gay Initiatives, 55 Ohio St. L.J. 491 (1994).

355. *Loving v. Virginia*, 388 U.S. 1 (1967).

356. See *Harris v. Forklift Sys. Inc.*, 114 S. Ct. 367 (1993) (interpreting Title VII of the Civil Rights Act); see id at (Ginsburg, J., concurring).

357. See Robert Cover, *The Uses of Jurisdictional Redundancy*, Wm & Mary

639 (1981), 22.

358. See Richard Kluger, *Simple Justice* (New York: Knopf, 1975).

359. See Roberta Suro, "Woman Fleeing Tribal Rite Gets Asylum, Genital Mutilation is Ruled Persecution," *Wash. Post,* January 14, 1996, A06.

360. *Romer v. Evans,* 116 S.Ct. 1620 (1996).

361. The Supreme Court agreed that the white firefighters deserved a chance to be heard and thus permitted a challenge to the prior settlement. *Martin v. Wilks,* 490 U.S. 755 (1989). The 1991 Civil Rights Act overrode at least a narrow version of the Supreme Court's decision. 42 U.S.C. 2000(e)-2A.

362. *Cooper v. French,* 460 N.W.2d 2 (Minn. 1990). See Maureen E. Markey, *The Price of a Landlord's "Free" Exercise of Religion,* 22 Fordham Urb LJ 699 (1995).

363. See Wendy Brown, "Wounded Attachments: Late Modern Oppositional Political Formations," in *The Identity in Question* ed. John Rajchman (New York: Routledge, 1995), 199; see chapter 3 (discussing "wounded attachments").

364. It is the longest running straight play since *Amadeus.* Kevin Kelly, "M. Butterfly, Miss Saigon, and Mr. Hwang,: *Boston Globe,* 9 September 1990, 92.

365. Ibid., at 93. In this way, the play challenges the audience to think not only about the gender of the character but also the gender of the actor, and thus the possibilities of

cross-gender casting. Cross-gender casting, while uncommon, is not without precedent. See Dan Sullivan, "Colorblind Casting: It's Not Yet a Tradition—When Black is White, Women are Men, And the Theater Is Challenging," *Los Angeles Times,* 2 October 1988, calendar section, at 50.

366. Kelly, "M. Butterly," at 93.

367. See Indian Child Welfare Act of 1978 (ICWA), 25 U.S.C. section 1901–1963.

368. See Randall Kennedy "Yes: Race-Matching is Horrendous," *ABA Journal,* April 1995, 44. Critics also emphasize data showing that race-matching policies also tend to keep nonwhite children longer in temporary care—awaiting same-race adoptive parents. See Elizabeth Bartholet, *Family Bonds* 86–117 (Boston: Houghton-Mifflin, 1993). But see Ruth-Arlene Howe, "Redefining the Transracial Adoption Controversy," 2 *Duke Journal of Gender, Law and Policy,* 131 (1995) (to do other than race matching is a form of genocide).

369. See Mary Joe Frug, "Post-Modern Feminist Manifesto," in *Postmodern Legal Feminist* (New York: Routledge, 1993), 38–48.

370. See generally Christopher Edley, Jr., *Not All Black and White: Affirmative Action, Race, and American Values* (New York: Hill and Wang, 1966). Note: individuals receive no federal protection against discrimination on the basis of sexual orientation, although some municipalities and states recognize this as a protected

group. In addition, the Supreme Court recently rejected Colorado's state constitutional effort to foreclose civil rights protections for homosexuals on local and state levels. *Romer v. Evans*, 116 S.Ct. 1620 (1996).

371. Such debates typically depend on confusion about the meaning "affirmative action," which I define here as private voluntary efforts or programs adopted under governmental rulings to alter the methods by which institutions recruit and select in order to eliminate barriers from past discrimination or failures to be inclusive and to promote diversity along racial, ethnic, and gender lines. For a more extended consideration of affirmative action, see chapter 6. Despite efforts to polarize Americans on this issue, usually by equating affirmative action with quotas, individuals including from the Neil Rudenstine, President of Harvard University, to Colin Powell, former head of the Joint Chiefs of Staff, endorse the basic fairness of promoting equal opportunity and the basic wisdom of strengthening institutions through diversity.

372. Wendy Brown, "Wounded Attachments," in *The Identity in Question*, ed. John Rajchman (New York: Routledge, 1995), 211.

373. Ibid.

374. Ibid. See also William Connolly, *Identity/Difference* (Ithaca, NY: Cornell Univ. Press, 1991).

375. Kristin Bumiller, *The Civil Rights Society* (Baltimore, MD: Johns Hopkins Univ. Press, 1988).

376. See chapter 3 (discussing "being regarded as" theories, such as the Americans with Disability Act, 42 U.S.C. § 12102(2)(C)).

377. Federal disability law also currently permits claims of erroneous identification as disabled; this approach, of course, reinforces the idea that there really are persons with disabilities and the category is bounded and clear. *NAACP v. State*, 775 F.2d 1403, 1427 (11th Cir. 1985).

378. Such an argument was proposed and rejected when a Jewish group sought protection against racial discrimination on the grounds that they were—wrongly—perceived to be a race. See *Shaare Tefila Congregation v. Cobb*, 107 S.Ct. 2019 (1987). The Supreme Court decided instead to accord protection by turning to a nineteenth-century dictionary definition of race in use at the time the civil rights law in question was adopted, and on that basis, treated Jews as a race. See Martha Minow, *Making All the Difference* (Ithaca, NY: Cornell Univ. Press, NY 1990), 55.

379. See Maria Puente, "Poll: Blacks' Confidence in Police Plummets," *USA Today*, 21 March 1995, 3A. See also Gerald F. Uelmen, "Perspective on Justice," *Los Angeles Times*, 24 January 1996, B9.

380. See Indira A. R. Lakshmanan, "Team Effort Slows Tide of Youth Violence in City," *Boston Globe*, July 22, 1996, A1. See also Kevin Merida, "Proposal Push to Try Juveniles as Adults," *Emerge*, November 1996, 26–27

(describing a Chicago probation program using counseling to help 80,000 urban youth; only seven percent committed future crimes). Another example that should trigger internal review by officials involved would be the over-representation of nonwhite children in segregated classrooms for children with disabilites. See *Hobson v. Hanson,* 269 F. Supp. 401 (D.D.C. 1967). For a call for expanded opportunities to challenge racism in the assignment of students to special education, see Theresa Glennon, *Race, Education, and the Construction of a Disabled Class,* 1995 Wis L Rev 1237.

381. Justice Thurgood Marshall, "Reflections on the Bicentennial of the United States Constitution," 101 Harv L Rev 1 (1987).

382. Michael D'Orso, *Like Judgment Day: The Ruin and Redemption of a Town Called Rosewood* (New York: Grosset/ Putnam, 1996).

383. C. Jeanne Bassett, *House Bill 591: Florida Compensates Rosewood Victims and Their Families for a Seventy-One-Year-Old Injury,* 22 Florida State U L Rev 503 (1994).

384. Ibid.; see also D'Orso, *Judgment,* 297.

385. Bassett, *Rosewood,* 521.

386. D'Orso, *Judgment,* 162–69, 306–17.

387. Id. at 318–20.

388. See ibid. at 93–106, 318–23.

389. 50 U.S.C. 1989b-b9 (1988 & Supp. IV 1992). See also the American-Japanese Evacuation Claims Act of 1948, 50 U.S.C. app. sections 1981-

1987 (1982) (providing for compensation for specified property losses). For an argument defending these reparations, see Mari J. Matsuda, *Looking to the Bottom: Critical Legal Studies and Reparations,* 22 Harv CR-CL L Rev 323 (1987). See also Anthony DePalma, "Three Countries Face Their Indians," *New York Times,* December 15, 1996, p.E9, Vol.1 (describing Canadian creation of Nanavut territory giving native peoples self-governance and proposals for further reparations).

390. Another example is the U. S. Indian Claims Commission, established in 1946 and closed in 1978, which heard claims concerning abrogation of tribal or other Indian property rights occuring prior to the 1940s. See Robert N. Clinton, Nell Jessup Newton and Monroe E. Price, *American Indian Law,* 3d ed. (Charlottesville, VA: Michie Co., 1991), 721–24. Yet reports of lawyers who manipulated the process to enrich themselves raise sober questions about designing and implementing such programs well.

391. See Boris I. Bittker, *The Case for Black Reparations* (New York: Random House: 1973) (finding black reparations constitutional but partial, and therefore at risk of unfairness; urging national debate on the subject); Rhonda V. Magee, *The Master's Tools, Note: From the Bottom Up: Responses to African-American Reparations Theory in Mainstream and Outsider Remedies Discourse,* 79 Virginia L Rev 863 (1993); Vincene Verdun, *If the Shoe Fits, Wear It: An Analysis of Reparations to African Ameri-*

*cans*, 67 Tulane L Rev 597 (1993).

392. Sri Lanka may be unique in sponsoring a truth commission that addresses abuses by a contemporaneous regime.

393. For an extensive consideration of the effects on collective memory of prosecutorial approaches to state-sponsored mass brutality, see Mark J. Osiel, *Ever Again: Legal Remembrance of Administrative Massacre*, 144 U Penn L Rev 463 (1995).

394. An example is the work of Professor Sarah Deutsch, at the History Department at Clark University.

395. See Melissa Faye Greene, *The Temple Bombing*. (Reading, MA: Addison-Wesley, 1995).

396. Harlon Dalton, *Racial Healing* (New York: Doubleday, 1995), 157.

397. Ibid., at 156 (referring to the work of D. Marvin Jones).

398. These settings should avoid the familiar tendency to put members of minority groups and women in the role of constantly having to explain themselves and their experiences to others, who should try to educate themselves without simply assigning the burden to those who have already been burdened.

399. Ibid. at 157–8. See also bell hooks, *Yearning* (Boston: South End Press, Boston) (discussing "home-place").

400. See Judith Herman, *Trauma and Recovery* (New York: Basic Books, York 1992).

401. Robert Cover, "The Folktales of Justice," in *Narrative, Violence, and the Law: The Essays of Robert Cover* eds. Martha Minow, Michael Ryan and Austin Sarat (Ann Arbor: Univ. of Michigan Press, 1992) (describing tribunal organized by philosophers Bertrand Russell and Jean-Paul Sartre).

402. See Robert Post, *Cultural Heterogeneity and the Law: Pornography, Blasphemy, and the First Amendment*, 76 Cal L Rev 320 (1988) (constitutional law protects the capacity of individuals to form new and different groups).

403. This discussion in part responds to the dilemmas of representation. See chapter 1.

404. 42 U.S.C. 1973 (1988).

405. See Bush Vera, 116 S. Ct. 1941 (1966) (opinion of O'Connor, J.); *Miller v. Johnson*, 115 S.Ct. 2475 (1995); *Shaw v. Reno*, 509 U.S. 630 (1993).

406. Lani Guinier, *Tyranny of the Majority*, (New York: Free Press, 1994), 120–22.

407. The term also had racist overtones. See Stephen Carter, "Foreword," in Guinier, *Tyranny*, vii, xix. President Clinton caved in to the smear campaign.

408. That both the Reagan and Bush administrations pursued remedies for Voting Rights Act violations using multidistrict and proportional representation rules seems to have escaped Guinier's critics. Carter, *Forward*, xi.

409. Ibid. at 149.

410. Ibid. at 149.

411. Ibid.

412. Ibid.

413. Similar temporary groups may come together as signatures for ballot access.

414. This approach is compatible with a more general argument made by Chantal Mouffe: "The issue is to create a new conception of citizenship in which the distinction of gender becomes nonpertinent... What I'm against is a certain type of identity politics that says what politics is about is the representation of all those identities as they already exist." Chantal Mouffe, "Discussion," in *Identity in Question*, 31.

415. Guinier also seeks a system that prevents entrenched majorities, so that no group can become indifferent to treating others fairly. See Lani Guinier, *More Democracy*, 1995 U Chi. LForum 13. A different approach may be required in a different context. See Jack H. Nagel, "New Zealand's Novel Solution to the Problem of Minority Representation," 5 *The Good Society* 25, Spring 1995 (describing mixed-member proportional system electing half the members of parliaments from single member districts but determining the relative strength of parties through a proportional representation system, and using one geographically based single-member district for the Maori minority).

416. Clarence Page, "The Political Reality of Separating Races, *Rocky Mountain News*, 14 September 1995, 63A.

417. See generally Ruth Colker,

234–40; Hollinger, supra, 22–38. See also Lise Funderburg, *Black, White, Other* (New York: W. Morrow and Co., 1994); Andrea D. Greene, "Racial Boxes Not Comfortable Fit for All," *Houston Chronicle*, 5 February 1996, 16. See generally *American Mixed Race*, ed. Naomi Zack (London: Rowman and Littlefield, 1995).

418. Linda Alcoff, "Mestizo Identity," in *Mixed Race*, 257–78; Gloria Anzaldua, *Borderlands/La Frontera* (San Francisco: Spinsters/Aunt Lute, 1987).

419. See Mike McName, "Should the Census Be Less Black and White?," *Business Week*, 4 July 1994, 40; Deborah Ramirez, *Race and Remedy in a Multicultural Society: It's Not Just Black and White Anymore*, 47 Stan L Rev 457 (1995). Similarly, census questions about disability could be reformed to permit people to identify themselves in ways other than perjorative categories, while still producing information relevant to the societal need for supports for persons with disabilities.

These questions suggest that there could be a practical side to what philosophers have called "attributive meaning," picking out an object simply for a present purpose but not for unrelated purposes. See Keith S. Donnellan, "Reference and Definite Descriptions," in *Meaning, Necessity and Natural Kinds* ed. Stephen P. Schwartz (Ithaca, NX: Cornell Univ. Press: 1975).

420. Michael Gorra, "Response" in Identities, in *Identities*, eds. Kwome

Anthony Appiah and Henry Louis Gates, Jr. (Chicago: Univ. of Chicago Press, 1995), 434.

421. See Colker, 239.

422. Colker, 245.

423. Ibid. at 246.

424. The current experimental tests affording people the option of identifying themselves as "multiracial" similarly have produced considerable confusion.

425. See Lise Funderburg, "Boxed In," *New York Times*, 10 July 1996, p. A15, col. 2 (similar recommendation by a person who identifies herself as both "black and white").

426. There is a difference between the use of a governmental classification to create castes and the use of that classification to pursue equality. See Christopher L. Eisgruber, *Political Unity and the Powers of Government*, 41 UCLA L Rev 1297 (1994).

427. *Batson v. Kentucky*, 476 U.S. 79 (1986). The challenger has to make out a prima facie case that the pattern of exclusions triggers an equal protection concern, and then the other side has the chance to offer non-prejudicial grounds for the struck jurors. Id. See also *Hernandez v. New York*, 111 S.Ct. 1859 (1991) (Kennedy, J., plurality opinion) (finding it a sufficient explanation for the exclusion of Spanish-speaking jurors—treated as a racial exclusion—that the jurors might have difficulty accepting the English translator's version of the Spanish testimony). The relative ease with which parties may defend against the prima facie

case renders the *Batson* test quite limited if the goal is to end invidious racial, ethnic, religious, or sex discrimination in jury selection. Jeffrey Abramson, *We, The Jury: The Jury System and the Ideal of Democracy* 259-260 (New York: Basic Books, 1995). See discussion, chapter 2.

428. *Edmonson v. Leesville Concrete Co.*, 500 U.S. 614 (1990) (extending *Batson* to civil cases); *J.E.B. v. Alabama ex rel. T.B.*, 114 S.Ct. 1419 (1994) (extending *Batson* to exclusion on the basis of gender).

429. Justice Thomas, joined by Justice Scalia, dissented from the Supreme Court's denial of review of a case in which the criminal defendant claimed that peremptory challenges should also be tested against exclusions based on religious bias. *Edward Lee Davis v. Minnesota*, 144 S.Ct. 2120 (1994) (Thomas, J., with whom Justice Scalia joined, dissenting). Justice Ginsburg wrote in her concurrence in the denial of the petition for a writ of certiorari that the state court had itself rejected the claim in part because it is usually improper even to ask questions about the jurors' religious affiliations and beliefs. Id. (Justice Ginsburg, concurring).

430. See Sheri L. Johnson, *Black Innocence and the White Jury*, 83 Mich L Rev 1611, 1691–708 (1985). Others have proposed affirmative selection to achieve similar representative ends based on group identity. See, e.g., Tracey L. Altman, *Note, Affirmative Selection: A New Response to Peremptory*

*Challenge Abuse*, 38 Stan L Rev 781, 802–12 (1986); Donna J. Meyer, *A New Peremptory Inclusion to Increase Representativeness and Impartiality in Jury Selection*, 45 Case W Res L Rev 251 (1994). Yet, such an approach may well increase the likelihood of hung juries. Hans Zeisel, *Comment, Affirmative Peremptory Juror Selection*, 39 Stan L Rev 1165 (1987).

431. *Strauder v. West Virginia*, 100 U.S. 303, 308 (1879); Tracy L. Altman, *Note Affirmative Selection: A New Response to Peremptory Challenge Abuse*, 38 Stan L Rev 781, 787–93 (1986).

432. See *Batson* (discussing history of exclusion of blacks); *Taylor v. Louisiana*, 419 U.S. 522 (1975) (discussing exclusion of women).

433. Lisa E. Alexander, *Vicinage, Venue, and Community Cross-Section: Obstacles to a State Defendant's Right to a Trial by Representative Jury*, 19 Hastings Const LQ 261, 261–62 (1991).

434. For a thoughtful discussion of the issue, see Abramson, *Jury*, 99–141. See especially id. at 132: "as ancient as the peremptory challenge's credentials are, the theory of impartiality that underlies its use (that both sides should be free to eliminate persons suspected of racial, sexual, or ethnic bias against them) is in conflict with the theory of impartiality in the cross-sectional ideal (that bias needs to be represented on an impartial jury because there is no way to escape from it, there are only ways to balance it)."

435. Toni M. Massaro, *Peremptories or Peers?—rethinking Sixth Amendment Doctrine, Image, and Procedures*, 64 NC L Rev 510 (1986).

436. The peremptory challenge began in England with the king's power to challenge any juror and was gradually accepted into the common law and carried over to the United States, with the endorsement of Joseph Story. See Jon van Dyke, *Jury Selection Procedures* (Cambridge, MA: Ballinger Pub. Co., 1977), 148–49. The federal government formally granted peremptory challenges to the prosecutor in 1872. Id.

437. See *Batson*, 476 U.S. at 102–3, 107–8 (Marshall, J., concurring) (arguing for the elimination of peremptory challenges in order to end discrimination in jury selection). In a recent decision, Judge Constance Baker Motley ruled that no peremptory challenges may be exercised in her courtroom. See Mark Hansen, "Peremptory-Free Zone," *ABA Journal*, August 1996, 26 (discussing *Minetos v. City University of New York*, No. 92 Civ. 8785). She found the entire process of peremptory challenges and efforts to monitor them rife with violations of equal protection. See also Abramson, *Jury*, 258–64 (recommending elimination of all peremptory challenges because *Batson* fails to guard against discrimination in jury selection even for groups gaining Equal Protection coverage as well as for groups lacking equal protection coverage).

438. Abramson, *Jury*, at 12, notes that lawyers use peremptory chal-

lenges "On the basis of some suspicion that young or old, rich or poor, white-collar or blue-collar, Italian or Irish, Protestant or Jewish jurors will be favorable to the other side"—but most of these stereotypes would elude Equal Protection scrutiny because they do not refer to "suspect classes" protected under the *Batson* test.

439. See Sheri Lynn Johnson, *The Language and Culture (Not to Say Race) of Peremptory Challenges*, 35 Wm & Mary L Rev 21 (1993).

440. See Altman, *Jury*, 800 (discussing possibility that people are more or less empathetic in relation to rules and institutional expectations).

441. Efforts to supplement voter registration lists may be necessary to produce inclusive jury pools, given the disparities in voter registration rates across groups. Kairys, Kadane and Leockzy, *Jury Representativeness: A Mandate for Multiple Source Lists*, 65 Cal L Rev 776 (1977). See also Nancy Gertner and Judith Mizner, *The Law of Juries* (forthcoming).

442. This discussion grows from a forthcoming paper, "Is 'Reasonable Person' a Reasonable Concept in a Multicultural World?" (August 1995 draft) in Austin Sarat, ed., *Everyday Practices and Trouble Cases* (Evanston, Il: Northwestern U. Press, Forthcoming), which I co-authored with Todd Rakoff. I thank him for the many conversations that inform the discussion there and here.

443. Is it so different to use "reasonable person who is blind" rather than "reasonable blind person" or "reasonable person who is Chicano" rather than "reasonable Chicano?" Two differences might emerge: the circumstances considered under the first formulation for each case would not stop with the group identity label, but would continue and thereby permit consideration of the intersecting experiences of gender, region, age and so forth; and the test would avoid treatment, as if solid and fixed, of an identity that is inevitably mutable and affected deeply by other unnamed dimensions.

444. Where a woman is a plaintiff, as in a sexual harassment suit, another alternative would set as the standard the treatment anyone would want for a sister, daughter, or wife. Thanks to Nell Minow for this formulation. Rakoff and I actually avoid in our paper the "hot button" issues such as sexual harassment and rape in which we think it fair to assert that contemporary social attitudes differ considerably along gender (and perhaps racial or ethnic) lines, and instead argue that in the more ordinary disputes over contracts, torts, and criminal law, "reasonable person" should be modified to reflect circumstances rather than to implement "reasonable woman," "reasonable Asian American," and so forth.

445. *Weirs v. Jones County*, 86 Iowa 625 (1892).

446. The first highly visible case was *Doe v. University of Michigan*, 721 F. Supp. 852 (E.D. Mich. 1989) (reject-

ing state university's hate speech code as a violation of the First Amendment). An analogous debate addresses proposed regulation of pornography. See Catharine MacKinnon, *Feminism Unmodified: Discourses on Life and Law* (Cambridge, MA: Harvard Univ. Press, 1987); Catharine MacKinnon, *Only Words* (Cambridge, MA: Harvard Univ. Press, 1993); Frank Michelman, *Conceptions of Democracy in American Constitutional Argument: The Case of Pornography Regulation*, 56 Tenn L Rev 291 (1989); Nadine Strossen, *A Feminist Critique of "The" Feminist Critique of Pornography*, 79 Virginia L Rev 1099 (1993).

447. The polarization extends to scholarly books. For the pro-First Amendment view, see Henry Louis Gates, Jr. et al. *Speaking of Race, Speaking of Sex: Hate Speech, Civil Rights, and Civil Liberties* (New York: New York Univ. Press, 1994). For the pro-regulation perspective, see Mari Matsuda, Richard Delgado and Charles Lawrence, *Words that Wound: Critical Race Theory, Assaultive Speech, and the First Amendment* (Boulder, CO: Westview Press, 1993). See also Thomas Grey, *How to Write a Speech Code Without Really Trying: Reflections on the Stanford Experience*, 29 U.C. Davis L Rev 891 (1996); Steven H. Shiffrin, *Racist Speech, Outside Jurisprudence, and the Meaning of America*, 80 Cornell L Rev 43 (1994) (discussing criminal sanctions against racially motivated crimes and the attendant debates over the meanings of America). A comparison

between the debate within the United States and Canada's practices is a healthy reminder of the possibility of alternative approaches. See Kent Greenawalt, *Fighting Words: Individuals, Communities, and Liberties of Speech* (Princeton, NJ: Princeton Univ. Press, 1995).

448. Richard Abel, *Speech and Respect* (London: Stevens & Son, 1994). He recommends informal processes that respond to racist speech with speech, including acknowledgment of harm and apologies. Id. at 145. He also argues that speech bans are bound to include exceptions for politics, art, and scholarship that engulf the rule, and evasions through parody, ambiguity, and romantic defiance. Id. at 93, 98, 105–7.

449. See Gottlieb, "Banning Bigoted Speech: Stanford Weights Rules," *San Jose Mercury-News* 7 January 1990, p. 3, col. 1 (reporting that Thomas Grey, drafter of the Stanford speech code, said "his rule probably wouldn't apply to one of the most publicized racial incidents at Stanford, when a white student left on a black student's door a poster of Beethoven drawn as a black caricature"); Mari Matsuda, *Public Response to Racist Speech: Considering the Victim's Story*, 87 Mich L Rev 2320 (1989).

450. Mari Matsuda, a leading defender of the hate-speech codes, has at times put the debate this way.

451. *R.A.V. v. City of St. Paul,* 112 S.Ct. 2538, 2548 (1992). The majority also found defective the prohibition of

some kinds of fighting words—those using race, color, creed, religion, or gender—but not others, such as "aspersions upon a person's mother." Id. at 2547–48. The Supreme Court later approved legislation that does not criminalize hateful expression itself but instead permits enhanced penalties for acts already criminalized if committed "by reason of the race, color, religion or national origin of another person or group of persons." Joel Zand, Hate Crime Laws: Disagreement in the Courts, ADL on the Frontline (Anti-Defamation League), October 1992, 7 (describing legislation upheld in *Ohio v. Wynant*, 61 U.S.L.W. 3830 (1993) (No. 92-568)).

452. Linda Greenhouse, "Defining the Freedom to Hate While Punching," *New York Times*, 20 December 1992, sec. E5.

453. Though I did so in Martha Minow, *Surviving Victim Talk*, 40 UCLA L Rev 1411, 1423 (1993).

454. I explore this argument more fully in Martha Minow, *Speaking and Writing Against Hate*, 11 Cardozo L Rev 1193, 1404–1408 (1990). Shiffrin develops a related argument that hate-speech regulations are likely to be counterproductive by mobilizing opposition and fanning racial resentment. Shiffrin, *Speech*, 98–103.

455. See Alexis de Tocqueville, *Democracy in America* ed. C. Phillips Bradley, 1835; reprint (New York: Alfred A. Knopf, 1972); Mary Ann Glendon, *A Nation Under Lawyers* (New York: Farrer, Straus and Giroux, 1994).

456. See Sanford Levinson, *Constitutional Faith* (Princeton, NJ: Princeton Univ. Press, 1988); Mouffe, supra; Walzer, Thick and Thin, supra.

457. Schools can be wonderful settings for exploring artistic expression, especially addressing the complexity of group identities. See Kathy Greeley, "Making Theater, Making Sense, Making Change," in *Social Issues and Service at the Middle Level*, eds. Samuel Totten and Jon E. Pedersen (New York: Garland, 1995) (discussing elementary school teacher's use of playwriting to help students grapple with past injustices and to take risks in self-expression and change).

458. Edward Guthmann, "Freida Lee Mock's Strong Clear Vision Director Says `Lin' Stands On its Own," *San Francisco Chronicle* 8 November 1995, D1 (describing film about Maya Lin, the memorial and the politics surrounding it).

459. See Robert Atkins, "When the Art Is Public, the Making Is, Too," *New York Times*, 23 July 1995), 2, p. 1, col. 1.

460. Jay Pridmore, "Revealing Displays Make Vietnam Museum Noteworthy," *Chicago Tribune*, 9 September 1994, 14 (describing Smithsonian Institution exhibit of objects left by mourners at the Vietnam Memorial). See Pamela Weinstock, Note: *The National Endowment for the Arts Controversy and the Miller Test*, 72 BUL Rev 803 (1992). The AIDS quilt, with squares made by suriving family members and friends of people who died of AIDS, is another example of a work of art that

has inspired more art, as well as opened occasions for people to engage in individual and collective mourning.

461. See Kathleen M. Sullivan, *Essay: Free Speech and Unfree Markets*, 42 UCLA L Rev 949 (1995) (discussing Jesse Helms and others who attack public funding of the arts).

462. See Ann Douglas, *Terrible Honesty: Mongrel Manhattan in the 1920s* (New York: Farrar, Straus & Giroux, 1995); Toni Morrison, *Playing in the Dark* (Cambridge, MA: Harvard Univ. Press, 1992); Patricia Williams, *The Rooster's Egg* 196 (Cambridge, MA: Harvard Univ. Press, 1995), 196 (" ... it is one thing to romanticize the notion of culture as fixed and pure, and quite another to ignore the legal and economic consequences of a dominant social gaze that habitually, repeatedly sees its own cultural production in such naturalized yet unreflectively nativistic terms that there is little vision for how much has been borrowed or given, little appreciation for the generosity of our interdependence.")

463. Gitlin, *Twilight*, 59. Then again, consider the compound identities explored by Salman Rushdie, Derrick Walcott, many Jews writing in Europe since the Enlightenment, and other non-Americans.

464. William Stafford, "Keepsakes," in *Stories That Could Be True: New And Collected Poems* (New York: Harper & Row, 1977), 128.

465. Michael Walzer, "Comment,"

in Charles Taylor, *Multiculturalism: Examining the Politics of Recognition* ed. Amy Gutmann (Princeton, NJ: Princeton Univ. Press, 1994), 101. Walzer continues: "I don't doubt that there is a tenison, sometimes open conflict between these official efforts at social reproduction and the unofficial efforts of minorities to sustain themselves over time." Id.

466. See Jonathan Messerli, *Horace Mann: A Biography* (New York: Knopf, 1972); Richard Prattie, *The Public School Movement* (New York: David McKay Co., 1973), 75–124 (describing rationales for public schools, including assimilation, equality, and preparation for jobs).

467. See, e.g., *Commonwealth v. Twitchell*, 617 N.E.2d 609 (1993) (Christian Scientist parents faced criminal sanction for failing to obtain medical treatment for their dying child); Layli Miller Bashir, "Female Genital Mutilation in the United States," 4 *Am. UJ Gender and Law* 415 (Spring 1996).

468. K. Anthony Appiah, "Identity, Authenticity, Survival: Multicultural Societies and Social Reproduction," in Taylor, *Multiculturalism*, 158.

469. See chapter 3 (discussing interracial adoption and Indian Child Welfare Act).

470. See Martha Minow, *In All Families: Loving and Owing*, 95 West Virginia L Rev 275 (1992–93) (discussing spiritual custody warded to one parent after divorce and visitation cases posing

conflicts over upbringing of children).

471. Elizabeth Kamarck Minnich, *Transforming Knowledge* (Philadelphia: Temple Univ. Press, 1990).

472. For an argument close to this view, see Stephen Gillers, *On Educating Children: A Parentalist Manifesto*, 63 U Chicago L Rev 937 (1996). Cf. Alexander Bickel, *The Least Dangerous Branch: The Supreme Court at the Bar of Politics* (Indianapolis: Bobbs-Merrill Co., 1962) (celebrating the "passive virtues" of courts that leave difficult issues to the political branches).

473. See Amy Gutmann, *Democratic Education* (Princeton, NJ: Princeton Univ. Press, 1987).

474. See Appiah, *Identity*, 158 ("we have it in our power to some extent to make our children into the kind of people who will want to maintain our culture").

475. Different nations, with different traditions, may also call for balancing but strike the balances differently. Canada, for example, has faced the desires of the majority in the province of Quebec to preserve the French language amid the pressures of a primarily English-speaking country. See Taylor, *Multiculturalism*, 55.

476. *Pierce*, 268 U.S. 510, 535 (1925).

477. *Kentucky State Board v. Rudasill*, 589 S.W.2d 877 (Ky. 1979). See also *State v. Whisner*, 47 Ohio St.2d 181, 351 N.E.2d 750 (1976) (similar result in Ohio).

478. E.g., *State v. Shaver*, 294 N.W.2d 883 (N.D. 1980).

479. 406 U.S. 205 (1972).

480. The law could be satisfied by attendance at private schools, subject to state approval. The Amish parents who were the subject of this case did not pursue this option. Id. at 207, n.2.

481. Ibid. at 207. Thus, the Amish parents declined to send their four-teen- and fifteen-year olds to school.

482. Ibid. at 209–11.

483. Ibid. at 216.

484. Ibid. at 224. The state may also have been influenced by the impact of enrollments on local school funding. See Madeleine Kimmich, *America's Children, Who Cares?* (Washington, D.C.: Urban Institute Press, 1985), 62 (local school funding often based on enrollments).

485. *Wisconsin*, 406 U.S. 205, 23–46 (1972).

486. The Court noted also that several states recognized the participation of Amish youngsters in family farming and business as vocational training. 406 U.S. 205, 236 & n.23 (1972).

487. 406 U.S. at 241 (Douglas, J., dissenting in part).

488. Compare *Parham v. J.R.*, 442 U.S. 584 (1979) (rejecting due process claim challenging parental authority to commit children to mental hospitals in light of traditional deference to parental decision making) with *Planned Parenthood v. Danforth*, 428 U.S. 52 (1976) (rejecting statutory requirement of parental consent prior to a minor's abortion). For a sustained

criticism of the usual deference to parents in the medical and educational decisions for their children, see James G. Dwyer, *The Children We Abandon: Religious Exemptions to Child Welfare and Education Laws as Denials of Equal Protection to Children of Religious Objectors*, 74 NC L Rev 1325 (1996).

489. *Yoder*, 406 U.S. at 241–42, 244–45.

490. Ibid. at 247–49.

491. *Yoder*, 406 U.S. 218 n.9 (1972). See also Albert Hirschman, *Exit, Voice and Loyalty* (Cambridge, MA: Harvard Univ. Press, 1970) (discussing options of exit, voiced disagreement, and loyal adherence to a given political order).

492. Charles Hamilton Houston, the architect of the civil rights litigation strategy that led to *Brown v. Board of Edcuation*, once said, "Do not bind the children within the narrow circles of your own lives." See Genna Rae McNeil, *Groundwork: Charles Hamilton Houston and the Struggle for Civil Rights* (Philadelphia: Univ. of Pennsylvania Press, 1983).

493. Note that the Amish sought only to exclude their own children from education beyond the eighth grade, not to forbid such education for all children. See Carol Weisbrod, *Family, Church and State: An Essay on Constitutionalism and Religious Authority*, 26 J Fam L 741 (1987–1988).

494. See William M. Gordon, Charles J. Russo and Albert S. Miles, *The Law of Home Schooling* (Topeka KS: National Organization on Legal Problems of Education, 1994).

495. See Jon S. Lerner, *Protecting Home Schooling Through the Casey Undue Burden Standard*, 62 U Chi L Rev 363 (1995).

496. See Lerner, *Home Schooling*, 388.

497. These avenues are likely to be more successful than individual court challenges by parents to public school curricula or texts. See *Mozert v. Hawkins County Board of Education*, 827 F.2d 1058 (6th Cir. 1987) (rejecting mother's religiously based challenge to the use of a textbook series). A few states also provide that a course must be taught if a requisite number of parents request it and at least a minimum number of students would enroll. See Mass. Gen. Laws Ann. ch. 71, sec. § 13 (West, 1996).

498. The landmark decision in this area was *Meyer v. Nebraska*, 262 U.S. 390 (1923), which overturned a state statute restricting public school instruction in German. Against the backdrop of a conflict between a minority group of German immigrants and a majority wanting to Americanize immigrants, the Court found the statute violated both the teacher's right to teach and the parents' rights to secure instruction for their children.

499. *Edwards v. Aguillard*, 482 U.S. 578 (1977); *McLean v. Arkansas Board of Education*, 529 F. Supp. 1255 (E.D. Ark. 1982); *Epperson v. State of Arkansas*, 393 U.S. 97 (1969).

500. *Cornwell v. State Bd of Educ.*, 314

F. Supp. 340 (D. Md. 1969); *Medeiros v. Kiyosaki*, 478 P.2d 314 (1982); *Smith v. Ricci*, 446 A.2d 501 (1982).

501. *Virgil v. School Bd of Columbia County*, 862 F.2d 1517 (11th Cir. 1989); see also *Bd of Educ., Island Trees Union Free Sch. Dist. N. 26 v. Pico*, 457 U.S. 853 (1982).

502. *Bd of Educ., Island Trees Union Free Sch. Dist. No. 26 v. Pico*, 457 U.S. 853 (1982) (plurality opinion).

503. In one case, a parent objected to the use of texts in a public school on the grounds that they presented sex roles, religion, and the supernatural in ways that contravened her beliefs and commitments in raising her children. See *Mozert*. The trial court agreed, and allowed her children to be excused from use of the texts; the appellate court reversed. For thoughtful and thorough explorations of the case and the surrounding history, see Stephen Bates, *Battleground: One Mother's Crusade, the Religious Right, and the Struggle for Control of Our Classrooms* (New York: Poseidon Press, 1993); Nomi Stolzenberg, *"He Drew a Circle that Shut Me Out": Assimilation, Indoctrination, and the Paradox of a Liberal Education*, 106 Harv L Rev 581 (1993).

504. Martha M. McCarthy & Nelda H. Cambron-McCabe, *Public School Law: Teachers' and Students' Rights*, 3d, ed. (Boston: Allyn and Bacom, 1992), 80.

505. See generally Stephen R. Goldstein, E. Gordon Gee and Philip T.K. Daniel, *Law and Public Education: Cases and Materials*, 3d ed. Char-lottesville, VA: Michie, 1995), 890–91.

506. 122 Ill. Rev. Stat. § 27-19 (1993).

507. Cal. Reorganized Educ. Code § 37226 (West, 1995).

508. Wis. Stat. Ann. § 40.46(8) (1991).

509. Several states require education to promote character traits such as courage, patriotism, citizenship, honesty, and respect for others. See, e.g., Alabama Code § 16–6B–2(h) (1995); Ark. Stat. Ann. § 6-16-111 (1995); Cal. Ed. Code, § 33032.5 (60200) (1996). See Thomas Lickona, *Educating for Character: How Our Schools Can Teach Respect and Responsibility* (New York: Bantam Books, 1991).

510. Rochelle Sharpe, "Efforts to Promote Teaching of Values in Schools Are Sparking Heated Debate Among Lawmakers," *Wall Street Journal* 10 May 1994, A20.

511. Melinda Fine, *Habits of Mind: Struggling Over Values in American Classrooms* (San Francisco: Josey Bass Publishers, 1995), 171–72.

512. See *Swann v. Charlotte-Mecklenburg Bd. of Educ.*, 402 U.S. 1 (1971); *Brown v. Bd. of Educ.*, 347 U.S. 483 (1954). Although federal courts are setting limits on the duration, *Bd. of Educ. of Freeman v. Pitts*, 112 S.Ct. 1430 (1992) (permitting cessation of school desegregation order over parts of the system that had become desegregated even though other parts remained segregated); *Oklahoma City Public Sch. v. Dowell*, 498 U.S. 237

(1991) (permitting end of plan despite segregation from demographic shifts after earlier phase produced desegregated schools) and geographic scope of school desegregation orders, *Milliken v. Bradley*, 418 U.S. 717 (1974) (disapproving school desegregation across urban/suburban district lines absent proof of discrimination in all the districts), state courts may also require desegregation under state constitutions. *Sheff v. O'Neill*, 238 Conn. 1, 1996 Conn LEXIS 239.

513. Some challenges to racial disparities in ability groupings and programs for children identified as disabled have succeeded, see, e.g., *Larry P. v. Riles*, 793 F.2d 969 (9th Cir. 1984); but some lose, see *Parents in Action on Special Education v. Hannon*, 506 F. Supp. 831 (N.D. Ill. 1980). Racial disparities in ability groups and special education classes persist, sometimes with evidence of intentional racial discrimination. See *People Who Care v. Rockford Bd. of Educ. Sch. Dist. #205*, 851 F. Supp. 905 (N.D. Ill. 1994).

514. See Tamara Henry, "Confusion Over Single-Sex Classes Fear of Lawsuits Makes States Leary," *USA Today* 3 July 1995, 6D.

515. See 20 U.S.C. § 1681 (1994).

516. *United States v. Virginia*, 116 S.Ct. 2264.

518. Ibid. at 2275 (quoting *Wengler v. Druggist Mutual Insurance Company*, 446 U.S. 142, 150 (1980)). The Court also warned against post hoc rationalizations for the exclusion.

518. See *Newberg v. Bd. of Public*

*Educ.*, 26 D&C 682 (1983), denied review, 330 Pa. Super. 65, 478 A.2d 1352 (Penn. Superior Court 1984); *Bray v. Lee*, 337 F. Supp. 934 (D. Mass. 1972); *Garrett v. Bd. of Educ. of Sch. Dist. of Detroit*, 775 F.Supp. 1004 (E.D. Mich. 1991).

519. See Mary B.W. Tabor, "Planners of a New Public School for Girls Look to Two Other Cities," *New York Times* 23 July 1996, § B1, col.2 (discussing proposed female public school in Harlem, and existing Philadelphia High School for Girls and Western High School in Baltimore). The Philadelphia and Baltimore schools do not exclude boys but no boys have applied. See also Derrick Bell, "Et Tu, ACLU?", *New York Times*, 19 July 1996, § A23, col.1 (distinguishing purposes behind exclusion of females by the Virginia Military Institute and all-girl school proposed in Harlem).

520. See Henry, *Single-Sex* (discussing single-sex schools in Texas, Colorado, Maryland, Michigan, Georgia, and District of Columbia). Senator Dan Coats of Indiana has proposed "The Mentor Schools Act," which would establish single-sex public schools, and "The Role Model Academy Act," which would permit residential academies especially to encourage role models for male students. See Chi Chi Sileo, "Social Policy Next After the Budget," *Washington Times*, 15 January 1996, 20.

521. Lynnel Hancock and Claudia Kalb, "Public Schools Try Single-Sex Classes," *Newsweek* 24 June 1996, 76

(describing efforts in Texas, Colorado, Michigan, and Georgia). Diane Ravitch emphasizes the success of British single-sex schools: "of the top 20 schools in the nation, 18 were girls' schools. Of the top 150 schools in Great Britain, only 14 were coeducational. Even among the top 50 public schools, only five were coeducational." Diane Ravitch, "Things Go Better in Single-Sex Schools," *Washington Post*, 31 August 1995, A23.

522. *Mississippi Univ. of Women v. Hogan*, 458 U.S. 718 (1982) (accepting a man's challenge to sex-based exclusion from a nursing school). Is it possible to articulate women's differences in ways that do not reiterate or refuel old stereotypes? For an incisive discussion of this issue in the context of *Hogan*, see Mary Joe Frug, *Postmodern Legal Feminism* (New York: Routledge, 1992), 30–52.

523. See Dwyer, *Children*, at 1342–43. Dwyer objects that children educated in parochial schools that teach sexist ideas experience denials of equal protection of the law. Id. at 1353, 1366–1453.

524. The Education for All Handicapped Children Act was enacted in 1975 (signed by President Gerald Ford), and incorporated after amendments into the Individuals with Disabilities Education Act, 20 U.S.C.A. §§ 1400–1485; Section 504 of the Rehabilitation Act of 1973, 29 U.S.C. § 706 (8) et seq. Most states in addition have their own laws, and special programs for gifted children are regulated

entirely under state and local laws and rules.

525. See Bonnie P. Tucker, *Federal Disability Law in a Nutshell* (St. Paul, MN: West Publishing Co., 1994), 266.

526. E.g., *Florence County Sch. Dist. Four v. Carter*, 114 S.Ct. 361 (1993); *Babb v. Knox County Sch. System*, 965 F.2d 104 (6th Cir. 1992); *Lascari v. Bd. of Educ. of Ramapo Indian Hills Regional High Such. Dist.*, 116 N.J. 30, 560 A.2d 1180 (1989).

527. See generally Seymour B. Sarason & John Doris, *Educational Handicap, Public Policy, and Social History: A Broadened Perspective on Mental Retardation* (New York: Free Press, 1979) (observing that the rise of tracking coincided with the rise in the number of immigrants).

528. See Kern Alexander and M. David Alexander, *The Law of Schools, Students and Teachers In a Nutshell* 2d. ed. (St. Paul, MN: West Publishing, 1995), 246–47.

529. See *Lau v. Nichols*, 414 U.S. 563 (1974); *Castaneda v. Pickard*, 648 F.2d 989 (CA-5 1981). The heated debates in this area are summarized in Rachel Moran, *The Politics of Discretion: Federal Intervention in Bilingual Education*, 73 Cal L Rev 1249 (1988).

530. The rationale of *Brown* and its progeny has been extended to Mexican American students, *Cisneros v. Corpus Christi Independent Sch. Dist.*, 467 F.2d 142 (5th Cir. 1972), cert. denied, 413 U.S. 922 (1973), and to American Indian students, *Natonabah v. Bd. of Educ. of Gallup-McKinley County Such.*

*Dist.*, 355 F.Supp. 716 (D.N.M. 1973).

531. Even ability grouping, or "tracking," cannot be used if its effect is to segregate. *Smuck v. Hobson*, 408 F.2d 175, 189 (D.C. Cir. 1969); *Hobson v. Hansen*, 269 F. Supp. 401, 443 (D.D.C. 1967), cert. denied, 393 U.S. 801 (1968). This principle is consistently breached in practice, however.

532. These choice programs reflect earlier debates over school vouchers. Progressives supported public "bounties" in the hands of low-income students to make those students attractive to private and suburban schools while conseratives supported public vouchers in order to subsidize private schools, but both kinds of proposals foundered over whether public vouchers could pay for private parochial schools. See Gordon MacInnees, *Wrong for All the Right Reasons: How White Liberals Have Been Undone by Race* (New York: New York Univ. Press, 1996), 136–44.

533. See Kimberly C. West, *Note: A Desegregation Tool that Backfired*, 103 Yale LJ 2567 (1994). See also Stuart Biegel, *School Choice Policy and Title VI: Maximizing Equal Access for K-12 Students in a Substantially Deregulated Educational Environment*, 46 Hastings LJ 1533 (1995).

534. See Diane Ravitch, "Schools That Specialize: Are They Democratic? Do They Work?" *Washington Post*, 28 July 1996, R01.

535. Graham Rayman, "New Direction for Vouchers," *Newsday*, 11 September 1996), A55.

536. 114 S.Ct. 2481 (1994). Although treated by the courts as an issue of religious establishment, the case also addresses the scope of private residential choice to influence schooling; it also echoes judicial discussions of race consciousness in the design of voting districts.

537. This incorporation followed procedures established by state law. 114 S.Ct. 2481, 2485–87 (1994). The procedure involved no substantive review of the justifications for desirability of a newly incorporated town. Indeed, the supervisor who approved the petition did so with regret about the lack of authority for a substantive basis for review, and criticized the incorporation as a misuse of incorporation to bypass the intense and litigated conflict over the Satmar's zoning violations. *In re Formation of a New Village to Be Known as 'Kiryas Joel,' Supervisor, Town of Monroe, Orange County, New York* (Decision on Sufficiency Petition), 10 December 1976, *reprinted in* Joint Appendix at 15–16, *Bd. of Educ. of Kiryas Joel Sch. Dist. v. Grumet*, 114 S.Ct. 2481 (1994) (No. 93-517) (challenging the validity of the village incorporation petition). The supervisor also treated claims by the Satmar of religious persecution as spurious.

538. Israel Rubin, *Satmar: An Island in the City* (Chicago: Quadrangle Books, 1972), 28.

539. Allan L. Nadler, *Piety and Politics: The Case of the Satmar Rebbe*, 31 Judaism 135, 145 (1982).

540. Jerome R. Mintz, *Hasidic*

*People: A Place in the New World* (Cambridge, MA: Harvard Univ. Press, 1992), 29.

541. To speak of this or any community as if it were united and homogeneous is a mistake. Indeed, deep and often extreme divisions of opinion and practice occur in Kiryas Joel and their existence poses a fundamental difficulty in any procedure that defers judgments to "the community."

542. Rubin, *Satmar*, 171.

543. Ibid. at 152.

544. William M. Kephart and William W. Zellner, *Extraordinary Groups*, 4th ed. (New York: St. Martin's Press, 1991), 161–75.

545. Rival private religious schools exist there, but only private schools.

546. 28 U.S.C. §§ 1400-1402, 1404, 1409, 1411-1414 (Supp. V 1993); N.Y. Educ. Law §§ 4004-4005 (McKinney 1995).

547. A set of cases forbids state aid to parochial schools and even the provision of state services, such as publicly funded services for students with disadvantaged backgrounds or with disabilities, on the grounds of parochial schools. In 1985, the Court ruled that public services such as remedial programs for disadvantaged students cannot be provided by employees of public schools on parochial school property. *Aguilar v. Fenton*, 473 U.S. 402 (1985). The Court similarly ruled in 1977 that although diagnostic services would be permissible on the site of a religious school, therapeutic and remedial services could only be provided on a neutral site off the premises of a sectarian institution. *Wolman v. Walter*, 433 U.S. 229 (1977).

In contrast, in 1993, the Court found no constitutional bar to the provision of a sign language interpreter for a deaf student who attended a parochial school. The Court reasoned that this public provision of a service defrayed none of the usual costs of the parochial school, nor did the interpreter participate in the actual instruction of the student. *Zobrest v. Catalina Foothills Sch. Dist.*, 113 S.Ct. 2462 (1993).

Justice O'Connor's concurrence in *Board of Education of Kiryas Joel Village School District v. Grumet*, 114 S.Ct. 2481, 2497 (1994) (O'Connor, J., concurring), suggested reconsidering *Aguilar* and *Wolman*. There may be reasons to support this view apart from obviating the motive for the statute at issue in *Kiryas Joel*. I will suggest, however, that problematic as it is, the statute affords a greater chance for connecting an insular religious community to others in society.

548. Some of the parents had tried this option in the neighboring Monroe-Woodbury school district. Earlier, the Satmar community had used an annex to the religious school for delivering special-education services, but this use of public funds was forbidden by Supreme Court decisions in the mid-1980's.

549. *Kiryas Joel*, 114 S.Ct. 2495.

550. This claim animated the lawsuit that became Monroe-Woodbury

Central School District v. Wieder, 527 N.E.2d 767 (N.Y. 1988) (alleging in adequate one-on-one services). In addition, some of the parents claimed that their children's language needs were not met. See Affidavit of Abraham Wieder in Support of Motion to Intervene, app. H at 127a, Attorney Gen. of N.Y. v. Grumet, 114 S.Ct. 1046 (1994) (No. 93-539).

551. The First Amendment to the Constitution combines a commitment to separate church and state and a guarantee to individuals that they remain free to exercise their own religion. These two goals often seem to conflict. An individual may ask the government to devise a special accommodation to permit free exercise of religion, but then the government faces objections that such an accommodation favors that religion, or favors religion over no religion. This tension has produced a variety of resolutions. See generally Laurence H. Tribe, *The American Constitutional Law* §§ 14–4 to 14–5, 1166–79 2d ed. (Mineola, NY: Foundation Press, 1988).

552. Some observers even question whether the Satmar compromised religious beliefs in order to gain public funds. The secular judiciary, committed to separating religion and state, should not inquire into mixed motives, except insofar as actual sincerity of belief may become an issue.

553. See, e.g., Nadler, *Piety*, 145–47; Ira C. Lupu, *Uncovering the Village of Kiryas Joel*, 96 Colum L Rev 104, 111–12 (1996). Viewers of CNN may

have acquired their own evidence on such matters while the case was pending. As the case was argued in the Supreme Court, members of the Satmar community vied for the opportunity to speak with reporters about fights internal to the community as well as views about the case. Oral tradition among the New York Jewish community also reflects these views of the Satmar. The story is told of one group of Satmar who, during a battle over incorporation of another village, were able to convince the Presiding Judge that they were patriotic Americans by naming their streets after U.S. presidents. Daniel D. Alexander, "Political Influence of the Resident Hasidic Community on the East Ramapo Central School District" (unpublished Ph.D. dissertation, New York University, 1952), 48. Meantime, Satmar individuals who disagree with the presiding rabbi face social shunning, and even risk more hostile acts, such as car burnings. Robert Hanley, "In the Ashes of Arson at Kiryas Joel, Tensions of Bitter Factionalism," *New York Times*, 29 July 1996, sec. B1, col. 2.

554. "Voter Fraud Discovered," *Newsday*, 23 September 1996), A28 (describing allegations of double voting as well as internal violence in Kiryas Joel).

555. Geraldine Baum, "Crossing the Line?," *Los Angeles Times*, 19 December 1993), p. 1, col. 2.

556. Suzanne Fields, "Public School District for Sect Denied," *Atlanta Journal & Constitution*, 30

June 1994, A2.

557. *Parents' Ass'n of P.S. 16 v. Quinones,* 83 F.2d 1235, 1238 (2d Cir. 1986) (recounting quotation from media coverage of the case).

558. Mintz, *Hasidic,* at 162.

559. A joke circulated within other Jewish communities about the Satmar, conveying another side of this story— the picture of the Satmar as self-righteous fanatics: a Satmar rebbe dies and goes to Heaven where the angels offer him a meal. The rebbe says, "Excuse me, who said this food is kosher?" "God himself," answers an angel. "Hmm, very interesting, could I maybe have a salad?" replies the rebbe (to avoid eating anything that is not kosher).

560. In court, on the record, the Satmars emphasized that separatism is not a tenet of faith. Before the Supreme Court of the United States, the Satmar specifically disputed the plaintiffs' claim that the Satmar faith requires its adherents not to mix with persons of other faiths. Brief for Petitioner at 4 n. 1, *Bd. of Educ. of the Kiryas Joel Village Sch. Dist. v. Grumet,* 114 S.Ct. 2481 (1994) (No. 93-517) ("The record does not support this contention, and it is wrong as a matter of fact."). The brief for the Satmars stated: "While we have never disputed that the Satmar prefer to live together, they do so to facilitate individual religious observance and maintain social, cultural, and religious values, not because it is 'against their religion' to interact with others."

561. Telephone interview with Nathan Lewis, Counsel for Kiryas Joel, 4 Nov 1994).

562. Affidavit of Steven M. Bernado, app. J at 115-17a, *Bd. of Educ. of Kiryas Joel Village Sch. Dist. v. Grumet,* 114 S.Ct. 544 (1993) (No. 93-517).

563. Brief for the Petitioner at 4 n.1, *Kiryas Joel* (No. 93-517). Consistent with their view that religious law is central, the Satmar also argued that their acceptance of co-education for disabled children is permitted by "Satmar religious observance." Id. This convenient answer to some may raise questions about sincerity, as did the change in Church policy following the Supreme Court's decision in *Bob Jones University v. United States,* 461 U.S. 574 (1983) (refusing a tax exemption to a religious institution that discriminated on the basis of race).

564. Siding with Kiryas Joel Village School District were Agudath Israel of America and other advocates for Orthodox Jewish groups, the Roman Catholic Archdiocese of New York, and a variety of other Christian groups. Against them were the American Jewish Congress, the Union of American Hebrew Congregations, the American Jewish Committee, the Anti-Defamation League, the National Council of Jewish Women, People for the American Way, a variety of other religious groups, groups committed to the separation of church and state, and teachers' unions. The opposition also included 500 members of the Committee for the Well-Being of

Kiryas Joel, a committee formed by village residents to support the rejection of the school district.

565. Along these lines, most Jews have traditionally opposed the introduction of prayer in public schools on the theory that it will not be Jewish prayer said there, whether implicitly or explicitly, and instead will be a boost to the majority religions. As Shakespeare told us, however, misery makes strange bedfellows; so does politics. Thus, some Jews join with the Christian fundamentalists to oppose a Supreme Court perceived as hostile to religion. Such coalitions were needed to get Congress to adopt the Religious Freedom Restoration Act, 42 U.S.C. §§ 2000bb–2000bb(4) (Supp. V 1993). Fundamentalist Christians have also solicited support from Jewish groups for their proposals to permit prayer in public schools and more generally enlarge the role of religion in public life. See, e.g., Mona Charen, "A Wise Effort to Unite Christians and Jews," *Tampa Tribune*, 1 April 1995, 7; Clifford D. May, "Separation Need Not Mean Alienation," *Rocky Mountain News*, 9 April 1995, available in 1995 WL 3186479; Steve Rabey, "Some Conservative Jews Join Hands with Religious Right," *Dallas Morning News*, 18 February 1995, 1G.

566. 579 N.Y.S.2d 1004 (N.Y. Sup.Ct.), aff'd, 592 N.Y.S.2d 123 (N.Y. App. Div. 1992), aff'd in part, 618 N.E.2d 94 (N.Y.), cert. granted, 114 S.Ct. 544 (1993), aff'd, 114 S.Ct. 2481 (1994). The trial court held that the state statute creating the special district violated the Establishment Clause of the U. S. Constitution. The appellate court affirmed, as did the highest court of the state. That court's majority reasoned that the statute created an unacceptable symbolic union of church and state, implying endorsement of Satmar Hasidim. The chief judge of New York's highest court is herself an Orthodox Jew; Chief Judge Judith Kaye wrote a concurrence rejecting the school district as too broad a measure to address the specific issue of the requirement to separate church and state because the statute created a special school district rather than simply a local school. 618 N.E.2d at 102 (Kaye, C.J., concurring).

567. Justice Souter delivered the opinion of the Court, maintaining (1) there is no assurance that another religious community seeking a special district would obtain one from the legislature, and (2) this accommodation of religion crossed the border into unacceptable establishment which could be avoided by other measures. 114 S. Ct. at 2491–95 (1994). Three Justices joined Justice Souter's additional theory that the state's delegation of authority to a group defined by its common religion produced an impermissible fusion of governmental and religious functions. Id. at 2487–9. Justices Blackmun, Stevens, O'Connor, and Kennedy also each wrote separate concurring opinions.

None of the Justices explored another twist in the case, perhaps because it is so complicated. The federal law concerning the rights of disabled children allows parents to opt, as the Constitution permits, for private schooling. Federal law specifically requires states to assure that special education and related services are extended to children placed by their parents in private schools. Bonnie P. Tucker, *Federal Disability Law: In a Nutshell* (St. Paul, MN: West Publishing, 1994), 334. But who is to pay for this: the parents or the public? This is an issue still in dispute in the courts. Id. at 337–38. If the private schools are religious, may parents obtain public support for the education and related services needed by their children who have disabilities? The parents here could not afford private tutoring. Petitioner's Brief at 23, *Kiryas Joel* (No. 93-517).

568. *Kiryas Joel*, 114 S.Ct. at 2504–05 (Kennedy, J., concurring in the judgment).

569. Concurring, but writing only for herself, Justice O'Connor worried about the appearance of a legislature that favored one religious group over other groups. Id. at 2495–2500 (O'Connor, J., concurring in part and concurring in the judgment). Her concurrence suggested ways to provide permissible accommodations, including a general statute permitting groups such as the Satmar to apply for permission to set up independent school districts. Id. at 2498. She also called for reversing prior Supreme Court cases forbidding public special-education services on the sites of religious schools. In his concurring opinion, Justice Stevens, joined by Justice Ginsburg, objected to shielding of the Satmar children from secular influences. Id. at 2495 (Stevens, J., concurring).

570. Ibid. at 2505 (Scalia, J., dissenting).

571. Act of July 6, 1994, ch. 241, 1994 N.Y. Laws 827. The statute directs that any municipality located wholly within but not coterminous with a single large school district can organize a new school district if certain conditions are met. Those conditions include regulation of both absolute student enrollment (minimum, 2000) and the reduction from the pre-existing school system (no more than sixty percent), assurance that the creation of the new district will not produce a school system (the new one or the remains of the old one) with per pupil expenditures below the statewide average, and required approval by a majority of the requesting municipality and a majority of the pre-existing school board. Id. The legislature also adopted an act that abolished the Kiryas Joel Village School District but ensured continuing operation of its school until consolidated with or replacement by a new or existing school district. Act of July 6, 1994, ch. 279, 1994 N.Y. Laws 888.

572. This new statute was challenged in court; the trial court rejected the plaintiffs' request for a preliminary injunction, *Grumet v. Cuomo*, 617

N.Y.S.2d 620, 632 (N.Y. Sup. Ct. 1994), while the appellate division court agreed with the challenge. Joseph Berger, "School District of Kiryas Joel is Ruled Illegal," *New York Times*, 27 August 1996, p.B1, col.5. The challengers claimed that the requirements of the new statute make it useful in practice only to the Village of Kiryas Joel; the state claims that many other municipalities could comply. The state attorney general was contemplating seeking further review as this book went to press. Id.

573. See Michael W. McConnell, *Accommodation of Religion*, 1985 Sup Ct Rev 1, 4; Michael W. McConnell, *Accommodation of Religion: An Update and Response to the Critics*, 60 Geo Wash L Rev 685, 716 (1992).

574. This argument, while similar to an Establishment Clause argument, also mirrors some equal protection analysis. See generally Martha Minow, *Making All the Difference: Inclusion, Exclusion, and American Law* (Ithaca, NY: Cornell Univ. Press, 1990), 41–48 (drawing parallels between equal protection and religious protection issues).

The argument more basically proceeds with this line of reasoning: At its core, our Constitution is a document against the domination of any religious groups by others or by nonreligion, against the domination of the individual by the state, and, perhaps, also against the domination of the states by the federal government. Legislative favoritism toward any one group is suspect. At the same time, neutrality is a mistaken way to articulate these goals, for the state is inevitably preferring one position among the entire possible range in evaluating claims of domination, inequality, or disadvantage. Therefore, the judiciary is charged with the important task of monitoring the legislative results to assure that no group systematically prevails over others.

This line of analysis is not especially easy to apply. Indeed, consider the difficulty of comparing the power and privileges of the Satmar Hasidic community, American Jews in general, and children with disabilities to resolve the challenge to the Kiryas Joel School District. At the same time, the analysis renders explicit the goals of a liberal state in a pluralist society.

575. The choice between separation and efforts to assimilate or at least mix with the larger community would fade, in practice, if the Court took up Justice O'Connor's suggestion to overrule its earlier precedents forbidding the provision of public services on the site of religious schools. Most likely, then, Kiryas Joel would dissolve its single public school and take the public funds to provide services for children with disabilities on the sites of the religious schools for boys and the religious schools for girls. This would result in more separation than the solution afforded by the special school district, and, given the arguments to follow, I

find it less satisfactory.

576. It is not entirely clear that "choice" is the right concept here, if members of a community like the Satmar feel compelled by, rather than "choosing," their way of life. See Michael J. Sandel, *Religious Liberty— Freedom of Conscience or Freedom of Choice?*, 1989 Utah L Rev 597. See also *Bowen v. Roy*, 467 U.S. 693 (1986) (Stevens, J.) (comparing a father's religious practice, forbidding him to write his daughter's Social Security number on a form, to a kind of disability). Yet, choice is a constant framework for analysis in U.S. law and culture, and one that even fundamentalist religious groups deploy when it is helpful to them. Thus, a third alternative that many, including many religious leaders, endorse would be vouchers which would permit parents to select their own preferred school. The separation of church and state question would arise immediately with vouchers if the parent selected a religious school. Efforts to construct a constitutional voucher scheme are underway in many parts of the country. For a review of the argument, see James B. Egle, *The Constitutional Implications of School Choice*, 1992 Wis L Rev 459, 495.

577. Perhaps, as Robert Cover has suggested, the state's interest in social control threatens and at times even destroys the meanings created by subcommunities. Robert Cover, "Nomos and Narrative," in *Narrative, Violence, and the Law: The Essays of Robert Cover,* eds. Martha Minow, Michael Ryan, and Austin Sarat, (Ann Arbor, MI: Univ. of Michigan Press, 1992), 19–23, 95.

578. 20 U.S.C. § 1400(c).

579. Tucker, *Disability*, 275.

580. To further complicate matters, the parents claimed that the public school failed adequately to meet the language needs of their children with disabilities. Petitioner's Brief, at 6, *Kiryas Joel* (No. 93–517).

581. See supra (discussing *Yoder*). It is noteworthy that concern for children's own choices arise more commonly when their parents are members of minority religions than otherwise. In contrast, even less solicitude for children's interests appears in cases outside religious contexts when parents seek to curtail their children's liberty. See *Parham v. J.R.*, 422 U.S. 584 (1979) (civil commitment of minors by parents does not require a due process hearing). In addition, reducing children's interests to their preferences fails to acknowledge both the large influence of their parents and life experience on what they imagine and desire—and the cost, to them, of posing choices that otherwise they would not see. Some think that putting choices to children—about schooling, or other important matters—undermines a conception of their lives as ordained, founded, or constructed by something larger than themselves. Of course, denying them choice also takes away options. Nonetheless, asking children to choose is only one way to attend to the children's interests.

582. *Kiryas Joel,* 114 S.Ct. at 2495 (quoting *Board of Educ. of Monroe-Woodbury Ctr. Sch. Dist. v. Wieder,* 527 N.E.2d 767, 770 (N.Y. 1988)).

583A. Id.

583B. 114 S.Ct., at 2495 (Stevens, J., concurring). If he meant to restrict this point to a quid pro quo notion—in exchange for public schooling, the children must be exposed to other kinds of children—I would find it somewhat more compelling, although this very refinement might drive even more parents away from public schooling and thus render less possible the vision of the common school, integrating all kinds of children. *Board of Educ. of Kiryas Joes Village Sch. Dist. v. Grumet,* 114 S.Ct. 2481, 2495 (1994) (Stevens, J., concurring). This was consistent with Justice Stevens' view expressed in Wallace v. Jaffree, 472 U.S. 38, 50–55 (1985), that protection of individuals'—here, the school-children's—freedom of conscience is the central focus of all the clauses of the First Amendment.

584. David A. Hollinger, *Postethnic America: Beyond Multiculturalism* (New York: Basic Books, York 1995), 4. As Christopher Eisgrouper notes, the residents of Kiryas Joel and the residents of neighboring Monroe-Woodbury "were apparently happy to be rid of one another." Christopher L. Eisgrouper, *The Constitutional Value of Assimilation,* 96 Colum L Rev 87, 100 (1996). The question remains whether this kind of voluntary separation is good for the society as a whole.

See infra (discussing residential segregation).

585. See supra tan 112 (discussing some religious views attributing membership beyond individual choice).

586. See Horace Kallen, *Cultural Pluralism and the American Idea* (Philadelphia: Univ. of Pennsylvania, 1959); Randolph Bourne, "Trans-National America," in *War and the Intellectuals: Essays by Randolph S. Bourne,* 1915-1919 ed. Carl Rese (New York: Harper and Row, 1964); Cover, "Nomos and Narrative."

587. See Benjamin Barber, *Jihad v. McWorld* (New York: Times Books, 1995).

588. *Woman on the Edge of Time* (New York: Alfred A. Knopf, 1976).

589. Petitioner's Brief, at 28, *Kiryas Joel* (No. 93–517).

590. See Joshua Halberstam, *Everyday Ethics* (New York: Viking 1993).

591. See Ira C. Lupu, Uncovering the Village of Kiryas Joel, 96 Colum. L. Rev. 104 (1996).

592. Absent specific state statutes, there is no duty for school authorities to take action to correct racial imbalances due to housing patterns, although school authorities may choose to do so. E. Edmund Reutter, Jr., *The Law of Public Education* 880-87 (Westbury, New York: Foundation Press 4th ed. 1994). It is difficult to estimate the number of public schools and communities largely homogeneous by religion, race, or ethnicity due to residential segregation, but they are not rare in the United States,

and they are common in central urban areas. Public and private choices both contribute to the patterns of segregation, so, once again, individual choice does not capture the full story.

593. See Gary Orfield, Susan E. Eaton and The Harvard Project on School Desegregation, *Dismantling Desegregation: The Quite Reversal of Brown v. Board of Education* (New Press: New York 1996); *Hart v. Community School Board of Education*, 512 F.2d 317 (CA 2 1975) (Coney Island school desegregation case reaches to include public housing authority practices); *Millikin v. Bradley*, 418 U.S. 71 (1974) (acknowledging interaction linking housing choices by individuals, school segregation, and unkown and perhaps unknowable factors).

594. *Milliken*, 418 U.S. 744–45 (1974). But see *Hart*, 512 F.2d 37 (2d Cir. 1975) (expanding the court's inquiry in school segregation cases to include an evaluation of the effects of segregated living patterns in public housing). I join those who have criticized the *Milliken* decision. See, e.g., David Chang, *The Bus Stops Here: Defining the Constitutional Right of Equal Educational Opportunity and an Appropriate Remedial Process*, 63 BUL Rev 1, 53 (1983); Carol F. Lee, *The Federal Courts and the Status of Municipalities: A Conceptual Challenge*, 62 BUL Rev 1, 57-73 (1982). Others with similar political objectives have refrained from criticizing *Milliken*, perhaps because of a more basic criticism of constitutional litigation as a means to achieve racial justice. See H.N. Hirsch, *Race and Class, Law and Politics*, 69 BUL Rev 457, 459–60 (1989) (discussing the failure to criticize *Milliken* in Derrick Bell, *And We Are Not Saved* (New York: Basic Books, 1987), and Harold Cruse, *Plural But Equal* (New York: William Morrow, 1987)). Contrasting with *Milliken*, interdistrict remedies have been approved where intentional segregation occurred because of actions and decisions by the relevant authorities in the affected districts. See, e.g., *Hoots v. Pennsylvania*, 672 F.2d 1107 (3d Cir.), cert. denied, 459 U.S. 824 (1982); *Newberg Area Council, Inc. v. Bd. of Educ.*, 510 F.2d 1358 (6th Cir. 1974), cert. denied, 421 U.S. (1975). The viability of this approach in light of recent Supreme Court rulings permitting the dismantling of desegregation efforts remains in question. See *Missouri v. Jenkins*, 115 S.Ct. 2038 (1995); *Freeman v. Pitts*, 503 U.S. 467 (1992); *Bd. of Edu. of Oklahoma v. Dowell*, 498 U.S. 237 (1991).

595. See Orfield, "Toward an Integrated Future," in *Dismantling*, 331, 334–6. In a disturbing development, the Court has ruled that such efforts should be limited in time even if segregation persists. *Missouri v. Jenkins*, 115 S.Ct. 2038 (1995).

596. Christine H. Rossell, *Applied Social Science Research: What Does It Say About the Effectiveness of School Desegregation Plans?*, 12 J Legal Stud 69, 94–95 (1983). But others have argued that only behaviors change, not the prejudiced attitudes that may underlie

behavior. John B. McConahay, "Reducing Racial Prejudice in Desegregated Schools," in *Effective School Desegregation: Equity, Quality and Feasibility* ed. Willis D. Hawley (Beverly Hills: Sage Publications, 1981), 35, 48.

597. Similarly, integrated housing, especially through programs that open white suburban communities with good schools to members of racial minorities, can promote stable, tolerant neighborhoods of diverse people. See David L. Kirp, John P. Dwyer, and Larry A. Rosenthal, *Our Town: Race, Housing and the Soul of Suburbia* (New Brunswick: Rutgers University Press, 1995); Susan E. Eaton and Elizabeth Crutcher, "Magnets, Media, and Mirages," in *Dismantling*, 265, 288–89; Orfield, "Segregated Housing and School Resegregation," in *Dismantling*, 291, 324–28.

598. McConahay, *Prejudice*, at 35.

599. Ibid. Such joint activities are more effective than instructing teachers about race relations and changing the curriculum to reflect multicultural traditions, although such measures might also be useful. Id. at 37, 44.

600. Robert J. Goodwin, *Public School Integration of Children with Handicaps After Smith v. Robinson: "Separate but Equal" Revisited?*, 37 Me L Rev 267, 272 (1985).

601. McConahay, *Prejudice*, at 41.

602. Ibid. at 38.

603. Rossell, *Research*, at 99–100.

604. Citywide drama classes, vocational classes, community service projects, youth councils, journalism programs, and music and sports groups already attract and sustain diverse students in many communities.

605. Examples include all-city orchestras and bands, all-city basketball and soccer teams, and journalism programs drawing students from different schools.

606. School provision of transportation, space, and release time could ease, and even promote, participation. Parents who home school their children may oppose such activities, but they may also welcome some of them. The point, then, would be to develop a sufficiently broad and attractive array of activities to engage a truly diverse range of students.

607. Lynda Richardson, "Off the Bench, Judges Unite to Fight Bias," *New York Times*, 22 July 1996, sec. B1, col. 1.

608. The participating judges were shocked to learn of the racial segregation in the city's schools. Id.

609. Ibid. at B3, col. 6.

610. One example is City Year. See Suzanne Goldsmith, *A City Year: On the Streets and in the Neighborhoods with Twelve Young Community Service Volunteers* (New York: New Press, 1993).

611. Some already do. See Indiana Code Ann. 22-9-1-7 (education programs to eliminate prejudice against minority groups).

612 See Thomas LaBelle and Christopher Ward, *Multiculturalism: Diversity and Its Impact on Schools and Society* (Albabny, NY: SUNY Press,

1994); Dinesh D'Souza, *Illiberal Education* (New York: Free Press, 1991); Richard Bernstein, *The Dictatorship of Virtue* (New York: Knopf, 1994); Todd Gitlin, *The Twilight of Common Dreams* (New York: Henry Holt, 1995) (chapter 1).

613. For those states that regulate only the outcomes, not the inputs, of schools or home schooling, assessment of students in knowledge in one of these areas could be required rather than direct instruction.

614. I am assisted here by Professor Lawrence Blum's useful identification of four distinct yet related values addressed by curricular efforts under the name of "multicultural education": antiracism, cultural respect, commitment to cultural pluralism, and interethnic or interracial community. Lawrence Blum, "Multicultural Education" (draft paper commissioned by the Harvard Task Force on the Ecology of Schooling, spring 1996).

615. *Testimony of Margot Strom, before the Subcommittee on Human Resources and Intergovernmental Relations of the Committee on Government Operations*, U.S. House of Representatives, 19 October 1977, 1.

616. See Melinda Fine, *Habits of Mind: Struggling Over Values in America's Classrooms* (San Francisco: Josey-Bass Publishers, 1995), 137–70.

617. See ibid. at 143–4; William Damon, *The Moral Child: Nurturing Children's Natural Moral Growth* (New York: Free Press, 1990).

618. See *Dismantling*; William Celic, III, "Study Finds Rising Concentration of Black and Hispanic Students," *New York Times*, 14 December 1993, A1 (reporting study by Gary Orfield). Even systems under judicial desegregation orders may be labeled in compliance with racial balance requirements if they take a small percentage of white students and spread them throughout an essentially nonwhite school population. Christine H. Rossell, *The Carrot or the Stick for School Desegregation Policy* (Philadelphia: Temple University Press, 1990), 55.

619. West, *Desegregation*, 2590.

620. Gary Orfield and Susan E. Eaton argue that the courts actually have sponsored a movement dismantling desegregation efforts. See *Dismantling*. Some contrary trends can be discerned, though. See id. at 347; see also *Our Town*.

621. Small numbers of students attend single-sex schools, while many students, disproportionately nonwhite, are in substantially separate special education classrooms. A different kind of segregation occurs for students in parochial schools, although Catholic schools increasingly enroll large percentages of non-Catholic students. See Christopher L. Eisgruber, *The Constitutional Value of Assimilation*, 96 Colum L Rev 87, 98 (1996) (suggesting that people flee to new homogenous communities when they dislike their neighbors).

622. See Christopher L. Eisgrouper, *Political Unity and the Powers*

*of Government*, 41 UCLA L Rev 1297, 1314–16 (1994).

623. Compare National Commission on Excellence in Education, *A Nation at Risk: The Imperative for Educational Reform* (1983) with Carnegie Task Force on Education in the *Early Years of Promise* (1996).

624. See Lawrence Steinberg, "Failure Outside the Classroom," *Wall Street Journal*, 11 July 1996, p. A14, col. 3 (reporting results of study explaining poor student achievement in terms of parental disengagement).

625. Thus, only 2.2 percent of Beijing's first-grade students scored as low as Chicago's average students in math; by fifth grade, only 1.4 percent scored that low. Harold W. Stevenson and James W. Stigler, *The Learning Gap: Why Our Schools are Failing and What We Can Learn from Japanese and Chinese Education* (New York: Summit, 1992), 28–30.

626. Lawrence Steinberg, *Beyond the Classroom: Why School Reform Has Failed and What parents Need to Do* (New York: Simon & Schuster, 1996). Similarly, gendered expectations contribute to underperformance by many girls. See American Association of University Women, *How Schools Shortchange Girls* (1995) (studies conducted by Wellesley College Center for Research on Women).

627. See Elaine Woo, "Immigrant, U.S. Peers Differ Starkly on Schools," *Los Angeles Times*, 22 February 1996, p. 1 (describing findings of Marcelo Suarez-Orosco and Carola Suarez-

Orozco, and similar studies by Ruben G. Rumbaut and others). The studies found that eighty-four percent of newly arrived immigrant children said that school was "the most important thing" in their lives, compared with forty percent of the white students and fifty-five percent of Mexican Americans already living in the country. Id.

628. See Michael Kinsley, "The Spoils of Victimhood," *New Yorker*, 27 March 1995, 62, 63; Patricia Smith, *Becoming Bad Boys* (Ann Arbor, MI: Univ. of Michigan Press, forthcoming).

629. See Carnegie Corporation, *Starting Points: Meeting the Needs of Our Youngest Children* (New York: Carnegie Corporation, Ap;ril 1994), 20.

630. See Kenneth R. Weinstein, *Truth-in-Testimony: Penetrating the Special-Interest Facade* (Heritage Foundation Reports June 28, 1996) (critiquing Children's Defense Fund's effort to mobilize support for children and children's governmental and nongovernmental programs); Alissa Rubin, "Stand Outs: Who Stands for Children?," *The New Republic*, 24 June 1996, 12 (noting conservative critics charged the rally used kids to camouflage a liberal, big-government agenda).

631. See Peter H. Stone, "The RNC Taps the Fat Cats," *National Journal*, 1 July 1995 (Republican National Committee seeks media blitz to support balanced budget in name of children's future). Similarly, children's interests are invoked by those who support U.S.'s endorsement of the U.N. Convention on the Rights of the Child and

by those who view it as a dangerous incursion on parents' abilities to make decisions for their children.

632. Irving B. Harris, *Children in Jeopardy: Can We Break the Cycle of Poverty* (New Haven, CT: Yale University Press, 1996), 4.

633. Ibid. at 25–26.

634. Ibid., at 26 (citing U.S. Department of Education, The Reading Report Card, 1971-88, National Center of Education Statistics, National Assessment of Educational Progress, April 1994).

635. See, e.g., Testimony on Education's Impact on Economic Competitiveness, Joseph T. Gorman, Chairman, Business Roundtable Education Task Force and Chief Executive Officer, TRW, Inc., before Senate Labor and Human Resources Subcommittee, 2 February 1995.

636. See Harris, *Children*, 106–10 (comparing homicide and incarceration rates of seventeen industrialized countries).

637. Other times, though, at least rival ours for this description. See Todd Gitlin, *The Sixties: Years of Hope, Days of Rage*, rev. ed. (New York: Bantam Books, 1993).

638. See Paul E. Peterson, "An Immodest Proposal," 121 *Daedalus* 151, 151–59 (1992) (arguing that the voting power of the elderly helps to explain why they moved out of poverty and benefited from expanded public programs during the same period that more children fell into poverty and federal and state governments cut programs for children).

639. Arthur M. Schlesinger, Jr., *The Disuniting of America* (New York: W.W. Norton, 1992), 113.

640. Ibid.

641. Ibid. at 123.

642. Ibid. at 80.

643. The debates surrounding the National Standards for U.S. History, developed by National Center for History in Schools in 1994, exemplifies these tensions. Compare Lynn Cheney, "Hijacking America's History," 146 *Reader's Digest* (January 1995): 89 with Garland L. Thompson, "History? Revisions in Teaching Spark Debate," 11 *Black Issues in Higher Education* (12 January 1995): 32. See generally Mary V. Bicouvaris," National Standards for History: The Struggles Behind the Scenes," 69 *The Clearing House* (Jan.–Feb. 1996): 136.

644. Ann Douglas, *Terrible Honesty: Mongrel Manhattan in the 1920s* (New York: Farrar, Strauss and Giroux, 1995); Michael Kammen, *Mystic Chords of Memory: The Transformation of Tradition in American Culture* (New York: Knopf, 1992): Arthur Mann, *The One and the Many: Reflections on the American Identity* (Chicago: Univ. of Chicago Press, 1979); Gunnar Myrdal, *An American Dilemma* 20th anniv. ed. (New York: Harper & Row: 1944, 1962); Aviam Soifer, *Law and the Company We Keep* (Cambridge: Harvard Univ. Press, 1995); Ronald Takaki, *A Different Mirror: A History of Multicultural America* (Boston: Little, Brown and

Co., 1993); Molefi Kete Asante and Diane Ravitch, "Multiculturalism: An Exchange," 60 *American Scholar* (Spring 1991): 267.

645. See, e.g., Takaki's *A Different Mirror.*

646. Eric Foner, *What Is an American?* (unpublished address, upon award as Scholar of the Year by the New York Council for the Humanities, 1995), 3.

647. Ibid. See also Diane Ravitch, "Multiculturalism: E Pluribus Plures?" *The American Scholar* (Summer 1990), 337.

648. Foner, *American,* 4.

649. Ibid. A group of professional historians, educators, and curriculum officials, supported by the National Endowment for the Humanities (NEH) and the federal Department of Education, developed proposed national standards for the teaching of history for kindergarten through eighth grade. Cheney, then head of the NEH, attacked the resulting three volumes as toeing a line of political correctness, neglecting such figures as George Washington, Ulysses S. Grant, and Robert E. Lee, while emphasizing the negative aspects of American history and the accomplishments of minority members. See Todd Gitlin, *The Twilight of Common Dreams: Why America is Wracked by Culture Wars* (New York: Metropolitan Books, 1995), 189–99. The standards seemed to depart from the triumphalist tone of most American history textbooks, but many historians defended them. Id. at 194.

During the first hundred days of the Republican Congress's 1995 "Contract with America," the U.S. Senate, by a vote of 99 to 1, condemned the standards; the one dissenter wanted a more draconian prohibition on the use of public funds to distribute the materials. Id. at 198.

650. See also James W. Loewen, *Lies My Teacher Told Me: Everything Your American History Textbook Got Wrong* (New York: The New Press, 1995) (critique of prevailing texts and alternative telling of American history to emphasize conflict, suspense, drama, and connection with contemporary issues).

651. See infra (discussing work of Michael Kammen). In addition, a thorough history would examine the roots and shifts in the meanings of nation and national identity. See Katherine Verdery, "Whither `Nation' and 'Nationalism'?," 122 *Daedalus* 37, 40 (1993).

652. See chapter 4.

653. See Lawrence A. Cremin, *Popular Education and Its Discontents* (New York: Harper & Row, 1990). Expanding that arena would require clear-sighted acknowledgment—in the media, by industry—of the patterns of racial segregation, economic dislocation AND growth—and of the honest agreements and disagreements over the specific details of those patterns.

654. E.g., Schlesinger, *Disunity,* 41–42, 130–31.

655. Ibid. at 38–39.

656. See ibid. at 113, 134, 138.

657. See ibid. at 230. Moreover, if indeed social division is pronounced, many astute observers trace it more to the growing economic disparities in the nation than to the debates over curriculum and conceptions of American history. See Michael Lind, *The Next American Nation* (New York: Free Press, 1995).

658. For discussions of pressures to conform to a particular version of American culture, see Gitlin, *Twilight*, 50–67. See also Verdery, *Wither*, 42: "National symbolization includes as well the processes whereby groups within a society are rendered visible or invisible. For the project of nation-building, nonconforming elements must be first rendered visible, then assimilated or eliminated. Some of this can occur quite physically, through the violence most recently associated with "ethnic cleansing" in Bosnia-Herzegovina. But short of this are other, symbolic violences through which difference is highlighted and obliterated. Notions of purity and contamination, of blood as a carrier of culture, or of pollution are fundamental to the projects of nation-making. They merit more attention than scholars have accorded them."

659. See, e.g., Lawrence H. Fuchs, *The American Kaleidoscope: Race, Ethnicity, and the Civic Culture* (Hanover, NH: Wesleyan Univ. Press, 1990) (pluralism, unifying civic culture of political ideals).

660. Philip Gleason, "American Identity and Americanization," in *Concepts of Ethnicity* eds. William Petersen, Michael Novak, Philip Gelson (Cambridge, MA: Harvard Univ. Press, 1980).

661. See Fuchs, *Kaleidoscope*.

662. See Kenneth Karst, *Belonging to America* (New Haven, CT: Yale Univ. Press, 1989). A more critical attack argues that American civil identity has always involved multiple, competing traditions, including nativist and inegalitarian as well as liberal republican strands. See Roger M. Smith, "Beyond Tocqueville, Myrdal, and Hartz: The Multiple Traditions in America," 87 *American Political Science Review* (September 1993): 549 and Jacqueline Stevens, "Beyond Tocqueville, Please!," 89 *American Political Science Review* (1995), 987.

663. Stanley Hoffman, "Thoughts on the French Nation Today," 122 *Daedalus* (1993): 63, 64.

664. See Charles Fried, *The Supreme Court, 1994 Term: Foreword— Revolutions?*, 109 Harv L Rev 13, 25 (1995); Mary Ann Glendon, *Rights Talk: The Impoverishment of Political Discourse* (New York: Free Press, 1991); Kenneth Karst, *Belonging to America: Equal Citizenship and the Constitution* (New Haven, CT: Yale Univ. Press, 1989); J.P. Mayer ed. Alexis de Tocqueville, I *Democracy in America* trans. George Lawrence (Garden City, NY: Doubleday Anchor, 1969), 270.

665. Sanford Levinson, *The Constitution in American Civil Religion*, 1979 Sup Ct Rev 125.

666. Glendon, *Rights*, 177.

667. See generally Hendrick Hartog, "The Constitution of Aspiration and 'The Rights that Belong to Us All,'" J Am Hist (December 1987), 1013.

668. Georgeton University Law Center develops curricular materials and classes on "street law" to teach young people about their rights and duties. Similiar programs exist in Tennessee.

669. Gitlin, *Twilights,* 161–62.

670. See Joan Beck, "Get the Facts Straight and Start Dealing with Racial Realities in the Once-a-Decade Head Count," *Chicago Tribune,* 11 July 1996, 23.

671. Michael Lind, "Are We a Nation?," *Dissent* (Summer 1995), 355, 356.

672. See also David Hollinger, *Postethnic America: Beyond Multiculturalism* (New York: Basic Books, 1995), 160 ("the distinction between civic and ethnic eventually breaks down because over the course of time civic affiliations can help to create those that are eventually recognized as ethnic").

673. See Judith Stacey, *In the Name of the Family: Rethinking Family Values in the Postmodern Age* (Boston: Beacon Press, 1996). The classic statement of this view is Georg Simmel, *Soziologie* (Berlin: Duncker and Humblot, 1968).

674. See Horace Kallen, *Cultural Pluralism and the American Idea* (Philadelphia: Univ. of Pennsylvania Press, 1959) (promoting view of Amer-ica as federation of cultures); Randolph Bourne, "Trans-National America," in *War and the Intellectuals: Essays by Randolph S. Bourne, 1915-1919* ed. Carl Resek (New York: Harper & Row, 1964) (democracy thrives on group differences, not sameness or artificial harmony); Michael Walzer, "Multiculturalism and Individualism," *Dissent* (Spring 1994) (advocating more particularized cultural groups and associations to produce greater, deeper sense of belonging for more Americans, not to single homogenized American culture, but to more meaningful affiliations that support sense of belonging and agency).

675. See Hollinger, *Postethnic,* 154.

676. R. Laurence Moore, *Religious Outsiders and the Making of Americans* (New York: Oxford Univ. Press, 1986).

677. Jodi Dean describes a way to pursue solidarity in a pluralist society: citizens should not try to see the stranger as the other of a citizen; but citizens should try to recognize themselves as strange. Jodi Dean, *Solidarity of Strangers: Feminism After Identity Politics* (Berkeley: Univ. Cal. Press, 1996) (describing Kristeva). For an insightful rejoinder to Kristeva, see Bonnie Honig, "Ruth, the Model Emigree," in *'There's No Place Like Home': The New Politics of Pluralism* (forthcoming) (criticizing Kristeva's advocacy of abstraction and failure to engage actual Others in her deliberations).

678. Gitlin, *Twilight,* 206–7.

679. Jodi Dean, *Solidarity.*

680. Joseph A. Maxell, "Diversity,

Solidarity, and Community" (forth-coming, in *Educational Theory*).

681. See Iris Young, *Justice and the Politics of Difference* (Princeton, NJ: Princeton Univ. Press, 1990); Iris Young, "Gender as Seriality: Thinking About Women as a Social Collective," 19 *Signs* (Spring 1994): 713; Jerry Frug, (draft) (calling for greater density in housing to promote such interactions).

682. See Maxwell, *Diversity, Solidarity, and Community*.

683. See James Clifford, *The Predicament of Culture* (Cambridge, MA: Harvard Univ. Press, 1988); Elizabeth Mertz, *Legal Loci and Places in the Heart: Community and Identity in Sociolegal Studies*, 28 Law & Soc. Rev 971 (1994); Regina Austin, *"The Black Community," Its Lawbreakers, and a Politics of Identification*, 65 So Cal L Rev 1769 (1992); Roy Wagner, *The Invention of Culture*, rev. ed. (Chicago: Univ. of Chicago Press, 1981); Lisa Fishbayn, "A People Is Not Conquered Until the Hearts of the Women Are: On the Group Law and the Colonization of Gender Relations Among the First Nations of Canada," unpublished draft thesis.

684. Clifford Geertz, *The Religion of Java* (Glencoe, NY: Free Press, 1960); Ritual and Social Change, (quoted in Maxwell, 10), 149, 168.

685. "Generally speaking, nationalist ideology suffers from pervasive false consciousness. Its myths invert reality .... It preaches and defends continuity, but owes everything to a decisive and utterly profound break in human history." Earnest Gellner, *Nations and Nationalism*, 124–5 (1983). See also Michael Walzer, *What It Means to be An American: Essays on the American Experience* (New York: Marsilio, 1992) (danger of a national community to individual liberty).

686. Verdery, *Wither*, 42, 44.

687. See Michael Kammen, *People Of Paradox: An Inquiry into the Origins of American Civilization* (Ithaca, NY: Cornell Univ. Press, 1980).

688. Ibid. at 70.

689. Ibid. at 82–85.

690. Ibid. at 85.

691. Kammen suggests the desire to reconcile restless pluralities coexisted with celebration of incompatible multiplicities in America: "conservatism *and* liberalism, individualism *and* corporatism; hierarchy *and* egalitarianism, emotionalism *and* rationalism, autonomy *and* co-operation are all integral to the mutuality of pluralism." Id. at 92. Partisan groups operating in the swirl of these multiple trends often take on the coloration of opponents and the paradoxes expand to include new groups and individuals. Id.

692. Aviam Soifer, *Law and the Company We Keep* (Cambridge, MA: Harvard Univ. Press, 1995), 52.

693. Kenneth Karst, *Belonging to America: Equal Citizenship and the Constitution* (New Haven, CT: Yale Univ. Press, 1989), 176.

694. Soifer, *Law*, 69.

695. Susan Bickford, "In the Presence of Others: Arendt and Anzaldua on the Paradox of Public Appear-

ance," in *Feminist Interpretations of Hannah Arendt* ed. Bonnie Honig (University Park, PA: Penn. State Press, 1995), 313, 330.

696. Lewis P. Hinchman and Sandra K. Hinchman, eds. *Hannah Arendt, Critical Essay* (Albany, NY: State Univ. of New York, 1994), 258.

697. See Hannah Arendt, *The Life of the Mind* (New York: Harcourt Brace Jovanovich, 1978), 200: "Since it is possessed by the citizen rather than by man in general, [political freedom] can manifest itself only in communities, where the many who live together have their intercourse both in word and in deed regulated by a great number of *rapports*—laws, customs, habits, and the like. In other words, political freedom is possible only in the sphere of human plurality, and on the premise that this sphere is not simply an extension of the dual I-and-myself to a plural We." One commentator on Arendt's work summarizes: "freedom is advanced when politics unfolds as the communicative interaction of diverse equals acting together as citizens." Mary Dietz, "Hannah Arendt and Feminist Politics," in *Hannah Arendt, Critical Essays*, 247–48.

698. See Hannah Arendt, *Between Past and Future* enlarged ed. (Grove, NY: Harcourt Brace and World, 1968), 226–27, 241–42; Hannah Arendt, *Men in Dark Times* 6–7, 23 (1968).

699. Hannah Arendt, *The Human Condition* (Garden City, NY: Doubleday, 1958), 167.

700. Bonnie Honig, "Toward an Agonistic Feminism: Hannah Arendt and the Politics of Identity," in *Feminist Interpretations of Hannah Arendt* ed. Bonnie Honig (University Park, PA: Penn. State Univ. Press, 1995), 135, 141. See also id. at 159: "a self that is never exhausted by the (sociological, psychological and juridical) categories that seek to define and fix it."

701. Ibid. 149.

702. Ibid. at 152–53 (discussing correspondence with Gershom Sholem). Honig suggests that Arendt neglected the possibility of contesting the meaning of the Jewish identity, not just contesting its centrality to her own identity. Id. at 155. Elsewhere, Arendt explained that for much of her life she answered who she was in terms of her Jewishness, because of the fact of persecution in Nazi Germany on that basis. From this she derived "the principle that one can resist only in the terms of the identity that is under attack." Arendt, *Men*, 18. See chapter 2, discussing role of oppression in definition of identities.

703. See also Bickford, "Presence," 313–35. Other theorists also warn of the dangers of an identity politics that leaves no room for differences and pretends that group identities are static. See, e.g., bell hooks, *Talking Back* (Boston: South End Press, 1989), 106–10.

704. See Lisa J. Disch, "On Friendship in 'Dark Times,'" in *Feminist Interpretations of Hannah Arendt*, 285–311, 295.

705. Disch, "Dark Times," 331.

706. See chapter 1.

707. Arendt, *Human Condition*, 181.

708. See Honig, "Politics of Identity," 140: "For the sake of 'who' it might become, [the self] risks the dangers of the radically contingent public realm where anything can happen, where the consequences of action are 'boundless' and unpredictable, where 'not life but the world are at stake.'" (quoting Hannah Arendt, "What is Freedom?", in *Between Past and Future* enlarged ed. New York: Penguin, 1977), 156. Through political action, the individual gives up the certainty of his or her "what," defined by roles in the private realm. Id. "In acting and speaking, men show who they are, reveal actively their unique personal identities and thus make their appearance in the human world . . . This disclosure of 'who' in contradistinction to 'what' somebody is . . . is implicit in everything somebody says and does." *Human Condition*, 179.

709. See Honig, *Identity*, 149.

710. Disch, "'Dark Times,'" 285–311, 288.

711. See Bickford, "Presence," 323–31.

712. See Bernard Yack, "Ethnos and Demos: A Political Theorist Looks at the Idea of the Nation" (unpublished essay). Yack argues that "participation is not the same thing as identification" and that "the idea of the civic nation was developed to counter the myths and illiberal practices associated with ethnonationalism" but civic nationhood does not well describe American political communities.

713. Disch, "Dark Times," 331.

714. Hollinger, *Postethnic*, 157.

715. Charles Taylor thus is partly right to discuss multiculturalism in terms of the search for recognition—see Charles Taylor, supra—but partly wrong, because this conception misses the needs for physical safety, material sustenance, and social reordering often at stake. Just an example, people are assaulted because they are, or are thought to be, gay, or black, or female. Something more than recognition is at stake for them, though identity politics may provide them a language.

716. Christine Chang and Renée Tajima, *Who Killed Vincent Chin* (documentary film first broadcast on PBS, "Point of View," (1988)).

717. See K. Anthony Appiah, "Identity, Authenticity, Survival: Multicultural Societies and Social Reproduction," in Charles Taylor, *Multiculturalism: Examining the Politics of Recognition* ed. Amy Gutmann (Princeton, NJ: Princeton Univ. Press, 1994).

718. See chapter 2 (discussing identities, and concerns that identities as a focus for politics lend themselves to reductionism, neglect intersections among identities, and imply coherence belied by boundary-crossing and other confusions about identities).

719. See Beck, "Racial Realities" (describing two million biracial or multiracial children counted in 1990 census and up to twelve percent inter-

racial marriage by Asian men, twenty-five percent for Asian women, sixty percent for Native Americans).

720. See chapter 3, discussing the role of law in making identities seem real and significant.

721. See Gerald Stern, "It's Not Right" (forthcoming in Porter Shreve and Susan Richards Shreve, eds., *Outside the Law: Narratives on Justice* (Boston: Beacon Press, 1997). Thus, the issue is not only slavery, but new forms of exclusion developed during Reconstruction and since. See generally George Lipsitz, "The Possessive Investment in Whiteness: Racialized Social Democracy and the 'White' Problem in American Studies," 47 *American Quarterly* (1995), 369-427.

722. See Michael Kinsley, "The Spoils of Victimhood," *New Yorker*, 27 March 1995, 62.

723. Richard Morin, "Across the Racial Divide," *Washington Post National Weekly Edition*, 16–22 (October 1995), 6.

724. See, e.g., Deborah Barfield, "Minority Legislators Fight State Budget Cuts," *Newsday*, 13 March 1996, A36; Sharon Cotliar, "Towns Make English Official," *Chicago Sun-Times*, 25 August 1996, 15; Robert D. Hershey, Jr., "Bias Hits Hispanic Workers," *New York Times*, 27 April 1995, sec. D1, col. 2; Irene Middleman Thomas, "Survival of the Fittest," 9 *Hispanic* (June 1996):32. State and federal efforts to restrict the use of Spanish reflect not only asserted goals of national unity and shared communication, but also potential discrimination on the basis of ethnicity or national origin, and imposition of one pattern of assimilation. See Martina Lewis, *English-Only Laws, Informational Interests, and the Meaning of the First Amendment in a Pluralistic Society*, 31 Harv CR-CL L Rev 539 (1996) (discussing *Yniguez v. Arizonans for Official English*, 69 F3d 920 (9th Cir. 1995) (en banc), cert. granted, 113 S.Ct. 1316 (1996) (discussing reasons why court of appeals affirmed rejection on First Amendment grounds of Arizona's constitutional amendment making English the official state language).

725. Peter Irons, *Justice at War* (New York: Oxford Univ. Press, 1983); Page Smith, *Democracy on Trial* (New York: Simon & Schuster, 1995); John Tateishi, *And Justice For All: An Oral History of the Japanese American Detention Camps* (New York: Random House, 1984).

726. Robert Williams, *The American Indian in Western Legal Thought* (New York: Oxford Univ. Press, 1990); Vine DeLoria, *Custer Died for Your Sins* (New York: MacMillan, 1969); Vine DeLoria, *American Indian Policy in the Twentieth Century* (Norman: Univ. of Oklahoma Press, 1985).

727. See *United States v. Virginia*, 116 S.Ct. 2264 (1996) (military academy); *Taylor v. Louisiana*, 419 U.S. 522 (1975) (jury service); Deborah Rhode, *Association and Assimilation*, 81 Northwestern U L Rev 106 (1986) (clubs and associations); Judith Resnik, *Asking About Gender in Courts*, 21 Signs 952

(1996) (violence, harassment, bias in courts); Reva B. Siegal, 'The Rule of Love': Wife Beating as Prerogative and Privacy, 105 Yale LJ 2117 (1996) (domestic violence).

728. See John P. De Cecco, ed., *Bashers, Baiters and Bigots: Homophobia in American Society* (New York: Harrington Park Press, 1985); People for The American Way, *Hostile Climate: A State-by-State Report on Anti-Gay Activity* (Washington, D.C.: People For The American Way, 1993).

729. The landmark case that successfully challenged conditions of confinement experienced by persons with mental disabilities in state institutions was *Wyatt v. Stickney*, 344 F. Supp. 373 (M.D. Ala. 1972); the case continues to the present as the state remains recalcitrant in complying with court orders. See generally Charles Halpern, "Half Way to the Millennium—an Historical Perspective," in *The Rights of Citizens with Mental Retardation* eds. Lawrence A. Kane, Jr., Phyllis Brown and Julius S. Cohen (Lanham, MD: Univ. Press of America, 1988), 77; Robert Burt, "Pennhurst: A Parable," in Robert Mnookin, *In the Interests of Children* (New York: W.H. Freeman, 1985), 265; David J. Rothman and Sheila M. Rothman, *The Willowbrook Wars* (New York: Harper and Row, 1984).

730. Adeno Addis, *Role Models and the Politics of Recognition*, 144 U Penn L Rev 1377, 1441 (1996).

731. In addition, stark racial differences occur in perceptions of equality in America. Most whites, in one national survey, said they believed civil rights are being enforced, while most blacks said they believe that racial discrimination is rising and a big problem. Morin, *Divide*. Hispanics and Asians agreed that blacks are far worse off than whites. Id.

732. See Sander Gilman, *Differences and Pathology: Stereotypes of Sexuality, Race, and Madness* (Ithaca, NY: Cornell Univ. Press, 1985).

733. Charles R. Lawrence, III, *The Epidemiology of Color-Blindness: Learning to Think and Talk about Race, Again*, 15 Boston College Third World LJ 1, 16–18 (1995) (discussing Marc Elrich, "The Stereotype Within: Why Students Don't Buy Black History Month," *Washington Post*, 13 February 1994, C1.

734. Elrich, *Stereotype Within*.

735. Ibid.

736. Louis Harris, "The Future of Affirmative Action," in *The Affirmative Action Debate* ed. George E. Curry (Reading, MA: Addison-Wesley Publishing, 1996), 326, 332–33.

737. For an especially chilling exploration of this process, see "Special Section," a film by Costa Gravas that explores the response of Vichy France's judiciary to the Nazis.

738. Lawrence, *Color-Blindness*, 6-7.

739. See chapter 4.

740. See chapter 4.

741. Here, then, I support the general idea of the "National Conversation on American Pluralism and Identity" launched by the National Endow-

ment for the Humanities in 1994, and especially the commitment to promote "frank and open exchanges about our differences as well as our common ground." *A National Conversation, A Handbook of Tips* (1995). I suggest more attention to producing collections of contrasting experiences rather than emphasizing "what does it mean to be an American."

742. See chapter 5.

743. Ursula K. Le Guin, *A Wizard of Earthsea* (1968), cited in *The Beacon Book of Quotations by Women*, Rosalie Maggio compiler, (Boston: Beacon Press, 1992), 237.

744. See Michael Lind, *The Next American Nation* (New York, Free Press, 1995), warning that the real threat is not fragmentation along racial lines but fissioning along class lines. In contrast, Arthur Schlesinger, Jr., identifies inequalities and segregation as sources for concern, but emphasizes the dangers of tribalisms. Schlesinger, *Disuniting.*

745. So a kind of secession emerges. For consideration of secession as a response to diversity, see Adeno Addis, *Individualism, Communitarianism, and the Rights of Ethnic Minorities*, 67 Notre Dame L Rev 615 (January 1992); Adeno Addis, On Human Diversity and the Limits of Toleration, (unpublished manuscript).

746. Actual race relations may look better than the residential and school patterns. In 1991, a survey found that two-thirds of whites and four-fifths of blacks surveyed knew "many members of another race well," and forty-seven percent of whites and sixty-three percent of blacks said they "socialized regularly with members of another race." "The New Politics of Race," *Newsweek* 6 May 1991, 30. Yet, polarizing events, such as the Clarence Thomas confirmation hearings, the beating of Rodney King, the O.J. Simpson murder trial, and the media's coverage of each, help exacerbate if not create distrust across racial groups.

747. See John P. Dwyer, David Kirp, and Larry A. Rosenthal, *Our Town: Race, Housing and the Soul of Suburbia* (New Brunswick, NJ: Rutgers Univ. Press, 1995).

748. See e.g., *Adarand Construction v. Pena*, 115 S.Ct. 2097 (1995); *Hopwood v. Texas*, 1996 WL 120235 (CA 5 1996). Some cases produce voluntary termination of quotas. See, e.g., Lauren Beckham, "Students Cite Merit Over Quotas," *Boston Herald*, 16 November 1996, p. 10 (school committee ends use of racial quotas in admission to Boston Latin High School). Recently successful at the polls, the California Civil Rights Initiative (Proposition 209) is the only state-level anti-affirmative actions initiative thus far to appear on a ballot. The referendum would bar race and gender preferences in state contracting, hiring, and public education; it would not touch private business programs, and it cannot displace federal obligations. The Proposition has been challenged in federal court as a violation of federal law.

749. See W.B. Gallie, *Essentially Contested Concepts*, 56 Proc Aristotelian Soc'y 167 (1955-56).

750. Exec. Order 10,925 26 Fed. Reg. 1977 (1961). Lyndon Johnson is often given credit for the phase which he used in the later Executive Order 11,246, and expanded to include sex discrimination in Executive Order 11,375.

751. See Katherine Newman, *Declining Fortunes: The Withering of the American Dream* (New York: Basic Books, 1993).

752. Stanley Fish put it well: "It is a travesty of reasoning to argue that affirmative action, which gives preferential treatment to disadvantaged minorities as part of a plan to achieve social equality, is no different from the policies that created the disadvantages in the first place." Stanley Fish, *There's No Such Thing as Free Speech* (New York: Oxford University Press, 1994), p. 61.

See also Kingsley, "Spoils." ("It is not possible either historically or analytically to draw a sharp distinction between 'good' civil rights and 'bad' affirmative action").

753. See Aleinikoff, supra. So do "neutral" workplace rules leave in place burdens on many women, members of minority religions and persons with disabilities. See Minow, *Difference*.

754. Consider here Charles Lawrence's analysis of a Supreme Court decision that a voluntary minority set-aside program in Richmond, Virginia, violates the Equal Protection clause because there was "no direct evidence of race discrimination [against minority contractors] on the part of the city" or against minority subcontractors by the city's prime contractors. *City of Richmond v. J.A. Croson*, 488 U.S. 469 (1989). Yet, witnesses to history, and scholars, attest to the white community's discrimination against African Americans in Richmond.

See Peter Charles Hoffer, *'Blind to History': The Uses of History in Affirmative Action Suits: Another Look at City of Richmond v. J.A. Croson Co.*, 23 Rutgers LJ 270, 289-95 (1992); Alexander Aleinikoff, *A Case for Race-Consciousness*, 91 Column L Rev 1060, 1072-74 (1991). Justice Marshall's dissenting opinion in *Croson* pointed out the insult given by the majority to black elected officials in Richmond who approved the set-aside program: the majority treated them as self-dealing or otherwise unable to govern fairly (109 S.Ct., 706, 754 (Marshall, J., dissenting), rather than testing on the facts _ the fairness of the program. See Drew Days, *Fullilove*, 96 Yale LJ 453, 480-83 (1987) (justifying factual inquiry into self-dealing issues).

Wishing it were so does not make Richmond's history color-blind. Yet, the courts, and general public opinion, prefer this way of viewing the past, and make it difficult to prove past discrimination by requiring evidence of intent or specific links between perpetrators and victims.

755. See Stephanie M. Wildman, *Privilege Revealed: How Invisible Preference Undermines America* (New York:

New York Univ. Press, 1996); Cheryl I. Harris, *Whiteness as Property*, 106 Harv L Rev 1710 (1993).

756. See supra note 112. Also under challenge is the use of set-asides or "race-norming" or "gender-norming" of tests, meaning procedures that take the top same percentage of applicants from each race but use, therefore, different racial cut-offs. As racially unfair as such a procedure may seem, it basically is a cheap way to deal with defective tests or screens. The Civil Rights Act of 1991, sect. 703, banned the use of such score adjustments in employment.

757. See Weekly Media Availability with Attorney General Janet Reno (and Deval Patrick, Assistant Attorney General, Civil Rights Division, Justice Department), *Federal News Service*, 14 November 1996; Jeffrey Weiss, "Affirmative Action Rules Muddled, Some Experts Say," *Dallas Morning News*, 2 July 1996, 9A.

At the same time, quotas and set-asides have apparently done little to help the most disadvantaged in the society. Gayle M.B. Hanson, "When Race or Gender Counts Most, Who Pays?", *Washington Times*, 21 October 1996, p. 17; Seymour Martin Lipset, "Two Americas, Two Systems," 7 *The New Democrat*, 9, 14 (May/June 1995); Carol M. Swain, "A Cost Too High to Bear," 7 *The New Democrat* 19 (May/June 1995). That a wide range of people, including Republican presidential candidate Robert Dole, endorsed preferential selection

methods based on economic disadvantage indicates that affirmative action is more likely to be reformulated than cast off.

758. "Weekly Media Availability," supra. Patrick continued: "And I think if we begin to talk about [integration], then you get some perspective on why affirmative action continues to be important in some contexts and done the right way today."

759. Thus, a diverse police force is more likely to serve effectively a diverse community; a diverse university student body is more likely to prepare people to live in a diverse world. See this rationale offered by the Xerox Corporation for its affirmative action plan, treated as "a corporate value, a management priority, and a formal business objective": looking at the demographic forecasts, eighty-five percent of new recruits between now and the year 2000 will be women or nonwhite men. "So firms with a good track record of producing non-white managers and managing people from different backgrounds will enjoy a growing advantage in recruiting and motivating workers" and in appealing to diverse customers and performing internationally. "Affirmative Action: Why Bosses Like It," *The Economist*, 11 March 1995, p. 29. The U.S. Army similarly maintains the same merit standards for promotion regardless of race but makes promotion decisions related to the pool of minorities in the group that could be considered for promotion to the next higher rank.

One white officer explained,
"Only fully qualified people are pro-
moted, but not necessarily the best-
qualified. But don't forget, we are
talking about micromillimeter differ-
ences in these cases." Charles Moskos,
"The Army Experience," 7 *The New
Democrat* 22 (May/June 1995). See
Gordon MacInnes, *Wrong for All the
Right Reasons: How White Liberals
Have Been Undone by Race* 190
(New York: New York Univ. press,
1996) (describing Army practice).
See also David E. Hayes-Bautista
and Gregory Rodriguez, "Preparing
for Post-Anglo America," 7 *The New
Democrat* 27-28 (May/June 1995)
(noting efforts by private universities
and businesses in California to recruit
Latinos because it is good business,
given changing demographics in
the state).

Adeno Addis makes an additional
argument for diversity in control
of communications and mass media,
to share the power over images and
narratives and redress mistaken
images of members of minority
groups. Adeno Addis, "On Human
Diversity and the Limits of Toleration"
(unpublished manuscript).

760. Consider Roger Wilkins' view:
"The idea of affirmative action is *not* to
force people into positions for which
they are unqualified but to encourage
institutions to develop realistic criteria
for the enterprise at hand and then
find a reasonably diverse mix of
people qualified to be engaged in
it." Roger Wilkins, "Racism Has Its

Privileges,"
*The Nation,* 27 March 1995, p. 409.

The U.S. Army is an exemplar of
an employer that values diversity and
altered its selection process to achieve
it—without sacrificing quality. See
Charles Moskos, *All That We Can Be:
Black Leadership and Racial Integration
The Army Way* (New York: Basic Books,
1996); Charles Moskos, *The Army
Experience,* 7 *The New Democrat* 22
(May/June 1995).

761. Wilkins, "Racism," 415–16.

762. See id. at 409–16. For a constructive effort to reframe the debate,
see Susan Sturm and Lani Guinier, *The
Future of Affirmative Action: Reclaiming
the Innovative Ideal,* 84 Cal L Rev 953
(1996).

763. Glenn C. Loury, "The Social
Capital Deficit," 7 *The New Democrat*
(May/June 1995): 28-29.

764. See Kathleen Sullivan, *The
Supreme Court—Comment, Sins of Discrimination: Last Term's Affirmative
Action Cases,* 100 Harv L Rev 78, 96
(1986); see also *Johnson v. Transportation Agency,* 480 U.S. 616, 646
(1987) (Stevens, J. concurring)
(quoting Sullivan).

765. See chapter 5.

766. Kiku Addato's research on
sound-bites in campaigns; candidates'
complaints that their speeches and
position papers get no coverage but
their gaffes and interpersonal tensions
dominate the news. Kiku Addato, "The
Incredible Shrinking Sound Bite,"
*The New Republic,* 28 May 1990, p. 20.

767. Ron Grossman, "Immigra-

tion," *Chicago Tribune* September
1996, p. 1, zone C.

768. Ibid.

769. See Susan Okin, *Political Liberalism, Justice and Gender* (Symposium on John Rawls), 105 Ethics 23 (Oct. 1994); Elizabeth Spelman, *Inessential Woman* (Boston: Beacon Press, 1988); Karen Engle, *Female Subjects of Public International Law*, 26 New Eng. Sch.of Law L Rev 1509 (1992) (on international women's rights and the subaltern).

# INDEX

<>

moral relativism, 130
Moses, 31
Mukherjee, Bharati, 43-46
Mura, David, 23-24
mutability of meaning, 52-53

narratives of harm, 91-93, 151
national cohesion. *See* unity and
    disunity
National Council of Churches, 21
Native Americans. *See* American
    Indians
Nazis, 22, 27, 46
negotiation of identity, 50-53
*New York Times*, 83
Non-Intercourse Act of 1790, 71

O'Connor, Flannery, 51
Oedipus, 31
otherness, 157

paternity determinations, 65,
    66-68, 69, 70
Patrick, Deval, 155
peremptory challenges, 98-100, 151
Phillips, Anne, 16
*Pierce v. Society of Sisters*, 110
Piercy, Marge, 125
*Pigs in Heaven* (Kingsolver), 77-78
politics. *See also* identity
    politics generally
    affirmative action debate, 153-56
    importance of, 143-47
    national cohesiveness, issues of.
        *See* unity and disunity
    problems of American politics,
        156-58
*Politics of Presence, The*
    (Phillips), 16
pornography, 22

*Post-Ethnic America* (Hollinger), 46
power and oppression, 46-48
    becoming what you hate, risk of,
        53-58
    control of identity under, 48-50
    negotiation of identity under,
        50-53
professors, hiring of, 8, 11, 12,
    13-14, 154
Pryce, Jonathan, 12

race, 41, 42, 46
    adoption, race matching in, 75,
        107
    affirmative action debate, 153-56
    challenges to categories, 62-64
    color-blindness to denial, 150,
        153
    internalization of negative
        stereotypes, 149-50
    law, effects of, 59-64
    narratives to legitimize
        exclusion, 148-51
    segregation in education, 127-28,
        131
    voting and, 16-19, 94, 96, 148
*Racial Healing* (Dalton), 92
Ranciere, Jacques, 54
rape, 17
"reasonable person" standard,
    100-101
religious community, 111-12,
    117-28, 137-38
remedies
    artistic expression, 102-4, 151
    census categories, 96-98, 151
    compensation for harm, 90-91, 151
    enforcement of antidiscrimination
        laws, 87-90
    hate speech on college campuses,

consumer culture, 139-40
criss-crossing commonalities,
    140-43, 152
current political problems,
    156-58
integration as goal, 155-56
pluralism, ideal of, 135, 137-38
politics and care, 143-47
remedies for harm done. *See*
    remedies
rights, emphasis on, 138-39
self-segregation, patterns of,
    152-53
University of Texas, 10
U.S. Supreme Court. *See* Supreme
    Court cases

women
  boundaries of identity, 41, 42-45
  sex discrimination, 17, 148

victimization, emphasis on, 55
Vietnam War, 103
Virginia Military Institute (VMI),
    115
voting, 16-19, 148
  temporary affiliation proposals,
    94-96, 151
Voting Rights Act, 16, 95

Walzer, Michael, 106
Washington, Mary Helen, 49
*Washington Post*, 149
Waters, Mary, 39
West, Cornel, 33, 56
Wieseltier, Leon, 39
"Wife's Story, A" (Mukherjee),
    43-46
Williams, Sherley Ann, 48-50
Williams, Tennessee, 15
Wilson, August, 13
*Wisconsin v. Yoder*, 111-12
*Woman on the Edge of Time* (Piercy),
    125